Treasury of Newfoundland Stories

Volume I

True Crime & Adventure

© 2015, Jack Fitzgerald

 Canada Council for the Arts   Conseil des Arts du Canada   Canada   Newfoundland Labrador

We gratefully acknowledge the financial support of the Canada Council for the Arts, the Government of Canada through the Canada Book Fund (CBF), and the Government of Newfoundland and Labrador through the Department of Tourism, Culture and Recreation for our publishing program.

Cover Design by Maurice Fitzgerald
Layout by Joanne Snook-Hann and Todd Manning
Printed on acid-free paper

Published by
CREATIVE PUBLISHERS
an imprint of CREATIVE BOOK PUBLISHING
a Transcontinental Inc. associated company
P.O. Box 8660, Stn. A
St. John's, Newfoundland and Labrador A1B 3T7

Printed in Canada
Second Printing – March 2016

Library and Archives Canada Cataloguing in Publication

Fitzgerald, Jack, 1945-, author
    Jack Fitzgerald's treasury of Newfoundland stories volume 1 : true crime & adventure / Jack Fitzgerald.

Includes bibliographical references.
ISBN 978-1-77103-069-4 (paperback)

    1. Newfoundland and Labrador--History--Anecdotes.
2. Newfoundland and Labrador--Anecdotes. 3. Crime--
Newfoundland and Labrador--History. 4. Disasters--
Newfoundland and Labrador--History. I. Title.

MIX
Paper from
responsible sources
FSC
www.fsc.org   FSC® C011825

FC2161.8.F595 2015   971.8   C2015-904829-X

Treasury of Newfoundland Stories

Volume I

True Crime & Adventure

St. John's, Newfoundland and Labrador, 2015

Dedicated to Jack and Ruth Phyne

TABLE OF CONTENTS

Introduction ix

Chapter 1   The Bus Ride 1

Chapter 2   Big City Crime in Small Town Newfoundland 15

Chapter 3   The Hunting Knife 35

Chapter 4   The Tong Murders 61

Chapter 5   Tough Guys and Killers 99

Chapter 6   Four Women, Three Hangings 111

Chapter 7   Executed by Guillotine on St. Pierre 135

Chapter 8   Unlikely Criminals 147

Chapter 9   The Arsonist Calls 155

Chapter 10   The Solving of Two Criminal Mysteries 173

Chapter 11   A Glimpse of Hell 187

Chapter 12   Horrid Gulch 223

Chapter 13   Sixty-five Trapped Inside Inferno 233

Chapter 14   Blizzards, Cyclones, Hurricanes and Avalanches 255

Acknowledgements 285

Bibliography 286

Introduction

Jack Fitzgerald's Treasury of Newfoundland Stories, Volume I: True Crime and Adventure is a collection of widely diversified Newfoundland stories and folklore, concentrating on epics related to crime and adventure.

These stories span more than a century and include captivating stories of some of the most outrageous and brutal killings in Newfoundland history as well as riveting sagas of adventure. Also included are revised stories from Fitzgerald's older books now out of print.

In Chapter 2, "Big City Crime in Small Town Newfoundland," the incredible story of a crime near Little Catalina where the outrageous sexual assault and murder of a woman became even more outrageous by the twists and incredible turns that took place during the police investigation and trial that followed is told.

"The Hunting Knife" is another story of rage and brutality and takes place on Regatta Day 1968 where the soon-to-be-killer wins a hunting knife. That evening he uses his prize to viciously kill the girl he had hoped to marry. This story is revised from *Where Angels Fear to Tread*. His attack on his victim was perhaps even more ferocious than that of the killer in "The Bus Ride."

Two of the most mesmerizing stories of Newfoundland's criminal history are contained in Chapter 4, "The Tong Murders." This chapter brings together the spellbinding stories of two Chinese men, tried less than twenty years apart on charges of murder within the small St. John's Chinese community. The first tale weaves slowly through the day in St. John's in 1922 when a Chinese laundry worker killed three of his fellow countrymen, then attempted to kill a fourth. The second story is the dramatic feature describing what was called a "ceremonial killing" inside a Chinese café in the west end of St. John's. In one case, the accused is hanged in the other he is set free and leaves Newfoundland. Both stories are revised from *Ten Steps to the Gallows*.

Women did not escape the services of the hangman in oldtime Newfoundland. In Chapter 6, "Four Women, Three Hangings" records the stories of four women sentenced to be hanged, however, one was shown mercy and was saved the walk to the gallows. Many people today feel that an injustice was carried out in the hanging of one of these ladies, Catherine Snow. Read it and judge for yourself! This chapter is based on stories published in *Ten Steps to the Gallows*.

In the area of adventure, Fitzgerald has selected several of the most riveting and gripping stories from Newfoundland's long historic past. In Chapter 11, "A Glimpse of Hell", the late Jack Ford describes Nagasaki on the day when he stepped away from his work station in a Japanese shipbuilding factory for a drink of green tea and an atomic bomb was dropped on the city. He was likely one of the few people in the city that day who got a glimpse of the bomb-carrying plane seconds before the bomb was released. This is taken from *The Jack Ford Story*, the biography of the Newfoundlander in Nagasaki when the Atomic Bomb was dropped in 1945. Other exciting chapters include "The Solving of Two Criminal Mysteries", "Sixty-five Trapped Inside Inferno", "Horrid Gulch", and a grisly account of a murder and execution by guillotine that took place on neighbouring St. Pierre. The powerful story of the deadly storm that struck St. John's in 1959 is revised from *Newfoundland Disasters*, and includes stories of other catastrophic weather events.

Future volumes of *The Treasury of Newfoundland Stories* will include tales from the strange and bizarre, sea adventures, oddities, and more crime. The set will give readers a personal archive of the best and most memorable stories from Newfoundland's history.

Chapter 1: The Bus Ride

When the remarkably attractive, sandy-haired and brown-eyed Joan Ash boarded the bus at Carbonear to return to St. John's on the evening of March 20, 1960, she had no idea that she would be dead in less than two hours, brutally murdered by a fellow passenger. Although Joan knew the passenger well and had been threatened by him on several occasions, she had not taken him seriously. Now, as the wheels of the bus rolled along the Conception Bay Highway, she was living out the last minutes of her life, which were slipping away like the sands of an hourglass.

Nineteen-year-old Joan Ash was employed by the Dietary Department of the General Hospital on Quidi Vidi Road, in the east end of St. John's. While in the city she boarded at the hospital residence adjacent to the hospital. She had gone to visit her parents in Carbonear that weekend, accompanied by her close friend and co-worker, eighteen-year-old Vivian Chard of Bonavista. As the bus pulled away to begin its journey, the killer was not yet on board.

During the previous two weeks, Donald Stone's secret passionate obsession with Joan Ash had begun to surface and he began making threats to kill her. She told her parents about him and his threats during the weekend visit, but gave no indication that she felt Stone was serious or even capable of harming her.

Stone was twenty-eight years old and Joan liked him well enough to have dated him frequently over the previous seven months. While his infatuation with her was growing and Joan was beginning to like him, she heard some alarming rumours that led her to break off their relationship. Friends who knew him told her, "Donald was oversexed."

Stone was broken-hearted by her decision and strongly pleaded with her to reconsider. When she refused, he made his first of several threats to kill her if she left him.

Donald Stone was originally from Bryant's Cove, a small community near Harbour Grace, but was boarding at a home on Carter's Hill, which coincidentally was next door to the Chinese Laundry where a triple murder had taken place in 1922. Donald had spent some time as a patient at the Waterford Hospital and moved to Carter's Hill when he was released. Donald and Joan first met in Carbonear seven months earlier.

A few minutes after departing from Carbonear, the bus pulled into a stop at Harbour Grace to take on more passengers. Among those stepping aboard the bus was Donald Stone, wearing a dark car coat with white markings, black pants, black zip gaiters and brown shoes. Joan was surprised but not at all afraid of him. He made eye contact with her just as he took a seat a couple of places in front of her but in the opposite aisle. There was no exchange of greetings between the two or any acknowledgement that they knew each other.

Joan's reason for ending her brief relationship with Donald was reinforced by his behaviour during the bus ride. While stopped for a break at Fury's in Holyrood, he followed Joan off the bus and into the store. Joan totally ignored him, and he did not make any effort to engage her in conversation.

As the bus rolled out over the highway heading towards St. John's, Joan chatted with Vivian, mostly about Joan's new boyfriend. Donald Stone listened intently to the conversation, anger slowly building up inside him. By the time the bus reached St. John's, his rage was ready to burst. Donald Stone was like a time bomb ready to explode. Joan had no idea that the man she recently dated had serious mental health issues.

Joan Ash may not have realized how serious Stone was about their relationship. Who knows? Perhaps if she had not told him how she felt, the tragedy awaiting her at the end of her return bus ride might never have happened. Events may have taken a different twist. But that was not to be.

If Joan was going to Carbonear that weekend, Donald Stone was also going with the hope of running into her. Stone's obsession with Joan had convinced him that he could win back her affections, however, for Joan the relationship was definitely over.

In the two weeks leading up to that fateful night, he had seen Joan every night. He explained later, "… I did not take her home. I saw her on Saturday at the hospital and she told me then she was going home for the weekend on the six o'clock bus."

He told police that when Joan told him of her plans he went to his boarding house and, after having supper, rushed to catch the six o'clock bus. He was going to his home in Bryant's Cove. Although he sought her out next day (March 19th) at Carbonear, he was unsuccessful.

When the time came to return to St. John's, Sunday evening March 20th, he caught the 7:00 p.m. bus at Harbour Grace. Vivian Chard told police:

> When Stone got on the bus he sat in the middle
> of the bus. He had no conversation with us. He moved
> later to the back seat opposite where we were sitting. I
> was on the inside seat and Joan on the outside.

Stone then did something that caught their attention   he pulled down the zipper of his pants and exposed himself. Vivian told police, "Sometimes he would look in our direction but he said nothing." The comments by Joan that followed must have sparked rage in Stone. According to Vivian, "Joan spoke loudly enough for Donald Stone to hear. I think she wanted him to hear. She talked about her new boyfriend." During this incident, Joan ignored Stone and opened a package of cookies and candy given to her by her mother before she left home.

Later, at police headquarters, Stone cooperated with investigators. He admitted that he had made a series threats against Ash. He stated:

> I have threatened Joan three or four times previous to this that if I didn't get her nobody would. I threatened her because she was going out with other fellows. Each time I told her she shrugged it off and said she wasn't afraid of my threats.

Joan Ash never considered Stone as being her boyfriend. He was nothing more to her than a friend. When Stone appeared to be taking the friendship far more seriously she started to back away from him.

The bus stopped on Plymouth Road, within range of the home where eighteen years before another young girl was bludgeoned to death by her boyfriend.[1] The boyfriend, who was convicted of the crime, became the last man to be hanged in Newfoundland. When Joan and Vivian stepped off the bus, Anne Hall, also an employee at the hospital, joined the girls in walking down Plymouth Road. Before they neared the end of the road, the first sign that danger was imminent emerged. It was also the first time Joan and Vivian felt fear. The fury growing inside Stone was ready to erupt.

---

[1] See *Ten Steps to The Gallows*, Jack Fitzgerald, (Creative Publishers) regarding the murder of Josephine O'Brine.

Perhaps the three girls were off guard because the trip had ended and they were within a short walking distance from their residence. But Ann Hall was just a little behind her two friends, close enough to participate in a three-way conversation, yet far enough to get a glimpse of Stone, whose behaviour alarmed her. He looked focused and angry. Ann felt he was following them. She shivered in fear. Stone's pace quickened. He was almost running.

Anne described the scene:

> He caught up to me, passed me and then caught up to Joan and grabbed her by the throat. She fell on the ground. He had hold of her throat. Vivian had said he was going to kill Joan and that he had threatened her. I screamed, 'Come on, he might kill us too!' We ran.

As the two frightened girls fled the scene, Vivian saw Stone knock her friend to the ground and drag her towards a nearby building. She was horror-struck by the brutality of the scene that was just starting. She recalled, "Stone had her on the ground and was choking her. I heard her call my name 'Vivian! Vivian!' There were no people around to offer help." For a brief moment, Vivian had thought about going to Joan's aid, but lost her nerve after recalling that Joan told her that Stone likely had a gun.

The crime scene on Plymouth Road was about a five-minute walk from the Orthopaedic Hospital, adjacent to the old General Hospital. Mrs. Mullett, the housekeeper, noticing the emotional state of the two employees as they entered the residence, realized that something terrible had happened. She responded immediately to their pleas for her to call the police.

After boarding the bus, the last couple of hours remaining of Joan's life were now reduced to minutes as her two friends rushed to get help for her. Meanwhile, back on Plymouth

Road, life or death for Joan Ash was literally in the hands of the passenger whom she had not taken seriously enough. By this time, his twisted mind was out of control and the rage inside him was venting, unrestrained. The spirited Joan Ash was anything but a submissive target.

After knocking her to the ground, Donald tried hard to strangle her, but Joan fought back. Outmatched in height, weight and strength, Joan struggled to resist him. Her brave efforts were rapidly draining her energy, and infuriating her attacker who had already decided that if he could not have her, no one would. Throughout the attack she showed no fear, repeatedly and defiantly shouting at him with contempt, "God damn you, Stone!"

The struggle was tiring. Donald Stone interrupted his attack just long enough to regain his strength. Now in a standing position, he changed his mode of attack from strangling to bludgeoning. He kicked Joan in the head over and over, again and again, so by the time he was finished only the bone at the base of her skull had remained unbroken. Her once beautiful face was now totally disfigured. There was no fight left in Joan and she slipped into unconsciousness.

Despite her unconsciousness, her attacker refused to stop his assault. He continued until he believed she had drawn her last breath. While he stood over her body at the end of the attack, a passing car pulled in alongside him. One of the three men in the car asked if there was a problem. "I killed my girlfriend, go call the police!" he answered. About five minutes later, after calming down, he walked to the corner of the building to urinate. Before he could finish, the three men were back with the police.

Investigator Donald Randell described the bloodied scene:

> We walked up to the girl. She was lying on her back, her feet towards the street and her head towards

the Department of Health building. I noticed that her face was badly bruised and battered, and the snow around her head and shoulders was saturated with what appeared to be blood. From the mark[s] on the girl's face, I felt sure that she must have been hit with a hard instrument.

The Criminal Investigation Department's Sergeant Vince Noonan described what he had witnessed, "I shone my flashlight on the girl's face and noticed it had been battered and bruised. The two eyes were closed and her tongue partially showed through her lips." Up to this time, it was assumed the girl was dead. But suddenly there was a sign of life that surprised Noonan and Randell. A slight vapour was rising from the victim's head. Noonan rushed a call for an ambulance but ran into an obstacle that may have hastened Joan Ash's death. Regrettably, the two on duty ambulances were out on calls, and Joan Ash, who fought bravely to survive the attack, slipped into a coma and died.

By this time Sergeant Ches Noftall had arrived at the scene in a police van. He took a blanket from the van and gently covered the victim's body. He was assisted by another police officer in lifting the corpse into the back of the van. From there she was delivered to the General Hospital morgue for an autopsy.

While this was happening, Stone, who had been crouched on the ground, addressed Constable Ralph Mercer, one of the policemen just arriving at the site, and said, "Here I am, she is my girlfriend. I think I've killed her."

Mercer escorted him to the police car where Constables Clarence Hollett and Kevin Hayward were waiting. The suspect was searched for a weapon before entering. Hayward asked Stone how he felt. Stone, who was crying, answered, "Not very well after that." He made it obvious to police that he was prepared to admit to the crime. He volunteered that he had been a patient at the Waterford Hospital and had threatened to kill Ash several times because she was going out with other men.

News of the crime unfolding over on Plymouth Road spread around the east end by word of mouth and brought hundreds to the area. This created a traffic problem for police. Constable Fred Wicks stepped in to take over traffic control. Police officers were arriving and leaving. District Inspector March joined Sergeant Noonan in conducting a close investigation of the murder scene. When that task was completed, Noonan assigned Wicks to cover the blood with snow. By this time crowds on foot were jostling to get as close to the scene as possible.

At this point Sergeant Noonan was ready to arrest Stone. He had just returned to the murder scene after seeking out a nearby telephone to call for an ambulance. While Randell sought out witnesses from among the gathering crowd, Noonan went to the police car where he gave the police caution to Donald Stone and placed him under arrest.

He described his prisoner's reaction: "Stone showed no sign of emotion and there was no further conversation in the patrol car at that time. At the police station he agreed to give a written statement." Randell provided him with pen and paper and he wrote without hesitation.

When he felt that all he had to say was on paper, Stone opened his hands and, while stretching his fingers, calmly commented, "My hands are stiff." He showed no sign of being distressed by the barbarous act he had just committed.

Constable Randell witnessed the statement, and then noticed that there were stains of blood spattered over the prisoner's pants and overshoes. When Randell asked him to show his hands, he said, "There is nothing on them, I was wearing gloves."

Just four hours after boarding the bus at Carbonear the battered body of Joan Ash was lying on a slab at the morgue inside the old General Hospital. She was being examined by Dr. John Butler, a thirty-one-year old graduate of the Royal College of Surgeons in Dublin. The signs that a vicious and brutal attack had been inflicted on the victim were visible all over her body. The long beautiful hair that made her so attractive was now blood soaked and matted. When Dr. Butler completed his preliminary observations of the victim, Dr. Joseph Edward Josephson, government pathologist, stepped in and proceeded with the official autopsy.

One of the unpleasant duties of an investigating police officer involved in a homicide investigation is to be present at the autopsy to assure that all evidence is turned over to the police. This particular autopsy revealed one of the most brutal killings in this province's criminal history. It was a gruesome experience for the seasoned investigator Sergeant Noonan. Later, he recalled:

> During the autopsy Dr. Josephson passed me a part of a dental plate with two full teeth and part of two others which I had seen him take from the vocal chords. There was also a small part of a dental plate and a part of a tooth which I had seen him take from some part of the stomach.

Dr. Josephson recorded in his findings:

> The face was flattened and distorted and the nose was crushed. The eyeballs receded behind closed, puffy and blackened eye lids. There was considerable bleeding from the nose and the mouth. The skin of the face showed numerous short and long scuffed or scraped

abrasions extending in many directions. Multiple blue contusions of varying sizes were present on different parts of the face and forehead and several short bleeding cuts were situated across the nose.

He also observed an oval superficial blue scuff mark on her neck, which he pointed out could have been caused by pressure. In addition, the autopsy confirmed more unimaginable brutality inflicted on the ill-fated young woman. Dr. Josephson explained:

> Within the mouth there were many sandy gravel particles and several larger black stony gravel fragments. False teeth were found in the throat over the vocal chords and blocking the windpipe. More gravel and a tooth were found deep in the windpipe. The aspirated tooth and the many gravel fragments found in the windpipe and bronchial tubes indicated a condition of terminal suffocation superimposed upon shock from the multiple facial and head injuries.

Commenting on the gravel fragments inside the victim's mouth and throat, Josephson wrote, "These could only have been introduced by force, such as being kicked in the mouth. The face marks could be consistent with a kick from a gaiter." Dr. Josephson reported that the cause of death was, "Multiple severe injuries to the face and head due to aspirated gravel and broken upper denture."

The murder of Joan Ash remains as one of the most inhumane and savagely inflicted killings in Newfoundland history.

The preliminary hearing to determine if there was sufficient evidence to commit Stone to stand trial for murder was held on April 21, 1960. Stone, tall with dark hair and wearing a blue striped shirt and dark pants, was visibly nervous when Judge

Mulcahey read the charge against him. Following presentation of the evidence, the judge asked him if he had anything to say. "I have no evidence to give and no witnesses to call, your honour," Stone replied in a quivering voice.

The court then committed Donald Stone to stand trial on the charge of murder at the criminal sessions of the Supreme Court of Newfoundland. The trial was very short.

At the trial, the Crown introduced the statement given to police by the accused suggesting he suffered from mental illness. In it, he stated, "I feel sick all the time and have no control over my feelings. I have been in the mental hospital twice. The first time it was for three months and the second time it was for two months."

A brief mention was made of the two girls with Joan the night of the murder. He stated, "The other two girls with Joan ran when I knocked Joan down. I did not say anything to them or touch them."

Judge Robert Furlong was the presiding judge at the trial. H.P. Carter acted as Crown prosecutor and James Higgins, QC, represented Stone. Jimmy Higgins had an effective record as a criminal defence lawyer. He had defended eighteen clients facing first degree murder charges and lost none.

In addition to Stone's confession and pictures of the victim and the murder scene, the Crown called sixteen witnesses to testify.

The trail left Higgins' record unblemished. On June 1, 1960, the jury returned the verdict of not guilty by reason of insanity. As Donald Stone was escorted from the courtroom, Sergeant Noonan reflected on a comment Stone made on the night of his arrest. "I would rather die than be sent to the Waterford Hospital."

This story took on a different twist in the years that followed. Just months after Donald Stone's admission to the

Waterford, he suffered a heart attack and died. As the years passed, the story of the man who was so devastated after killing the love of his life that he died of a broken heart emerged. Memory of the murder's brutality faded and in its place grew the tale of a love story with a tragic ending.

Notes

The meaning of the terms: "not guilty by reason of insanity," and the defence of "temporary insanity due to use of drugs or alcohol" are often misunderstood among the general public.

To obtain a clear, definitive explanation of the above terms, many years ago I interviewed Dr. Douglas Paulse, the Director of Forensic Psychiatry and consultant to the police and correction services in the province of Newfoundland and Labrador, at the Waterford Hospital regarding the Donald Stone trial. Dr. Paulse referred to *Section 16 of the Criminal Code of Canada* to provide the definition of insanity. He explained insanity is present if, "… a person is suffering from a disease of the mind which renders it impossible for him or her to appreciate the nature and quality of the act or to know it is wrong, or if he is motivated by a specific delusion which if, in fact, were true would have justified his action, or if natural imbecility makes it impossible for him or her to appreciate the nature and quality of the act."

Persons accused of committing a serious crime such as murder usually undergo a psychiatric evaluation to determine if that person is fit to stand trial. Dr. Paulse explained that being declared unfit to stand trial means, "The defendant is not able to instruct counsel, understand the proceedings or show an awareness of what his situation is in the court hearing, nor is he capable of understanding the charges laid against him."

According to Paulse, the popularly held belief that temporary insanity due to use of drugs or alcohol as a legal defence is incorrect. He debunked this theory by explaining that insanity, as defined by the law, is a disease of the mind, not influenced by alcohol or drugs.

Chapter 2: Big City Crime in Small Town Newfoundland

The repulsive, macabre slaying of forty-nine-year-old Mona Johnson in Little Catalina shocked her neighbours and friends. The trial of her killer absolutely amazed them. Newfoundlanders have rarely witnessed a crime as ghastly and despicable as the killing of Mona Johnson. Our courts have rarely seen such a bizarre murder trial as the one that followed. Small-town Newfoundland is not the place where one would expect to see big city crimes, especially in the 1970s.

When a routine house fire in the middle of the night led to the discovery of the brutal murder of a middle age woman, police were shocked and immediately set out to track down the killer or killers.

This peculiar justice story began during the early morning hours of February 4, 1976. Two employees of the Department of Transportation and Communication, Clarence Murphy and Wallace Trask, both of Elliston, Trinity Bay, were in the vicinity of Mona Johnson's home at about 2:00 a.m. Mona lived alone in a small bungalow on a side road in Little Catalina. Her nearest neighbour was 300 feet down the road.

Murphy and Trask were startled by a sudden burst of flames venting through the back area of the house. They pulled into the driveway of Mona's neighbour, where they were able to call for emergency help. Within fifteen minutes the community's volunteer fire department, led by Chief Ancel Johnson, was at the scene battling the flames. The firemen's main concern upon arriving at the site was to locate and rescue the occupant. Everyone in the community knew Mona lived there alone. While the firemen poured water onto the flames and searched for Mona, neighbours gathered outside. "Good Lord, poor Mona!" cried one lady. "Maybe she's gone out for the night!" exclaimed another. It was a small community and Chief Johnson was aware that Mona often went on overnight trips to visit family members who lived nearby.

Firefighters battled the blaze until they brought it under control at 4:30 a.m. By 6:30 a.m. they were able to search the ruins and found a body lying face down on the bedroom floor.

Constable Edward Dunn, the first police officer on the scene, along with Chief Johnson turned over the body and immediately recognized the victim as Mona Johnson. It did not take long for them to encounter some alarming evidence. What they witnessed turned the incident into an even greater mystery. It was obvious from observing the body that foul play was involved. As they examined the scene it became even more bizarre.

What seemed to be plastic coated wire was tied around the wrists and throat of the victim. She was partially naked and covered in debris. Constable Dunn noted that her arms were spread out from her body, with the wire used to tie her right wrist to her throat. The area was immediately sealed off and a search of the ruins was conducted to gather evidence. The routine investigation of a fire site had abruptly changed into a murder investigation, which exposed even more bizarre revelations.

The RCMP investigators began probing into Mona Johnson's life. They learned that after her divorce she had lived for a short time with relatives in Little Catalina. Police went to the home of these relatives to gather background information on the victim. They had no idea when they approached Mrs. Anne Chaulk that a person in her house would soon set them on the right path towards arresting Mona Johnson's killer. Even seasoned police officers were scratching their heads over the twists and surprises in the case that followed.

While police discussed Mona Johnson with Anne Chaulk, her thirty-one-year-old grandson, Andrew Scott Reid, was in an upstairs room listening attentively to every word being said. Without any invitation to participate in the interview, Reid came down from his room and informed police he had some information that they might find important. The police were interested.

He told Corporal Green that he had been in the vicinity of Mona's home at about 1:00 a.m. that morning, just an hour before the fire started. He claimed he saw a dark-coloured car, which he had not seen before, parked in her driveway. Green recorded the information and left the Chaulk's home to question the other witnesses. However, Reid's tip became more significant as the day progressed.

When several witnesses contradicted Andrew Reid's story, Corporal Green became suspicious. He returned to Chaulk's to clarify his concerns and partway through the questioning invited Reid to accompany him to RCMP headquarters in Bonavista for further questioning. Reid expressed concern over what people in the community might think if they saw him with the police but agreed to the invitation.

An indication of the story that was about to unfold came when Reid commented, "I doubt if people are going to believe what I have to say."

"I could arrange for you to take a polygraph," Green suggested.

"That's a good idea," Reid answered.

By 12:20 p.m. that day Andrew Scott Reid was at the RCMP office in Bonavista. He gave police two statements, which were similar to the verbal statement he gave earlier that day at his grandmother's home.

Reid told police that the night before he was in a car drinking with friends. "We bought a dozen beer and then sat in the parked car and drank and sang songs. I had three or four beers before the group broke up and went home. They dropped me off near Mona's house at about 1:00 a.m.," he said.

Reid told police that he considered going in to visit his cousin (Mona) but after seeing a dark blue car in the driveway decided against it. Instead he walked home and went to bed.

During the interrogation, Staff Sergeant Vince O'Donnell, in charge of the investigation, arrived at the police office. He instructed Corporal Green to ask Reid about the clothes he wore on the night of the fire and to explain the scratch on his nose. When confronted with this line of questioning, Reid's mood changed and he asked to use the telephone.

After the call, he agreed to give the sergeant a written statement. This statement was taken at 9:15 a.m., February 6th. Reid told police that he was walking home past Mona's during the early morning on February 4th. He had been dropped off near there in a car by the friends he had been drinking with earlier that night.

Reid said it was a cold night and he decided he would drop in to visit his cousin, Mona Johnson. Mona answered the knock on the door and Reid claimed he asked her if he could come inside because it was cold out. She invited him inside. According to Reid, once in the house, he saw Rose, a girl he had at one time been engaged to, holding his son in her arms. Reid described Rose as a girl he met in Toronto about five years earlier. He explained, "We were engaged. She broke it off. It was the worst thing that ever happened to me."

Reid told police, "I asked her if she still loved me?" Instead of replying to the question, Reid claimed she held a plastic shoe horn in her hand and shoved it down the child's throat answering, "This is how much I love you."

In anger, Reid responded by seizing a telephone cord and strangling her with it. He then set fire to the bed, gathered his blood-stained clothes, and left the house. He tossed the stained clothing into an outdoor toilet. As the investigation unfolded, evidence gathered eliminated any speculation by investigators that Reid's visual impairment, only having only ten percent vision, might have caused him to have mistaken Mona for Rose.

The police again suggested to Reid that he take the lie detector test and he agreed. O'Donnell put the wheels in motion immediately to arrange a polygraph test for the suspect. Accommodations were arranged at the Albatross Hotel, Gander, and Sergeant John Neil, a polygraph expert from Halifax, was flown there to administer the test. Two officers from the General Investigating Service of the RCMP, Corporal Ed McHugh and Sergeant Larry Power, were assigned to take the suspect to Gander. Corporal John Green and Constable Fred Graham were assigned to guard the prisoner in Gander.

Andrew Reid was a musician and played with a local band in Little Catalina. During the trip to Gander on February 6th, Reid was calm and in a casual mood. His concern appeared not to be with the murder investigation but with a dance in Little Catalina that night. He expressed concern to the police officers over the possibility of being late for the dance. When Corporal McHugh asked him how he got the scratch on his nose he replied, "I got that playing with my dog."

The police and suspect arrived at the Albatross at 5:30 p.m. They waited in the lobby for the arrival of the polygraph expert who showed up shortly after 6:00 p.m. When Sergeant Neil went into a room to set up the polygraph machine Reid's casual mood changed. He began to display nervousness. Reid told McHugh, "If they ask me certain questions I'm not going to answer them." McHugh asked, "What type of questions?" Reid answered, "For instance, if they say: 'Did you kill or murder Mona?' I'm not going to answer."

Corporal McHugh noted the change in Reid's behaviour. He commented, "He was not casual anymore. He was showing signs of worry and concern. From his questions and appearance I formed the opinion Reid was responsible for Mrs. Johnson's death."

McHugh was concerned that the agitated mood of the suspect might adversely affect the polygraph test. He asked Sergeant Power, "... to rush things because of the change in the accused." From past experience he had learned that people taking the polygraph should be as calm as possible.

Sergeant Power told McHugh that police had found a blood-stained parka and shirt in an outhouse near Reid's home and they suspected that both belonged to Andrew Scott Reid. Power explained the blood stains were similar to the blood of Mona Johnson.

Police moved quickly to administer the polygraph test. Corporal McHugh took Reid to Sergeant Neil's room shortly after 6:00 p.m. and the testing went on until 9:15 p.m. At that time Sergeant Neil emerged from the room to inform McHugh that Reid had confessed to the crime and wanted to speak with him. McHugh described the mood of the accused at that time: "He was more upset than he had been before and from his appearance it was plain to see he had been crying."

His first words to McHugh were, "You knew it all the time, but I couldn't tell you." Corporal McHugh noted that the accused was an intelligent person. He asked Reid if he knew he would now be charged with murder. Reid sobbed and answered, "Yes." The investigator then read to the accused the police caution and placed him under arrest.

McHugh asked Reid what he did with the clothes he wore the night of the murder. He answered, "I put the parka and shirt down an old toilet." The officer then asked if Reid had sex with Mona. Reid was irritated over the question and replied, "No! No! I never touched her! I never touched her!"

Reid was held in custody in Gander overnight and returned to Bonavista the next morning. During the ride to Bonavista, McHugh asked Reid to point out where he had hidden the parka and shirt. He directed the police to an outhouse near his grandmother's house in Little Catalina. Reid was not aware that police had already recovered the clothing.

While in Little Catalina, Reid lay down on the back seat to avoid being seen by anyone in the community. He told the police he did not want to be seen and remarked, "I thought and I thought but I can't figure out why I did it."

During the drive to Bonavista, Reid began discussing what happened that night. He said, "I had to get rid of her. I took the cord off the telephone. I cut it with a knife. I hit her. There was blood all over the place. There was blood on my clothes. I knew I had to get rid of her. When I tied her up I didn't think she was dead but she didn't move. I got the wire and tied it around her neck to make sure she was dead."

As sort of an afterthought Reid commented, "Would you believe I don't know how I got the scratch on my nose? I had to make up the story that the dog did it. I had to tell you something."

On February 7th, in a Bonavista court, Andrew Scott Reid was charged with non-capital murder in connection with the death of Mona Johnson. He was remanded to the Hospital for Mental and Nervous Diseases in St. John's for a psychological examination to determine if he was fit to stand trial.

Following a ten-day assessment Reid was brought to Magistrate's Court in St. John's. Magistrate Hugh O'Neill listened attentively to doctors as they explained the results of the assessment. He then ruled that the accused was fit to stand trial. A preliminary hearing was scheduled for March 25th in Bonavista.

Robert Wells appeared in court on behalf of Reid and Barry Hill represented the Crown.

St. John's lawyer, Randy Earle, filled in for Robert Wells at the preliminary hearing. At the conclusion of the hearing the judge set June 2nd as the date for the accused to be arraigned in Supreme Court. At the arraignment Reid pleaded not guilty and Justice Arthur Mifflin set the trial date for June 14th, two weeks later.

By the trial date, Reid gave the appearance of being calm and in control. The twenty-six-year-old, blond-haired fish plant worker sat attentively in the prisoner's box flanked by two RCMP officers. He wore a sports coat, checked shirt and dark slacks. Occasionally he jotted down notes and sometimes glanced at his wife, Viola, who sat among the spectators.

The Crown prosecutor, Barry Hill, told the court he would present evidence showing that Andrew Scott Reid had gagged, bound, sexually assaulted and strangled Mona Johnson with a telephone wire. Mr. Hill said the accused then set the house on fire in a desperate attempt to destroy the evidence. He said he would call expert witnesses to present evidence connecting the accused to the crime.

The defence attempted to stop the Crown from introducing statements given by the accused to police as evidence. Reid had given five statements. Three of these were written statements and two were given orally. These statements said that, when he strangled Mona Johnson, Reid believed he was killing a former girlfriend. A Voir Dire, which lasted five days, determined that all statements given to police by the accused were admissible. The Crown had lined up thirty-seven witnesses.

Meanwhile the defence would rest its case on one witness, the accused himself, Andrew Scott Reid. Reid would deny killing Mona Johnson and startle the court with a bizarre account of what happened.

Sixteen-year-old Maxwell Rumbolt, who gave evidence for the Crown at the preliminary hearing, accidentally drowned before the trial date. His testimony was therefore read into court records by Mr. Hill. The Crown was developing its story as to circumstances surrounding the death of the victim and suggested the fire had started in the bedroom where the body was discovered.

Maxwell Rumbolt lived down the road from Ms. Johnson. He was up late on February 4th watching the Late Show on television. A sudden light piercing the darkness outside caught his attention. Rumbolt went to the window and identified the source of the light as flames coming from the house of Mona Johnson. He testified that these flames were coming from the rear of the Johnson house, where the victim's bedroom was later located.

Another Crown witness indicated that the victim had been receiving harassing telephone calls. Fred Rumbolt, a neighbour who often dated Mona Johnson, testified that he could not make contact with Ms. Johnson on February 3rd. He said that at 10:00 a.m. he talked with her by phone and she told him she had the flu and was not feeling well. Later that day he decided to pay a visit to Ms. Johnson. He went to her door at 5:30 p.m. and knocked, unsuccessfully, several times before leaving. He tried to gain entry but discovered the door had been locked from the inside. At 9:30 p.m. he tried again to reach Ms. Johnson by phone. There was no answer.

When cross-examined by Mr. Hill, Rumbolt said it was strange for the door to be locked from the inside. He added that it was also unusual for her not to reply to his telephone call at 9:30 p.m. He concluded that she must have gone out.

Because Mona had been receiving harassing telephone calls, she and Fred used a special code to phone each other. Rumbolt explained to the court that when calling her he would let the phone ring once and then hang up. Mona would return his call. Mr. Rumbolt testified that he was up late that night waiting for his son's return from Bonavista. He said at 3:00 a.m. he noticed flames coming from Mona's house.

His testimony was followed by evidence supplied by Dr. Peter Markesteyn, a forensic pathologist from the General Hospital, St. John's. Spectators leaned forward to hear the gruesome details revealed in his autopsy report.

This report disclosed that Mona Johnson had been badly beaten about the face and strangled with a plastic-covered telephone wire. Dr. Markesteyn observed that the body had been exposed to fire and smoke and there was plastic coated wire around the wrist, neck and part of the mouth. He believed that two cords were used around the victim's throat.

Some traces of textile found on the wire in the mouth showed that a gag had been applied to the victim's mouth. The witness concluded that death was caused by strangulation rather than fire because there was no soot in the woman's air passages, therefore, no evidence she was breathing while the fire was in progress.

When cross-examined by Mr. Hill, Dr. Markesteyn explained that it is extremely rare for a person to suffocate from this unless the tongue was pushed into the back of the throat. He said Ms. Johnson's tongue was protruding through her teeth and he did not believe the gag had caused her death.

Commenting on evidence that the victim was bleeding from the neck the witness explained, "This was the result of a force being applied and sustained to her neck. I reached the conclusion that the application of the wire around her neck caused strangulation."

The doctor could not say for certain if a hideous head injury had been caused before or after the death. He noted:

There was a large hole in the victim's scull and her

brain was visible. I could not reach a conclusion based on the x-rays and examinations on whether it was caused by something that occurred before the death. It is not uncommon for such an injury to be caused by the extreme heat of a fire. The x-rays showed there were no other bones broken.

The pathologist told the court that Mona Johnson had been raped before death. He stated that, "... sexual intercourse did take place prior to death. Not by mutual consent." He explained that the elastic material found on the victim's legs was apparently her underclothing and it had been there before the fire began. He concluded his testimony stating that he had taken specimens from the victim's vaginal area and blood samples which were forwarded to the RCMP crime lab in Sackville, New Brunswick.

Lucy Bishop, an expert with the RCMP crime lab in Sackville, told the court that the blood stains on Andrew Reid's clothing were similar to Mona Johnson's blood. The crime lab had also determined from the victim's blood samples that she had not been drinking alcoholic beverages. There were no traces of alcohol in the victim's body.

Sergeant John Neill, who administered the polygraph test on the accused, testified that during the process, Reid broke down and cried before confessing to strangling Mona Johnson and setting fire to her house. He told the court that Reid had volunteered to take the polygraph. The witness said that he explained to Reid how the polygraph worked and reminded him that he did not have to take it. Reid said he wanted to take it and Sergeant Neill read him the police caution before beginning the test.

Neill described Reid's mood while being tested. He said, "Reid appeared rational but concerned. He was a cunning individual because he thought out the answers to all his questions."

During the session, Reid said that he had not slept since the death of Mona Johnson. When the conversation touched on his relationship with a former girlfriend he had met five years previously in Toronto, Reid became upset. He said, "We were engaged but she broke it off."

The accused then went on to give a bizarre account of a recurring dream he was having. He claimed he had dreams of his son choking on a piece of plastic shoehorn that someone was putting down his throat.

The police officer noted a rapid change in Reid's mood when he began recounting the story he told police earlier about seeing a dark car in Mona's driveway. Sergeant Neill explained, "I formed the impression that he committed the crime from his gestures. He was crouched in his chair in a bent over fetal position, grasping both of his arms. He had his feet underneath his chair in a defensive position. There were outward signs of nervousness and he was stammering."

Reid interrupted his story to inform Neill that his wife Viola was in hospital in St. John's awaiting an operation. Neill allowed him to make a telephone call to her. He testified:

> Reid was visibly shaken when he spoke to her and said, 'stick with me, I love you. Do you love me? I'm here with the police about Mona.' He began crying loudly and I took the telephone. A woman was hysterical and crying aloud. I told her she would be contacted as to the results of the investigation and he then hung up the telephone.

The witness continued. He said that after a few minutes Reid settled down and the polygraph testing was resumed. Neill picked up a pen and drew a circle on a piece of paper. He showed the circle to Reid and commented, "You have told me part of the story, but it has not gone the full circle."

Neill began questioning Reid about his relationship with Rose. At this point, according to the witness, the accused became upset and showed signs of agitation. When Sergeant Neill suggested that Reid believed he was seeing Rose and not Mona Johnson, Reid exploded. He began crying and shouting, "It was Rose! It was Rose!" Neill described the physical effects of the suggestion on Reid. He said, "Reid's body was shaking and he was stammering and crying aloud at that point."

Reid blurted out, "She was laughing at me! She had my baby in her arms and was jamming a plastic shoehorn down his throat. He was choking. I hit her! I hit her! She fell down and I set fire to the house and ran."

Neill made no comment. He watched the accused's reaction and listened carefully to every word uttered. After a pause in telling his story, Reid looked at the police sergeant and commented, "Oh my God! What's Viola going to think? I don't want to be locked up!" Reid thought for a moment then added, "Rose looked like Mona. I hit her, she fell back."

The police officer sensed the inner torment and anguish building up inside Reid. He grabbed Reid's arm with one hand and with the other squeezed his hand. At this point, Neill stated, "The blood drained from his face and he appeared to lose consciousness for several seconds. When he regained composure, he was sweating profusely from his forehead." Neill encouraged Reid to take a break and rest awhile. He helped the accused to a bed in the room.

Under cross-examination, the defence lawyer asked Sergeant Neill if Reid had mentioned at any time having sex with the victim. Neill replied that he felt if the accused did have sex with the victim he would have found it disgusting because of his wife, and he would not have wanted to talk about it.

The court was distracted at this point by the actions of the accused in the witness box. Reid jumped to his feet and attempted to address Justice Mifflin, "My lord! My lord!" he shouted. But Judge Mifflin sternly interrupted and ordered him to sit down. He told Reid that his lawyer would speak on his behalf. He then called a recess to allow the witness time to settle down.

When the trial resumed a witness who was with Reid on the night of February 3rd testified. Seymour Dalton told the court they were together drinking and shared three dozen beer with two other friends. After that, he said, they dropped Reid off on a road near the home of Mona Johnson. It was 12:40 a.m. He stated, "Andrew Reid was perfectly all right when dropped off." The prosecution called several witnesses who testified that they were in the area that night and did not see any car at Mona Johnson's.

A key piece of evidence came from Henrietta Reid, who lived near Andrew Reid. She told the court that she saw the accused sometime after 4:40 a.m. on February 4th: "I looked out my window and saw Andrew Reid running from his house with something in his left hand. He went into an outhouse."

This led police to their recovery of the parka and pants, which Reid had disposed of shortly after the murder. The blood stains found on these items were similar to Mona Johnson's blood type. Forensic experts later found seminal fluid in specimens taken from Ms. Johnson's vagina.

Forensic expert Lucy Bishop told the court that both Andrew Reid and Mona Johnson had rare blood types. She noted that Mona Johnson's blood type is found, "... in only eight percent of the population. Andrew Reid's blood type is found only in seven percent or seven in one hundred (sic)."

When cross-examined by the defence, the witness said that blood types are likely to be similar in small communities. Mrs.

Bishop concluded her testimony by telling the court that, "No traces of alcohol were found in blood samples of the victim."

Another witness from the RCMP crime lab, Doug Shields, gave evidence regarding the wire used to strangle Mona Johnson. Mr. Shields, a chemistry expert, testified that careful analysis of the wire found around the victim's neck was similar to the wire found on a telephone in the Johnson home.

Levi Warren, a linesman with Canadian National Telegraph, told the court that the cord he installed linking the telephone to a connection box on the wall measured five and a half feet in length, the exact length as the wire found tightly wrapped around the victim's neck.

With the prosecution's case concluding, the defence called Andrew Scot Reid to the stand. Reid had completed high school in Little Catalina and then moved to St. John's to take an accounting course at the College of Trades and Technology. He also completed several upgrading courses at the Canadian National School for the Blind in Halifax, Nova Scotia. Reid was visually handicapped due to an impaired optic nerve, which left him with only ten percent of his vision. When Reid stepped into the witness box, sudden silence in the courtroom followed. Journalists at the press bench briskly recorded the accused's account of the events that took place behind closed doors at Mona Johnson's house the night she was mercilessly and brutally slayed.

At first he appeared to be calm and confident while revealing a story which had no resemblance to the statement he had given police. Yet, the more he talked the stranger and more bizarre his evidence became.

He testified that two unknown assailants had overpowered him when he visited Mona Johnson on the night of the murder. Reid claimed that before leaving they demanded his silence with threats to kill his wife and child if he ever told authorities that they killed Mona Johnson and burned her house. This was in contradiction to his statement to the police that he murdered Johnson because he believed she was his ex-fiancé and trying to kill his child. The witness was composed and confident as he delved deeper into his account of the night of the murder:

> I was hanging out with three friends in a parked car the night of the murder. We were drinking beer and singing songs. When we picked up my guitar at my house we downed three quarters of a flask of moonshine. Then we all got into the car and went for a drive to the spot where we stopped to drink the beer.

By 1:15 a.m. they were ready to call it a night. Reid asked his friends to drop him off on the road near Mona Johnson's. He told them he would hitchhike from there to Melrose to stay at his mother-in-law's house because his infant son was there.

Continuing his testimony, Reid explained that the cold winter night caused him to change his mind. After being dropped off he waited awhile, but there were no cars on the road. By then he was feeling the effects of the liquor he had consumed: "I had problems walking, so I decided to drop in at Mona's house to telephone my brother for a drive home." The witness said that the victim was his cousin but he had not seen her in about two years.

He stated that he walked to the back door of the Johnson house and noticed the outside door was ajar. He said:

> I knocked. There was no answer. I walked in. The kitchen was dark. The next thing I knew I was knocked to the floor by someone. I was pinned partially face down and I heard voices saying, 'Hurry up we got to get out of here. We got to get out of the province tonight.'

Reid continued:

> Then a man with dark hair and wearing a brown leather jacket came on the scene. The man rushed into the bedroom while the other man had me pinned to the floor. He returned from the room with something in his hand. He pushed what seemed to be clothing in my face and there was something wet on it. The man holding me said 'hurry light the fire.' When the other man went into the bedroom I saw the flickering light. The man set fire to the bedclothes. When he came out he said, 'let's get out of here.'

The accused then alleged that he was threatened by the assailants. He recalled:

> Before they left, one man grabbed me by the hair and hauled my head back. He told me the best thing for me to do was to 'get out of the house. If you say anything you won't have a wife or kids for long.' The two men then fled through the kitchen door.

Meanwhile, according to Reid, he was trembling with fear and was suffering agonizing pain in his arm. He said he got to his feet and went into the bedroom but the bed and wall were ablaze. He added, "There was a body on the floor but I couldn't tell who it was because it was face down."

He described his effort to help the woman by placing his hands under her and trying to lift her. He claimed that as he did, the woman fell against his chest and he saw blood and something around her neck. "I really got scared," Reid said, "I dropped the body and ran. I just ran until I got home."

When asked under cross-examination why he did not report this to someone immediately, he answered that the killers' threatening words kept coming into his head. Reid explained that when he arrived home he looked into the bathroom mirror and noticed he was covered in blood. He testified, "There was blood on my face, jacket and shirt. I took off the jacket and shirt and I washed the blood off my face."

The accused said he went to bed, but he couldn't sleep. He was restless and tossing and turning. He couldn't get the murder scene off his mind. The bloody clothing tormented him. He got out of bed and set out to hide the blood-stained items where he felt they would not be found.

Reid recalled the day the two police officers came to his house and he had offered to cooperate with them. "I intended to tell them what happened. However, I remembered the warning they gave me and I was scared. That is why I did not mention all this before."

Reid said when the police first suggested that he take a polygraph test he agreed. However, after some careful thought he decided it would be better to refuse it. He finally agreed to the test when he realized that not taking it would make the police even more suspicious of him.

The witness recalled that emotions began building up inside him when the door to the polygraph room closed and he was left alone with Sergeant Neill. Unknown to Neill, the true memories of the night of the killing were tormenting his suspect.

Reid said he became even more agitated when Neill began asking personal questions. He said the story about Rose trying to kill his son originated with the police expert. He told the court he went along with the sergeant's suggestion that he killed Mona because he believed she was Rose, his ex-fiancé.

The witness explained that Neill told him if what he thought happened was true it would be manslaughter not murder. He added that he decided it would be better to go to jail for manslaughter than to have something happen to his son.

By the conclusion of the trial the prosecution had called thirty-seven witnesses while the defence called only one, Andrew Scot Reid.

In his summary to the jury, Robert Wells argued that the Crown had not proven its case. He suggested that the Crown's case was based on the theory that the accused visited Ms. Johnson on February 4th for sex. However, the evidence did not clearly show that the accused had sex with the victim. Mr. Wells stressed that at no time in talking to police did the accused admit to having sex with the victim.

The Crown prosecutor, Barry Hill, felt the evidence spoke strongly for the guilt of Andrew Reid. Hill argued, "It's an insult to the intelligence of everyone here. Never before have you been subjected to such an arrogant story. Andrew Reid went to Mona Johnson's for sex and the sexual portion of the crime was too repulsive for him to admit."

In his address to the twelve all-man jury, Judge Mifflin described the killing of Mona Johnson as, "... a horrible and horrendous crime." He told the jury he did not believe the testimony of Andrew Reid. However, he explained, while it is not unusual for a trial judge to express his opinion on the evidence, "You the jury are in no way bound to abide by my opinion."

Judge Mifflin stated that Reid had tried to extricate himself from the crime by offering to assist the police in their investigation when they came to his home on the morning of February 6th.

The judge described Andrew Reid as, "... a pretty sophisticated individual. At one point he thought he could even beat the polygraph test, which the police had arranged for him to take."

He continued, "Reid was clever enough to know when he was trapped and he seized on the illusion of his ex-girlfriend Rose when it was suggested by police." The judge added, "He still thinks he can deceive you or me today. He's a rather imaginative person. His testimony is too ridiculous to talk about." Judge Mifflin concluded that there was no obligation on the Crown to show what prompts a person to commit an offence.

The jury convened on Friday, June 25th, to consider the evidence and arrive at a verdict. Their work took only one hour and twenty minutes. Alex Miller, foreman of the jury, announced the verdict of guilty as charged. The conviction carried a mandatory life sentence.

Judge Mifflin then advised the jury they could recommend a parole date if they chose. He explained that the convicted man must serve at least ten years before becoming eligible for parole. However, the jury could recommend anywhere between ten and twenty years. The jury chose not to make a recommendation leaving that decision to the court.

The judge expressed his gratitude to the jury for their work and told them, "... it was the only decision you could come to."

Judge Mifflin then asked Reid to stand to be sentenced. Reid was in tears as the judge sentenced him to life in prison. His wife, Viola, also broke into tears and was escorted from the building by friends. She had sat in the courtroom patiently and attentively throughout the nine-day trial. As police officers escorted Reid from the courtroom, he lost consciousness and stumbled. A short while later, he was on his feet and led from the courtroom to begin serving his life sentence.

Chapter 3: The Hunting Knife

In 1968, the delay of the Royal St. John's Regatta from Wednesday, August 7th to Thursday, August 8th, certainly did not dampen the spirits of the city's population, who turned out in droves to witness the event. Stores were closed the town seemed to be emptying in an exodus towards the east end of St. John's. Men, women and children, travelling in cars, buses, cabs, bicycles, and even shanks-mare (feet) were cheerfully heading east.

It was as though a "carnival atmosphere" had suddenly swept the town and why not? It was the 150th Anniversary[1] of the St. John's Regatta a day of celebration like United States' Fourth of July, France's Bastille Day or a traditional Newfoundland Christmas Day.

Among the tens of thousands of fans at Quidi Vidi Lake that day were Gerard Parsons and Audrey Ballett not at all unknown to each other. Although they never chanced to meet at lakeside, before the stroke of midnight Audrey would be lying in a pool of blood with Gerard Parsons standing over her clenching in his hand a knife dripping in blood – the same knife he had won as a prize hours before at the Regatta Wheel of Fortune.

Earlier that day a gleeful Gerard Parsons was enjoying himself at a Wheel of Fortune. He had purchased tickets, one of which bore the number thirty-two. While waiting for the spinning wheel to stop, his eyes fixated on the assortment of prizes on the shelves awaiting the winner's choice. There were dishes, cooking utensils, dolls, plush toys and a hunting knife.

[1] This was not the 150th running of the Regatta but the anniversary of the first rowing competition on St. John's Harbour now recognized as the official starting date of the annual St. John's Regatta.

The spinning wheel slowed to a stop and the ticket hawker shouted, "The lucky number is thirty-two! That's thirty-two! Who got thirty-two?"

Gerard Parsons, waving his ticket in his hand, shouted to make sure he was heard among the din of the crowd, "I got it! Here, I got it!" The hawker did not have to ask the winner to consider which prize he wanted; Parsons had already made that decision while the wheel was still spinning. Pointing to the top shelf, he again shouted, "I'll take the hunting knife!"

A mere coincidence or did the choice reveal something sinister in his nature? Time continued ticking away and both Parsons and his newly acquired piece of lethal property had a destiny to meet.

Gerard and Audrey's Relationship

The relationship between Gerard and Audrey began on Easter Sunday 1965, when a mutual friend set them up on a blind date. They hit it off from the very beginning and their relationship blossomed. He was proud and delighted when Audrey appeared on stage in the locally produced musical *Oliver.* Unfortunately for Audrey, Gerard became obsessed with her. He was even seriously considering marriage but felt he was not financially secure enough to take on the responsibility.

Audrey felt marriage could wait until things improved for them financially. They planned to save enough money for a down-payment on a house. For the present moment her dreams lay elsewhere. After the musical ended she decided to move to Toronto and seek work, intending to continue her relationship with Gerard by mail. He was not expecting her to make such a move so quickly and his best efforts to persuade her against it failed. This sent him into a depression, which drove him to alcohol. Parsons already had problems with alcohol and now it had worsened.

His torment was so severe that he made several suicide attempts, which led to a series of admissions to the psychiatric wards of city hospitals. In 1959 and 1968, he was admitted into the Waterford Hospital where he received treatment for alcohol abuse and depression.

Parsons went through a difficult and demanding emotional period when Audrey moved to Toronto. At the beginning of the summer of 1968 he suffered a series of blackouts including a suicide attempt. He recognized he needed help and voluntarily signed himself into the Waterford Hospital. He was not eating and was losing weight. Parsons was worried after losing forty pounds in a short period of time. For two days he fought his demons, hour after hour, until he felt trapped, and just as he had voluntarily signed himself in for treatment, he now signed himself out. He turned to the bottle to escape his torment. He just did not have the control and self-discipline to overcome his demons.

He felt he was at rock bottom when he began seeing things that were not there. This time when he voluntarily went to sign himself into the Grace Hospital psychiatric unit, two doctors chose instead to sign him in, to ensure he would stay for treatment. When he attempted suicide at the Grace Hospital, he was transferred back to the Waterford Hospital.

He responded well to his treatment there and in a short time showed enough improvement to be released. He was prescribed eight Librium tablets daily to treat his anxiety. Like the previous attempts to help him, drug therapy failed and despite his on-going depression he returned to work with hopes that working would help.

Gerard Parsons was fighting a losing battle with his tortured mind. During this period things worsened. He developed manic depression symptoms, and experienced alternating periods of acute depression and elation. In an effort to help

Parsons, the management at Canadian National switched him to less demanding work.

At his Prince of Wales Street home, a week before the Regatta and his reunion with Audrey Ballett, Parsons decided he could take no more. He grabbed a knife from the kitchen drawer and attempted to cut his wrists. He may have succeeded if not for the intervention of his brother and mother who managed to restrain him.

On the morning of Regatta Day, Parsons was suffering from a hangover from the night before. He was determined not to miss work. He had not eaten in days and passed up having breakfast that morning. He took two Librium and left for work.

Audrey Ballett arrived back in St. John's from Toronto on the night before the Regatta to begin her two-week vacation. She was eagerly looking forward to attending the Regatta with old friends before visiting Gerard Parsons. Audrey had learned of his drinking and stays at the Waterford. She felt he was spending his savings on booze and was having second thoughts about their relationship. She wanted to meet with him face-to-face to set him straight about her feelings and possibly end their relationship.

On the morning of Regatta Day, Audrey telephoned Gerard but he had already left for work. She left a message with Mrs. Parsons to tell him she was back in town. When Gerard arrived home for dinner, he was in his usual depressed mood. That changed instantly when his mother told him, "Audrey called you this morning. She is back in town."

Suddenly, Gerard's mood improved. He became very excited, wanted to know more, and the sadness that hung over him for a year was lifted. He called the number Audrey left and made arrangements to meet with her later in the day. Meeting with Gerard was less important to her than it was to him. Audrey's priority for the day was to meet with a few of her old friends and go down to the Regatta for some fun. She agreed to meet with Parsons at around 6:15 p.m.

This arrangement was not enough for Gerard who was so keen on meeting with Audrey that he decided to book the day off work and go down to the Regatta to look for her. To calm himself, he stopped at Hotel Newfoundland to have a few beers and then walked down to lakeside. He spent two hours pushing his way through shoulder-to-shoulder crowds scanning faces in hope of finding Audrey. He found himself at the head of the pond standing next to one of the Wheels of Fortune so popular on Regatta Day.

He really felt things were getting much better for him that day when one of the numbers he was holding came up on the wheel and he won the hunting knife. It was around 4:30 p.m. and he had not found Audrey. His thoughts then turned to meeting her as they had arranged at 6:15 p.m.

He managed to track down a taxi by 5:30 p.m., which took him home. The first thing he did when he entered the kitchen was place the hunting knife in a kitchen drawer. His planned meeting with Audrey was at 6:15 p.m. and he needed to shower and change his clothing.

Parsons was in an upbeat mood as the time for her visit approached. Audrey had other plans. She intended to accompany her friend, Margaret Ploughman, to visit a friend at the Grace General Hospital. At 6:00 p.m. the phone rang in the Parsons' home and Gerard rushed to answer it. It was Audrey, calling to inform him that she couldn't meet with him at the time planned. She promised she would be right over after the hospital visit.

Gerard's anxiety soared until he was feeling too impatient to wait. He found an excuse to accidentally meet up with her at the hospital. He remembered he had a friend who was a patient at the Grace, "I'll go visit him, and while there I'll look for Audrey," he reasoned. However, when he arrived at the hospital, he learned his friend was already discharged.

He was disappointed, but when he turned around he saw Audrey and her friend coming down a hallway. Parsons was seeing her for the first time in a year and he was almost inarticulate when he greeted her. Maybe it would have been wiser for Parsons not have met her under these circumstances. The combination of beer and pills he had consumed during the day made the two girls suspect that he had been drinking.

Ploughman described the encounter: "He seemed quite excited and was talking rapidly, saying it was a long time since he had seen Audrey."

Audrey was reluctant to go with him at this time in the condition he was in. She told him to go home and she would visit him at 8:15 p.m. He agreed, but she did not show up as promised. He left his house and went out looking for her. He encountered both girls at the corner of Prince of Wales Street and Gear Street. From there things moved smoothly along. The trio returned to Parsons' house where Audrey gave Gerard a new shirt and his mother a kitchen ornament.

Margaret Ploughman left and went on her own way. Mrs. Parsons went next door to visit with her friend Mrs. Gertrude Fleming. Gerard and Audrey were left alone. They had a lot to talk about.

Margaret called at 9:30 p.m. and Audrey told her everything was going fine. When she called again at 11:15 p.m., a policeman answered. She sensed something terrible had happened. The police were brought to the house by a call from Mary Parsons, Gerard's mother who returned home at 11:00 p.m. and found the doors locked and the lights out. She stood on the steps and leaned over to peek into the living room window. There was sufficient light from an outside light pole for her to see Audrey Ballett's body lying partly on the chesterfield and partly the floor.

She called upon her neighbour, Mrs. Fleming, to go into the house with her through the back door. Mrs. Parsons switched on the lights in the kitchen and hallway. Mrs. Fleming remained in the kitchen while Mrs. Parsons cautiously walked down the hallway to the living room. She didn't need to switch on the light because the light from the window was enough for her to see that Audrey's body was covered in blood. In fact the trail of blood led from the living room, along the hallway and to the outside front steps.

"Audrey! Audrey!" Mrs. Parsons screamed as she shook the dead body in disbelief. The bloody scene was horrific. She rushed back to the kitchen exclaiming, "My God, she's got her throat cut." The two women returned to Mrs. Fleming's house and called the Newfoundland Constabulary (RNC).

The first police officer to arrive on the scene was Detective Eric Penny. Penny was nearing the end his shift and in the process of driving fellow detective Len Simms home when a call came from the dispatcher at headquarters to proceed directly to 38 Prince of Wales Street.

They recognized immediately that they had a major crime on their hands. Entering the house, Penny and Simms observed that blood was spread on the walls inside and out; the interior showed evidence of a struggle and then the blood-soaked body of a young woman, the same young woman who had begun that day in joyous spirits at the Royal St. John's Regatta.

Within minutes police car sirens were heard all over town as police responded to a call to the murder scene. As this was happening, the murderer was making his getaway. He hailed a taxi near Queen Street in downtown St. John's, but when the driver learned he wanted to go to Flatrock, he passed the fare over to his son, Ted Hollohan, at the same taxi stand.

"I didn't know it was Parsons," Ted recalled. He added, "On the way to Flatrock we chatted about the weather and the

Regatta." There was nothing unusual about his behaviour, "He didn't appear to be drinking 'though it was possible he could have. We stopped at a tavern along the way, so Parsons could pick up some beer, then I drove down to Flatrock."

After Parsons paid his fare and was leaving the car, Ted noticed blood on the legs of his pants:

> I was not suspicious when I saw the blood. He could have been drinking and in a fight. He could have cut himself. There could have been any number of reasons why he had blood on his pants.

When Ted Hollohan later learned of the grotesque crime committed by his passenger, he was amazed at how calm Parsons was that night. He said:

> He was not nervous, as a matter of fact he was as cool and calm as a person who had just returned from a trip to Florida. I heard Parsons wiping his hands on the back seat. He said his hands were sticky from eating chicken and chips. I had no reason to suspect anything was wrong.

The taxi stopped at Parsons' father's home in Flatrock, where he attempted to borrow a car. When his father refused, he asked Hollohan to drive him to a girlfriend's house. He then paid the taxi fare and Hollohan returned to St. John's. Ted resumed his shift work at the taxi stand and gave no more thought about his fare to Flatrock. However, before the end of his shift the seemingly casual contact with Gerard Parsons would be emblazoned in his memory for a lifetime.

Back on Prince of Wales Street, Sergeant Don Randell was supervising the murder scene. The body was as Parsons had left it. Audrey's head was resting on a chesterfield cushion with one of her legs on the coffee table, the other beneath it. Constable Ed Mercer examined the body and found no sign of life. As Randall studied the scene, his thoughts likely flashed back eight years to the murder of Joan Ash on Plymouth Road and the brutality he confronted while investigating that crime.

It appeared to Randell that Audrey might have been leaving the house when Parsons began his knife attack. He followed his suspicions and confirmed that the victim was attacked with a knife while on the outside steps and then dragged back into the living room. This would account for the blood on the hallway walls. Multiple stab wounds were inflicted on the victim indicating her attacker was in a vicious rage. Simeon Wentzell, an identification expert with the Constabulary, moved into the murder scene and began gathering the physical evidence. Information gathered outside by Detective Eric Penny revealed that a man with blood on his clothing was seen earlier walking down Prince of Wales Street. The informer paid little attention to him because he thought he was, "Probably coming from a fight and going downtown."

This lead was enough to put Sergeant Randell on his tail. By this time every available police officer in the city was aware of the discovery of the body of a young woman in a home on Prince of Wales Street. Perhaps the killer had gone to a downtown bar. Maybe he took a cab. It was certainly a promising lead to follow.

Randell sent out an order for officers to search the downtown bars and every taxi stand in town. At 2:00 a.m. Randell walked into the OK Taxi stand on Waldegrave Street, where Ted Hollohan was still on duty. When Randell described the man he was looking for, Hollohan instantly identified him as the customer he had taken to Flatrock earlier. They searched Hollohan's cab and found blood stains left there by Parsons.

Just three hours had passed since the murder and the investigation was moving rapidly. There was even hope that by daylight the Constabulary would have their man. Unfortunately, three hours was plenty of time for Parsons to lengthen the trail between himself and the police.

By daybreak on Friday squads of police converged on the village of Flatrock and set up roadblocks in the north-east of St. John's. An RCMP police dog was brought in to aid in the search. The public was left in the dark as to what was going on. Concern and fear spread throughout the area when people saw the combined effort of the Constabulary, the RCMP and a police dog. While the police officers worked quickly and diligently, the top level had decided to keep a lid on what was unfolding. No information was forthcoming to explain the roadblocks, why both police forces were in the Flatrock area, or, particularly, any description of who they were looking for. These decisions hindered the police investigation by causing heavy traffic congestion by the curious public, which obstructed police work and later proved to be an embarrassment to the Constabulary.

Before the story broke in the media, rumours that a terrible murder had taken place on Prince of Wales Street were rapidly spreading throughout the city. Newsmen working on the story were being stonewalled by police. On Friday, August 9th, Head Constable Nick Shannahan got an arrest warrant from Magistrate Hugh O'Neill for thirty-three-year-old Gerard Parsons. The press was unable to confirm that a murder had taken place until Sunday. At the same time they learned that a massive manhunt in the north-east end of the city was underway.

The search was concentrated in the Flatrock area. Parsons knew that area well; he was born there, schooled there, grew up there and could easily evade police for weeks. Police checked for missing boats, stolen cars and homes that may have been broken into. Roadblocks stopped all cars entering and/or leaving Flatrock. There were also many small shacks and vegetable gardens for police to search. Even with the help of the RCMP, the search area was an overwhelming prospect to face. As for food, the fugitive could easily survive on berries, vegetables and fish all very plentiful in that area. The three-hour lead Parsons had for his getaway turned out to be a major obstacle in the investigation. Would the immediate release of the suspect's description have shortened the investigation? Perhaps not! By then, he was very likely already well-hidden.

Despite the best efforts of investigators, Parsons was still on the loose Monday morning. By then police had released an accurate artist's sketch of Gerard Parsons. He was 5 feet 9 inches tall, weighed 140 pounds and had black bushy hair. When last seen, he was wearing light green pants, a light green sports jacket, a green shirt and tan and dark shoes. There were blood stains on the pants. Hundreds of tips poured into police headquarters of sightings of the fugitive. Every available police officer was called in to participate in the manhunt. The RCMP became involved in the search effort.

Gerard Parsons evaded this massive police hunt for four days before being captured. Considering the time involved and the very large and difficult area to search, Parsons could have evaded arrest for a much longer time. On Monday, August 12th, at 10:20 a.m., Parsons was captured by RCMP Constable Everett Carrol. He wore the same blood-stained clothing worn on the night of the killing. Parsons asked Carrol, "Will you button up my coat? I don't want to look at it." He was referring to his blood-stained shirt.

When arrested, Parsons looked very tired and hungry. Police thoroughly searched the area for evidence before bringing their captive to police headquarters at Fort Townshend to be fingerprinted and photographed. By this time, police had determined that their prisoner had not been helped by anyone.

Shortly after the capture, news of the arrest was being broadcast. Reports stated that Gerard Parsons was to be arraigned in court that day. Traditionally, murder cases attracted overflowing crowds to the courthouse on Duckworth Street. The nature of this crime and the spectacular involvement of roadblocks and a massive police hunt assured that there would be higher than normal interest and there was!

People came from everywhere and waited in line for five hours to get a glimpse of the killer being brought into the building and, if possible, to gain admission to the courtroom – a courtroom that could only hold a small portion of the people waiting to be admitted.

The Evening Telegram reporter, Jim Stratton, covered the trial from beginning to end for his newspaper. Stratton reported, "Nobody would leave the line-up. They sent kids for Pepsi and chips. They wouldn't risk leaving, afraid they might lose their vantage point."

Police struggled to keep order among the crowd and to keep the kids off the walls, steps and driveway. Stratton noted, "On more than one occasion kids and adults came close to injury when they struggled ahead each time a police vehicle arrived." He added, "One police officer was overheard saying, 'Stupid! Don't they know it's a sick man they're bringing here, not a freak?'"

When the police car arrived, a hush swept through the crowd as Head Constable Nick Shannahan removed the prisoner from the car to escort him into the courthouse. The excitement among the spectators was suddenly reduced to near silence while heads strained to get a glimpse of the criminal who had been the target of such a massive police hunt. The accused's name and the details of the victim's death were not yet released to the public. Yet, the rumours of the blood-covered front steps and the interior of the house fed the public imagination.

The next day, *The Evening Telegram* published an editorial damning the police under the heading, "Police Caught in Own Web." The police should have confirmed the obvious from the beginning. It stated:

> From the description of the wounds and the brutal treatment of the woman's body, it would be obvious to the most junior policeman that the crime was murder. Yet, the police refused to confirm that any crime had been committed at all until late on Friday morning.
>
> From the moment the body was discovered some-where between 9:30 p.m. and 11:30 p.m. on Thursday night until 1:30 a.m. on Friday morning, it was as if every action of the police was designed to give the wanted person more time to escape or to commit another crime. The police refused to confirm that a person was being sought, refused to give a description of the person and behaved generally as if the news media were interfering in the pursuit of justice by asking questions. The description of the man was not released until more than twelve hours after the crime was committed, although they must have been aware of the identity of the person they were seeking within minutes of discovering the body.
>
> The obvious step would have been to broadcast a description of the man on the early morning news broad-casts and to publish his description and pictures in both daily newspapers on Friday. If the full description of the wanted man had been given out, as it could have been, in the early hours of Friday morning, he might well have been in custody within hours of its publication.

The most scathing criticism levelled by the editorial charged:

The Minister of Justice can hardly be blamed for inheriting such a police force but he can be faulted for not having done something about it in the time he has been in office.

In court Parsons was charged and the judge ordered him to be sent to the Waterford Hospital for psychiatric evaluation. This assessment determined that he was fit to stand trial. Twenty-one witnesses appeared at the preliminary hearing, which got underway on October 11th. During this era Newfoundland had the Grand Jury system. Instead of being committed to stand trial, the preliminary inquiry sent the case to the Grand Jury. The Grand Jury reviewed the evidence given at the preliminary and made a decision on whether there was enough evidence to go to trial. They returned, "… a full bill of indictment against Parsons."

The trial got underway on November 18th in Supreme Court with Justice Robert Furlong presiding. Parsons was represented by Robert Wells, and the Crown by James Power, Director of Public Prosecutions.

The twelve jury members were: Cyril O'Neill, Ira Bailey, John Cooper, Emmanuel Billard, Leo King, Frank Mullett, Harry Curtis, Walter Pottle, Harris Clark, Victor Batstone, Clement Dunphy and Douglas Kearsey.

Evidence presented by the Crown showed that a violent scuffle had taken place with the victim struggling hard to free herself from her attacker. When Randell entered the house, he examined the living room where the body was found. He noted that all the blinds were closed and found an empty sheath-knife case on the chesterfield. The police officer picked up two letters from the floor addressed to Parsons and signed by Audrey Ballett. It was evident to him that the girl had strongly resisted her attacker.

Sergeant Randell provided graphic evidence describing the struggle that took place. He testified:

There were blood stains on the lock of the front door, on the railing leading to the veranda of the house, on the house itself. There were also some blood stains on the adjoining house, number 38A. I concluded she was stabbed on the veranda of the house and dragged inside. During the struggle they knocked the hall stove out of position. She held onto the door jamb and tried not to be dragged into the living room.

The heavy oil stove in the hall was shifted about two inches. The stove pipes were disarranged and hanging on the stairs leading to the second story. The light switch in the hallway near the living room had stains of blood on it. The door jamb leading to the living room was also smeared in blood.

Sergeant Randell was present during the autopsy and testified in court that the autopsy confirmed sixty-four stab wounds on the victim's body. Fourteen of those were on her arms and hands which she suffered while defending herself.

More evidence of the amount of blood at the murder scene was provided by Constable Simeon Wentzell who arrive d there at 11:15 p.m. He told the court:

There was blood on the floor near where she was sitting. Her clothes had bloodstains on them and the chesterfield was saturated with blood. A towel in the bathroom was also saturated with blood.

Pathologist Dr. Young Rho who issued the death certificate for the victim explained where the sixty-four stab wounds inflicted on the victim were spread. He told the court:

These were found in the neck, chest, abdomen,

thighs, hands and arms. The chest wound penetrated the heart, and the abdomen wounds had penetrated the stomach and liver. The fatal wounds were the ones on the chest which penetrated the heart and the ones which penetrated the stomach and liver. The arm and hand wounds resulted from the deceased trying to defend herself.

Dr. Young Rho said that the wounds were inflicted with enough strength to penetrate the skin and muscles of the victim. He added that those on the neck and the other minor wounds were inflicted after the fatal wounds were administered. The pattern of the attack indicated that the killer was in a rage.

Throughout Dr. Rho's testimony the courtroom was remarkably silent. Spectators showed intense interest in the doctor's evidence, occasionally exchanging glances with others when the graphic brutal details of the killing were mentioned. One spectator was so disturbed that he collapsed and had to be carried out of the courtroom.

While witness after witness gave evidence telling the story of what happened Regatta night at the Parsons' home, the accused stared straight ahead as though in a trance with his mind and body elsewhere. Occasionally his attention returned to the courtroom and he would bow his head slightly and close his eyes. In the public gallery, visitors' eyes shifted from the person testifying to the accused whenever riveting details of the brutality of the murder were being revealed.

Handwritten notes Parsons made while hiding out in the woods near Flatrock were read in court. These showed he was not aware at that time that Audrey was dead. He wrote:

> It was not her fault. It was mine and drinking. She wanted to get married three years ago and go to

Toronto. I hope she is not dead or hurt. I do not remember all that happened or why. All my property I
have I want left to my mother. I am mentally sick and
now am sicker.

Constable William Taylor was in Shoe Cove near Flatrock
when Parsons was captured. The prisoner was inside an RCMP
car when Taylor opened the door and identified himself as he
entered the vehicle. He gave the customary police caution to
Parsons, which the accused understood. Parsons then asked, "Is
she dead?" followed by a confession, "I stabbed her once. I
think some more, but I don't remember too well. I found the
knife in my pocket and threw it down in the water near where
I was picked up."

When Taylor was providing this evidence in court, defence
lawyer Robert Wells objected. He argued that the accused had
spent five days [sic] in the open and was in no position to understand the police caution. Upon hearing Wells' argument
Judge Furlong ordered the jury to leave and he held a Voir Dire
(trial within a trial). Its purpose was to explore the defence position on the validity of the confession given to Constable Taylor. Wells put Parsons on the witness stand and asked him if
he had been cautioned by Taylor.

"I don't remember any caution from Constable Taylor." He
added that he did recall being asked by Taylor why he did it.

Wells asked, "Did you understand that you did not have
to speak if you didn't want to?"

"I was not aware of it. Although I did become aware of it
later," answered Parsons.

At the conclusion of the Voir Dire, Judge Furlong ruled
that the evidence presented by Constable Taylor was admissible. The jury was recalled into the courtroom and the trial resumed.

Constable Art Pike testified next. He told the court that Parsons confessed to him that he stabbed Audrey Ballett three or four times in the stomach. He said that Parsons told him that Audrey was breathing heavily and lying across the chesterfield when he left.

The bartender who served Parsons at Hotel Newfoundland on Regatta Day testified that Parsons was drinking beer and showing others the knife while boasting he had just won it at the Regatta. He offered it for sale, but there was no interest. The bartender, Hedley Preston, said he did not recall how many beer Parsons drank. John Payne, the taxi-driver who took Parsons home from the hotel on the day of the murder, testified that Parsons showed him the knife he won and asked, "How much do you think I can get for it?" Payne recalled, "Parsons seemed to have a few drinks in, but apart from that his behaviour seemed normal." When Parsons arrived home, he went into the kitchen and placed the hunting knife and its case into the silverware drawer.

Head Constable Nick Shannahan was the last witness for the Crown. He read the statement taken from Parsons on the day of his arrest and testified that Parsons was given the police caution before he volunteered his statement. In the statement Parsons filled in details of the day of the murder leading up the deed.

When Parsons and Ballett were left alone in the house, they talked about their relationship until an argument erupted. She asked him how much money he had. He answered, "$1,400." Audrey was upset by his reply. "You had more than that last year!" she said.

"Yes, but I spent most of that in going up to see you last October," Parsons explained.

An agitated Parsons got up from the chesterfield and went upstairs where he found a bottle of whiskey and two bottles of beer. He drank the beer and had two drinks from the whiskey before returning to the living room where he again lay alongside Audrey on the chesterfield. Parsons recalled fighting with Audrey but did not remember why. Although he remembered wrestling with her, he did not remember the stabbing.

Gerard Parsons was the first defence witness. On the stand he testified that he became impatient when Audrey failed to show up at his house at 8:00 p.m. as she had promised earlier in the day. "I got depressed. I can't describe the feeling I had. I thought she was not going to show up," he said. Gerard decided to go downtown for a few drinks.

At the intersection of Gear Street and Prince of Wales Street, he met Audrey and Mary Ploughman, her friend. "I was overjoyed when I met her. We went to my house," he recalled.

As his testimony turned to the hours leading up to the murder, there was a sudden change in his tone. He began to hesitate, he stammered, he showed confusion, his voice became high pitched.

When asked about the discussion he and Audrey had about the amount he had saved, he answered, "I told her I got expenses to meet, such as a retirement insurance plan which she had asked me to take out. She told me I had no money because I spent it on alcohol."

The argument was temporarily interrupted when the telephone rang. Parsons answered the call but it was Mary Ploughman asking for Audrey. When their conversation ended, Audrey resumed discussing Gerard's savings and suggested that with enough savings they could buy a house. He responded:

> I told her I had no money. I'm not sure if she was lying down or sitting up. She said she knew I was in hospital for drinking and told me I was lower than a

snake. She said if I didn't stop drinking liquor once and for all, she wouldn't see me again.

At this point, Parsons was edging towards rage. He remembered, "I recalled some things for her, like double crosser, and I said she was taking advantage of me. She looked like she was going to spit on me. I don't remember after that." He had likely reached the point of no return.

From there things happened so rapidly that when his fury was completely expended he found himself standing over Audrey, who was covered with blood and sitting on the chesterfield with her feet on the floor.

"She was breathing hard and I went over and put my arms around her and I called her name. She didn't move," Parsons told the court. He said he picked up the phone to call an ambulance but must have panicked because his memory went blank after that. But not completely blank; he testified, "I left the house. The next thing I remembered is getting out of the taxi at Flatrock."

When asked by Wells to describe his feelings at that time, he answered, "I don't know, I didn't have any feelings, because everything was blank – a daze – I was in a state of shock."

His next memory of the episode was of a few days later hiding out in the woods near Shoe Cove. Parsons was all alone holding the murder weapon in his hand. As he studied the knife his mind may have returned to the Wheel of Fortune and the happy crowds crushing him at the Regatta. Maybe he thought of how happy he felt at his luck in winning a hunting knife. When the realization of the knife's significance set in, he went to the water's edge and tossed the prize he had tried to sell at Hotel Newfoundland into the sea below. But his pain was not so easily discarded.

"I was wet and tired but I didn't feel hungry," he said. The tormented fugitive of justice then sat down and wrote a note telling what he had done because he was afraid he would die of hunger or be shot by police.

Asked by Wells if he remembered what had happened, Parsons replied, "I have no memory of killing or stabbing the girl with the knife. I don't remember how I got the knife in my hands."

Having denied any memory of killing Audrey Ballett, Gerard Parsons provided a contradictory answer while answering a follow up question. "What are your feelings towards Audrey Ballett?" asked the defence lawyer.

"I would sooner be dead than here now. When I killed her, I killed myself," responded Parsons.

Under cross-examination by prosecutor Power, Parsons was asked, "Do you recall telling Constable Pike on the morning you were captured that you stabbed Audrey Ballett in the stomach?"

"I remember talking to the police but I don't remember telling him that," answered Parsons.

"Why did you leave her in a bleeding condition?"

"I didn't know she was dying. At the present time I think it was a cruel and callous thing to do. I'm not capable of doing it now and wasn't capable before. It's a mystery to me, the same as it is to everyone else," the accused replied.

The defence attempted to show the jury that Parsons' use of alcohol and drugs had contributed to his brutal action. Wells called to the stand the superintendent at the Hospital for Mental and Nervous Diseases, Dr. J. Frazer Walsh.

At this point the drug Librium came under close scrutiny because the accused had been using it. Dr. Walsh described this drug:

> Librium is used to treat alcoholics. The drug is a minor tranquilizer and is used to relieve tension and anxiety. It allows a person suffering from alcoholism to carry

on without undue panic. In extreme cases of alcoholism a dosage of up to two hundred mgs per day could be prescribed. When abused by taking with alcohol, or abused beyond prescribed dosages, trouble begins. Anyone combining the drug Librium and alcohol over a long period of time could expect anything to happen.

Under cross-examination, Power asked Dr. Walsh to explain the effect that abuse could have on memory. He answered:

> There has to be a mental explosion. If he cracked, he wouldn't be able to act rationally and would overreact to the situation. He wouldn't be able to control himself. A person may be able to recall some things but wouldn't know exactly what he did.

Dr. Walsh pointed out that all his comments applied to a particular person in a particular case. Power interrupted the witness to ask:

> This is a situation in which a man had stabbed someone sixty-four times and says he could not remember. Is this the effect of the drug and alcohol or was it the accused just saying he could not remember?

"It could be either. A person taking Librium and alcohol may react in the opposite way to a situation. Instead of calming down he could become excited and act in an irrational manner," answered Dr. Walsh.

The Chief of Medical Services at the Waterford Hospital, Dr. Francis Gillespie, had interviewed Parsons during his assessment after the murder. He testified:

He has a personality disorder and it has been in-
grained in him for a long time. Parsons suffered from
alcoholism and is immature with a life-long tendency
to become frustrated and impulsive. Parsons is psycho-
pathic in that he did not learn from the past. He has
been treated a number of times for alcoholism.

This answer brought the prosecutor to his feet again, asking, "If Parsons, because he had been drinking excessively and
taking the drug, would he know what he was doing?"

"He would, up to a point. There is a cut-off point before he
would fall asleep and this is a shaded area," responded Gillespie.

"Would stabbing Audrey Ballett be beyond Parsons' control?"

"Maybe he didn't know what he was doing. Maybe he
did."

Judge Furlong had a final question for Dr. Gillespie. He
wondered, "If Parsons after being treated for alcoholism had
reverted to his old ways upon release, could he have committed
a murder before under the right conditions?"

"There is no way of knowing," concluded Gillespie.

With the presentation of evidence completed, the court
proceeded with the final summations by defence and prosecution. Robert Wells argued that Parsons on the day of the murder
was irrational and not aware of what he had done. He suggested
that his client was guilty of manslaughter and not capital murder. He told the jury, "By having blackouts, by being an alcoholic, by taking Librium and alcohol Parsons was not a rational
person. His behaviour was irrational on the day of August 8th."
He stressed that Parsons was unable to control himself due to
his using Librium and alcohol on that day. Wells argued:

It was an indication of the state of mind Parsons
was in, that when Audrey Ballett did not show up at

his home at 8:15 p.m. as promised, Parsons could not control himself and he had to go out. Parsons had been despondent and elated all day. Why else could Parsons consciously kill the girl he loved?

In conclusion, the defence lawyer asked the jury to consider the evidence and bring in a verdict of not guilty of capital murder, but guilty of manslaughter.

James Power argued for the Crown to convict Gerard Parsons of non-capital murder. He said, "Parsons' behaviour before August 8th makes no difference. All that matters are the things he did on the evening of August 8th." Power continued:

Two people were left alone in a room and the events that happened covered a short period of time. Parsons had to leave the living room to go to the kitchen and get the knife. While Parsons' memory is very vague on the events of the death, he is very clear on what happened before and after. There was more deliberation than the accused admits. The taxi drivers who had driven Parsons to his home and to Flatrock considered he was acting normally. Mrs. Ploughman, who met him at the hospital, testified that although she smelled alcohol on his breath, she considered him to be normal. Parsons' story of not remembering events was completely self-serving.

It was not alcohol that killed Audrey Ballett. It was Gerard Parsons.

All that was left now was for the judge to instruct the jury before they began their deliberation. He cautioned:

A great responsibility rests on your shoulders. The Crown had to prove beyond a reasonable doubt that

Parsons intended to kill the girl. The jury had to be satisfied that Parsons either did not know what he was doing or did not know that what he was doing was wrong.

He then reviewed the evidence that had been presented during the trial and told the jury:

> You have the following options: First, to find him guilty of non-capital murder, second, not guilty of non-capital murder, third, not guilty by reason of insanity and fourth, if he did not intend to kill Audrey Ballett you can find him guilty of manslaughter.

Parsons showed no emotion as the jury stood and filed out of the courtroom. His eyes rose towards the clock on the wall which showed it was 11:55 a.m. The jury ran into problems throughout the afternoon and returned to the courtroom to have the law explained or to review expert testimony.

Many spectators left to go home for supper and began lining up outside again at 5:00 p.m. By this time those who had been inside throughout the trial had become familiar with each other and there was much discussion and speculation about how it would end. The opinions varied with some people feeling the charge of capital murder would not stand. Others felt it would be a verdict of not guilty by reason of insanity or manslaughter.

At 5:45 p.m. word came from inside the courthouse that a verdict had been reached. The doors opened and people struggled to be among those fortunate enough to get inside. A large crowd was forced to wait outside to hear the outcome of the trial.

The court crier called for all to stand as Judge Furlong entered and took his seat. All others followed suit.

"Gentlemen of the jury, what is your verdict?" asked Judge Furlong.

The jury chairman stood and facing the judge replied loudly and clearly. "We find the accused not guilty as charged but guilty of manslaughter."

A shuffling sound swept across the courtroom as spectators shifted to look at each other, the jury members and Gerard Parsons, who showed no emotion towards the verdict.

"So say you all, gentlemen of the jury," said Judge Furlong.

"So say we all," responded the jury.

Gerard Parsons was asked to stand. "Do you have anything to say?" Judge Furlong asked.

"No, Sir," replied Parsons.

Parsons showed no emotion as the judge announced his sentence of fourteen years in prison. The maximum penalty was twenty years. Before leaving the courthouse, the defence lawyer made it known he would not be appealing the sentence.

Gerard Parsons was released on parole before the fourteen-year sentence expired.

Chapter 4: The Tong Murders

During the first half of the twentieth century in Newfoundland, four sensational murders took place within the Chinese community of St. John's that made international headlines and stirred speculation that Tong wars had taken place.

The first three of these involved a shooting spree on Carter's Hill[1], which ended with the slaying of three Chinese laundrymen, the attempted killing of a fourth and an unsuccessful suicide attempt by the Chinese gunman who carried out the deeds.

The fourth was the bizarre slaughter of the owner of a Chinese café at the west end of Water Street, which was described as a "ceremonial killing" and possibly the work of the Tong.

To begin, I will take you back to 1922 when the country was shaken by the news of a triple murder in the traditionally peaceful city of St. John's. Momentarily, I will reveal to you the final moments of the whole grisly episode before unfolding the spectacular series of events preceding it. The scene unfolds on the gallows inside Her Majesty's Penitentiary and the last moments of the man responsible for the triple murders:

> While waiting for the final act in the terrible affair,
> Wo Fen Game trembled for a second or two, as if he
> were feeling a chill morning air, and slowly turned his
> head toward the right where the hangman was preparing to spring the trap. Sheriff Blandford then gave the

---

[1] The portion of Carter's Hill today where the murders took place was known as Murray Street in 1922.

signal, and amidst a quietness that could be felt, the trap was sprung, and Wo Fen Game was sent into eternity.

-*Daily News*, December 16, 1922

This Story Begins And Ends In 1922

The peaceful atmosphere of old St. John's was shattered on the evening of May 3, 1922, when violence erupted in the centre of town among some members of the Chinese community, leaving three men dead and a fourth man seriously wounded. The newspapers of the day speculated that a Tong war had broken out in the city. This spectacular series of events had its beginning at the Jim Lee Laundry on Carter's Hill.

While the events leading up to the explosion of bloodshed were unfolding at the Jim Lee Laundry, the local population, unaware of what was taking place, went about their usual business. Crowds had braved the heavy winds and wet snow that battered the city that night, to attend various movies and concerts being staged at city theatres. There was a line-up outside the Casino Theatre on Water Street to view a play entitled *Chimes of Normandy*, being staged by pupils and ex-pupils of Holy Cross and St. Patrick's Hall schools. The Majestic Theatre was featuring its own Majestic Orchestra, giving its rendition of the latest foxtrots and waltzes. World-famous Hollywood producer, St. John's-born John Murray Anderson, was making final preparations to depart for New York City the following morning on the S.S. *Rosalind*.

At the Jim Lee Laundry, thirty-one-year-old Wo Fen Game was engaged in an argument with the laundry owners; this would set off the evening's tragic events. Wo Fen Game, who had served two years in France during the First World War as a member of the Chinese Labour Battalion, had been in Newfoundland only a year when the murders took place. A native of Sai Tang Village in Canton, China, Fen Game was brought to Newfoundland by his brother-in-law, Hong Kim Hi, a partner in the Jim Lee Laundry. Upon arriving in the city, he had his name changed from Wo Fen Gen to Wo Fen Game by Kim Lee, patriarch of the seventy-member Chinese community.

Fen Game left his wife, daughter, mother and father behind in China, and joined six other Chinese immigrants on the long journey to start a new life in Newfoundland, a country on the other side of world.

The $700 trip from Hong Kong to St. John's was made possible by Hong Kim Hi. Kim Hi offered Fen Game $12 a week to work at the Carter's Hill laundry and loaned him the $700 for travelling expenses. The offer was an attractive one for Fen Game who, at the time, was employed in a Hong Kong shipyard earning $8 per week. His enthusiasm was soon dampened when the laundry owners failed to pay him any salary at all.

After four weeks with no pay, an angry Wo Fen Game demanded payment for his work. Kim Hi, having consulted with his partners, agreed to pay Fen Game $4 per week. They did not pay him for the first four weeks because he did not know the work, and they were not satisfied with his effort. The owners did promise him an increase and a short while later his salary was raised to $8 per week.

Despite the efforts of Kim Hi, Fen Game became very unsettled and angry over the long hours and poor pay. He felt betrayed by the laundry owners who had promised him much more if he left China. His discontent began to show in his work. He frequently slept until mid-day and left his place of work when he felt like it.

Fen Game did not mix well with the Chinese community in St. John's. He was a regular visitor to King Restaurant on Water Street, which was owned by Charlie Fong. His cousin, Wo Fen Chat, and a fellow villager were employed at the King. These were his only close friends in the city.

On the day of the triple murders, it was Charlie Fong, accompanied by Rich Hong, who visited the Carter's Hill laundry in an unsuccessful effort to settle the dispute between Fen Game and the owners of the Jim Lee Laundry, and to try and get Fen Game back to work. The dispute came to a head earlier that day when Hong Loen made it emphatically clear to Fen Game that he was fired from his job, and no longer welcome to stay at the Carter's Hill residence.

This was like being condemned to death by starvation for the dejected Wo Fen Game. He was in a strange country, unable to speak the native language, and the slave-like conditions of the Chinese community at the time would make it virtually impossible for him to find work. Because Fen Game had been brought to Newfoundland by Kim Hi, he was considered to belong to him. If any other member of the Chinese community gave him work, it would certainly cause trouble.

The firing of Fen Game came as no surprise to him. His employers had, on many occasions during the preceding days, hinted that they wanted to get rid of him. He had felt they wouldn't take such a drastic step because he still owed Kim Hi $630 and surely Kim Hi would want this amount repaid first.

On the day prior to the triple slaying, Hubert Carter, a sales clerk with Martin-Royal Hardware Stores on Water Street, noticed a Chinese man in the store. This man was showing an unusual interest in a nickel plated .38 calibre revolver. When Carter approached him, he identified himself as Fong Kim of New Gower Street, and asked the purchase price of the weapon. When Carter told him $14, he seemed surprised at the high price. His motions indicated he could not afford the gun and he left the store. Carter later identified Wo Fen Game for the police as the man he served that day.

Kim Hi, destined to become the second victim in the triple murder, had been holding a small sum of money belonging to

Fen Game. Determined to buy the gun, Fen Game got his money from Kim Hi, and, just hours before the fatal attack upon his comrades, he went to the Martin-Royal stores, and purchased a revolver. Hubert Carter, in a move that was later to be revealed at Fen Game's murder trial, recorded the gun sale in the store records using the phony name given him by Fen Game, and identified the gun by its serial number 471442. Tucking the gun inside his coat, Fen Game hurried from the store and headed straight for the King Restaurant.

Charlie Fong gave him the bad news. Hong Loen was unshakable in his determination to fire Fen Game, and was insisting that he move out of the Carter's Hill residence. A downhearted Wo Fen Game left the King Restaurant and trod slowly up the hills and streets of St. John's towards the Carter's Hill laundry. Entering the laundry, Fen Game came eye-to-eye with his brother-in-law, Hong Kim Hi. "You brought me here and you must keep me here to work until I pay you back the money you sent me to come here!" demanded Fen Game.

Kim Hi had already discussed Fen Game's situation with his partners and they had both concluded that Fen Game would not be taken back. Replying to Fen Game's demand, Kim Hi said, "No, you must go somewhere else to work." Depressed by this news, Fen Game shouted, "If you do not give me work, there is no use to live and I will kill myself!"

Fen Game then went to the kitchen, crying. According to testimony given by Fen Game later at the hospital, Hong Loen laughed and said, "There is no use in your crying; you have to die sometime. I and Hong Wing will shoot you sometime."

Hong Wing was one of four owners of the Hop Wah Laundry on Casey Street and had come to St. John's from a rival village to Fen Game's. Family feuds had gone on between the two villages for years. Fen Game later suggested to the police that Hong Wing had threatened to kill him because of the trouble back in China.

Fen Game rushed upstairs to his room where he loaded the gun with cartridges purchased when he bought the gun. Returning to the laundry area and standing in a door between the shop and the next room, Fen Game fired his gun at Hong Loen who was standing side-on to him. The bullet entered Loen's body between the second and third ribs, two inches from the centre of his chest, and penetrated the left lung. It also pierced the aorta near its origin and penetrated the right lung, lodging in the chest wall between the ribs. Hong Loen dropped to the ground in a semi-conscious state. On hands and knees, he crawled out through the front door, and about forty feet up Carter's Hill before collapsing.

Hong Kim Hi, another partner in the laundry, startled at the violent actions of his brother-in-law, tried to subdue him. He threw his arms around Fen Game, and the gun went off. The bullet entered Kim Hi's body between the third and fourth ribs, two inches from the sternum, and penetrated the heart.

The third partner and victim, So Ho Kai, was ironing curtains in a washing room at the rear of the store. He was shot at such close quarters that his apron was blackened with gunpowder. The .38 calibre bullet hit Ho Kai between the eighth and ninth ribs, and entered his stomach and liver causing hemorrhaging, resulting in death.

The explosion of gunfire aroused twenty-four-year-old Ches Noseworthy, who lived next door to the Chinese laundry. He rushed to his front door just in time to see Fen Game leave the laundry and to hear the moans of Hong Loen as he lay near death up the street. As Noseworthy rushed up to the St. John's Store on LeMarchant Road for assistance, Fen Game headed for the Hop Wah Laundry on Casey Street with a fourth target in mind.

Fifty-three-year-old Hong Wing had been in Newfound-land for twenty years. His three partners Hong Yuen, Hong Sung and Hong One were in the store when Fen Game barged through the door. Hong Wing was in a back room of the laundry at the time. Fen Game shouted Wing's name. When Wing came to the front of the store, Fen Game fired two shots. The bullets struck a white enamel dipper in Wing's hand and one bullet, after striking the dipper, entered his right shoulder. Hong Yuen, who had greeted Fen Game as he entered the store, was terrified by what he saw. He ran into a back room just as Fen Game was turning to leave the laundry.

Twenty-two-year-old Frank Martret of George Street saw the blaze of gunfire through the laundry window, and heard the shots from where he was standing on the corner of Barron and Casey Streets. A pole light at the corner made it possible to see Fen Game as he ran down the steps of the laundry, crossed Casey Street and stopped in the middle of Barron Street. Martret watched in disbelief as Fen Game raised the .38 slowly to his head.

By now, the seriousness of what he had done was having its impact on Wo Fen Game. Holding the gun to his right temple, his hands trembling, Fen Game pulled the trigger. It was his trembling hand, to his regret, that saved him from death that night. The bullet deflected off his cheek, entered his breast, cut through the lung, and lodged between the fourth and fifth ribs on his left side. In spite of the bullet wounds, Fen Game managed to empty the gun and place it in his pocket. To Martret's amazement, Fen Game, followed by a trail of his own blood, stumbled down Barron Street and turned east at New Gower Street. Martret followed from a safe distance, puzzled by what he was witnessing.

The wounded man stopped at the door of the Jim Gay Laundry, located on New Gower Street between the intersection of Casey Street and New Gower Street, and the intersection at Deady's Lane and New Gower Street. Heavy pounding on the door startled the occupants inside the laundry. Fen Game shouted that he had shot himself as a crowd began to gather around him.

Twenty-nine-year-old Ling Sing opened the door slightly, and saw Fen Game fall to the ground in a pool of blood. He quickly shut the door. Ling Sing later told police he was afraid that the crowd would rush into his store and attack him. At the time, he was not aware of the triple-tragedy that had taken place.

Martret and Robert Mayo, a twenty-three-year-old long-shoreman from William Street, carried Fen Game to the office of Dr. Roberts, which was located in the building later known as the Brownsdale Hotel at the corner of Brazil Square and New Gower Street. As they attempted to lift Fen Game, a gun wrapped in a handkerchief dropped from the victim's pocket. Mayo recovered the gun and handkerchief and turned it over to Constable Churchill, who had been called to the office by the doctor.

Meanwhile, Ches Noseworthy of Carter's Hill, in his search for help for the dying Hong Loen, met Sergeant John Nugent nearby on LeMarchant Road. Nugent was on patrol in the higher levels area of the city that night. This duo persuaded Dr. John McDonald, a resident of LeMarchant Road, to come with them. Arriving at Carter's Hill, Dr. McDonald immediately examined Loen. He was too late. The Chinese laundry-man had succumbed to the bullet wounds.

Accompanied by Dr. McDonald, Sergeant Nugent entered the laundry. Opening the front door, they got a startling view of Kim Hi lying on his back, feet pointing towards the door with blood spattered all over his clothing. Dr. McDonald quickly examined the body, but Kim Hi was beyond help. Sergeant Nugent cautiously entered the adjoining washing room and was further startled by the sight of yet another body. A blood-spattered Ho Kai, in a kneeling position with one arm clenching a washtub, added to the eerie scene that greeted the doctor and detective inside the laundry.

Police Inspector General Charles Hutchings[2] was enjoying a social evening at the Shrine Club when he was interrupted by a telephone call from Sergeant Nugent. Alarmed at the news of the triple slaying, the inspector general grabbed his overcoat and boarded a taxi to rush to the Carter's Hill laundry. After viewing the murder scene and ordering a search of the house, the inspector general assigned Head Constable John Byrne to investigate the triple murder and assault.

While still puzzled over the mystery surrounding the murders, Hutchings received word of another shooting at the Hop Wah laundry located on Casey Street near Sheehan Shute Lane. Detective Lee accompanied the inspector general to the Casey Street laundry. By that time, neighbours in the area had come to the aid of the injured Hong Wing. They also assisted Hong Yuen, a partner in the laundry, in carrying Wing to an upstairs bedroom.

The General Hospital on Forest Road had been alerted about the shootings and an ambulance was dispatched to the Brazil Square office of Dr. Roberts, where Fen Game was being treated. Both Fen Game and Wing were taken to the hospital for treatment. Fen Game was in critical condition and was not expected to recover.

The murder weapon was taken by Constable Churchill to the city lockup and turned over to detectives to be held as evidence for the trial. Fen Game regained consciousness for a short time that night. In broken English he uttered the words,

[2] Inspector General Hutchings was the grandson of Captain William Boig, a prominent figure in locating the hiding place of the Lost Treasure of Lima on Cocos Island, with his partner in the project Captain John Keating.

"Me sin, me die tomorrow," to Dr. Wilson, a female hospital doctor.

As Fen Game lay near death at the General Hospital, city police were conducting an intensive investigation and putting the pieces together in an effort to reconstruct what had happened. Wing was not in serious condition; doctors removed the bullet from his shoulder, and he was released from hospital sixteen days later.

Funeral Director J.T. (Jimmy) Martin, who operated a funeral service on the corner of New Gower and Notre Dame Streets, was called to Carter's Hill to remove the bodies.

The wake that followed was far from a traditional Newfoundland wake. Actually, it was more like something from the Wild West and likely done to facilitate the immense public interest in the rapidly developing morbid episode. St. John's people had never witnessed anything like it. The bodies of the three slain Chinese men were placed in wooden coffins and displayed in a slanted position in the front window of the funeral home. Lines of curious people passed the spectacle in a manner usually reserved for prominent dignitaries lying in state.

Head Constable Byrne arranged for city photographer J.C. Parsons to take photographs of both laundries where the shootings had taken place. A government surveyor was also called in to make diagrams of both places and of the streets where they were located. Doctors Anderson and Grieve conducted the post mortems on the victims and the full report was given to Head Constable Byrne.

Reverend W.B. Bugden, minister of Wesley United Church on Patrick Street, conducted the graveside services for the three victims, who were laid to rest at the General Protestant Cemetery on Waterford Bridge Road in St. John's.

On the morning of May 4th, Inspector General Charles Hutchings, Justice of the Peace John McCarthy and local interpreter Kim Lee visited Fen Game at the hospital. Because Fen Game was not expected to live, Hutchings asked him if he felt he was dying. He replied that he did. Hutchings then proceeded to draft a confession for the accused. Fen Game outlined his problems with the three victims, and described how he actually killed them and wounded Hong Wing. Kim Lee read the statement back to him and then had him sign it.

When this statement was later introduced as evidence at Fen Game's trial, defence lawyer L.E. Emerson objected to it. The grounds for the objection were that it was not a deathbed confession because Fen Game had not died, and Fen Game was not properly cautioned by the police before the statement was taken. Emerson's objection was upheld by the court, and the statement was not accepted.

In preparing for the trial, the police decided that an independent interpreter was necessary. The local Chinese community was suspected of being hostile towards the accused, and could not be trusted. This, of course, included Kim Lee. On May 31, 1922, the Newfoundland Justice Department contacted their counterparts in Ottawa for assistance to find an interpreter who was expert in the Cantonese dialect. The famous Pinkerton Detective Agency in New York was also contacted regarding an interpreter. It could not provide one right away, as their expert was already involved in a New York Chinese slaying trial.[3]

While at the hospital, Wo Fen Game wrote two letters, which he asked the police guard on-duty to mail for him. Acting on instructions from Inspector General Hutchings, the guard passed the letters over to the police. Hutchings sent the letters to W. Shack Horne of the Pinkerton Detective Agency, New York, for translation. This effort revealed that one of the letters addressed to Fen Game's cousin, Wo Fen Chat, at the

---

[3] The New York slayings were believed to be Tong killings.

King Restaurant, contained an admission of guilt. The letter read:

> My dear cousin,
>
> I wish you everything well up to this. I am sorry I did this last night. I now find myself mistaken. You please tell all of my countrymen in the city I never intended to shoot my brother-in-law, but he came and put his two hands around my body when I shot Hong Loen. I am sorry Hong Kim Hi was unlucky. The bullet went into his body and killed him. I am so sorry, sorry. When I started to work, four times Hong Loen would not let me work. He put his two hands up and shoved me away. I turned back to work again and then all tell me to pick up my things and go clear of the place. They wouldn't allow me to pick up my things and go clear of the place. They wouldn't allow me to stay here. I did not go. Next day Hong Loen and Hong Wing both say we will shoot you to death. Now, cousin Wo Fen Chat if you will write home and write Havana and tell everything, everybody will read. Cousin, if you have time you may come down and see me.
>
> - (Sgd.) Wo Fen Game

An indication that justice officials in Newfoundland had hoped Wo Fen Game would die from his self-inflicted wounds, thereby saving the costs of a trial, was contained in the letter sent to Ottawa requesting an interpreter. It read:

> One of the members of the community ran amuck, and killed three of his countrymen and attempted to kill another and then UNFORTUNATELY made an ineffectual attempt to commit suicide.

Arrangements were made with George Hart, an investigator with the Chinese branch of the Department of Immigration in Ottawa, to act as interpreter. Hart arranged to be in Newfoundland for the trial by taking his holidays from immigration to coincide with the trial date. His $75 fee plus expenses were paid by the Newfoundland Government.

Before the charges were laid in Supreme Court, Fen Game had gone through the ordeal of a magisterial enquiry, which lasted three months. At 11:00 a.m., November 4, 1922, Wo Fen Game was arraigned in the Newfoundland Supreme Court. He pleaded not guilty to the three charges of murder and a fourth charge of wounding with intent to kill. The trial date was set for November 20th.

On November 7th, ninety-six residents of St. John's were summoned to the courthouse for the jury selection process. This process resulted in the following twelve members being selected: Alfred McNamara, Robinson's Hill; Silas Moore, 48 Pennywell Road; William Edwards, 112 Circular Road; Thomas Kelly, 7 Gear Street; Thomas Voisey, 3 York Street; Sam Vavasour, 117 Freshwater Road; A.G. Osmond, 26 Cookstown Road; Joseph Power, 91 Pennywell Road; Patrick J. Casey, 74 Hamilton Street; J.J. Neville, Blackmarsh Road; Patrick Maher, Barnes Road; and Herbert Hudson, 17 Freshwater Road.

The trial opened on November 20, 1922, with Chief Justice Horwood, Justice Johnson and Justice Kent in attendance. The Deputy Minister of Justice, P.J. Summers, had been appointed to prosecute the case, but because of illness, he was replaced by H.A. Winter. The court then appointed city lawyer L.E. Emerson to defend Wo Fen Game.

Thirty-five witnesses were called to the stand during the six-day trial. Most of them were from the Chinese community. This presented a problem to the court because several of the witnesses were Confucians, and in being sworn in, could not accept the required Christian oath-swearing. These witnesses were permitted to take the oath according to their own beliefs. This was done by each person writing his own name on a sheet of paper, lighting a match to it, and holding the burning paper in his hand until it burned out.

Interest in the trial centered on whether or not the defence would show that the four shooting victims conspired to kill Wo Fen Game. The strength of the prosecution's case rested with two admissions of guilt made by Wo Fen Game, one in a statement given to police and the other contained in the letter written to Wo Fen Chat.

In addition, the prosecution called on Hong Wing and a number of local Chinese witnesses to show that the alleged feud and conspiracy to kill Wo Fen Game did not exist. The only indication of any such feud or conspiracy came in the testimony of the accused.

All Chinese witnesses testified that they were not aware of any feud or other trouble between the accused and the victims. Emerson tried to discredit them by showing they did not know Wo Fen Game and therefore were not aware of the feud.

He also brought out the point that Hong Wing had been sought out and shot by Fen Game, while the other three other Chinese men present in the laundry were left unharmed. Emerson felt this action indicated Hong Wing was involved with the other three in a plot to kill Fen Game. The defence also showed that two of the victims, Hong Kim Hi and Hong Loen, each had revolvers which they purchased at Clouston's Hardware on Water Street less than two years prior to the slayings.

Some of the witnesses called during the brief trial included: Fred Candow, 14 Cabot Street; John Bishop and Ches Noseworthy, 5 Carter's Hill; Robert Mayo, William Street; Sergeant John Nugent; Superintendent Pat O'Neill; doctors Thomas Anderson and John McDonald; Constable John Walsh, Sergeant

George Bennett; John Cleary, Michael Emberly, Arthur Chafe, Cyril Seaward, Ed Cahill, Hubert Carter; and Frank Martret of George Street.

They testified to finding bullets and blank cartridges on Carter's Hill, Casey Street and Barron Street, witnessing the accused's suicide attempt and other activities after the shootings. Press reports claimed that throughout the trial, Fen Game tried to give the impression that he was mad. At times, he cowered on the floor, moaned out loud and distracted the court to the point where the chief justice ordered him moved to the rear of the courtroom, within hearing distance of the proceedings.

During the final day of the trial, Fen Game collapsed while giving his testimony. He was taken to a small room adjoining the courtroom, and the proceedings were adjourned temporarily. Dr. John Murphy examined the accused, and found him to be suffering from nervous prostration. He administered a shot of morphine. Fen Game was then returned to the courtroom and the trial continued.

In his final summation to the jury, Emerson stressed that Fen Game was an ignorant man, "Coming as he does from the lowest type of ignorant men in his own country." The defence lawyer claimed this ignorance made preparation of a proper defense very difficult. To illustrate the likelihood that Fen Game was telling the truth, Emerson asked the jury to consider why the accused attempted to murder Hong Wing. Pointing out that if the other three victims had been killed solely over a wage dispute, he posed the question, "Why was Hong Wing of the Casey Street Laundry, attacked?"

The prosecutor in his summation dismissed the defence claim of ignorance because, "It was contradicted by the evidence of the letters written by the prisoner himself." Winter noted there was no evidence to show self-defence. He said, "While the prisoner's coat was torn by one of the victims, this did not justify the killing."

He then dealt with the possibility of provocation. Winter said, "It would require a very great amount of provocation to cause a man to commit such butchery." With regard to the defence's claim of a feud between the accused and shooting victims, prosecutor Winter noted there was no evidence to support such a claim. He pointed out, "The demeanor of the Chinese witnesses was that the idea was too trifling."

The chief justice instructed the jury that a verdict on each count was required. He said, "There was strong evidence to show the murders were planned. There was the evidence given by the accused himself, the letter, written by the accused to his cousin, and the statement given at the preliminary enquiry."

He explained that provocation sufficient to incite to kill must be gross if it is to result in the reducing of the charges to manslaughter. Nothing short of grave provocation is sufficient.

The chief justice continued:

> On the question of self-defence, a person assaulted is not justified in using firearms against his assailant, unless he is in such a position as to make him consider his life is actually in danger. Your duty is to declare the verdict according to the evidence; and ours is to declare sentencing according to the verdict.
>
> The jury retired to consider its decision at 4:35 p.m. on November 24th. While awaiting the verdict, Wo Fen Game was taken to an anteroom inside the courthouse, where he cursed the law and its officers in English and in Chinese. At 5:25 p.m., after less than one hour deliberation, the jury returned to the courtroom with its decision. There was a deep silence in the court as the registrar, after completing the roll call of jurors, asked if a decision had been reached. Alfred McNamara, jury foreman, stood up, and following a short

hesitation, announced, "We find the defendant, Wo Fen Game, guilty on all counts."

The prisoner was informed of the verdict through interpreter George Hart. As though in a deep trance, Fen Game's face remained expressionless. The judge asked three times if there was any reason why the sentence of death should not be imposed. The accused remained silent.

The trial was adjourned until the following day for sentencing. That night at the penitentiary, Fen Game staged an escape attempt in which a prison guard was almost killed. After the accused had been brought back to the prison, he sat in his cell, a pitiful sight, looking dejected. Warden Rose, on duty at the time, must have felt sorry for him. When the prisoner asked for a cup of tea, indicating he was feeling sick, Rose obliged. When Rose entered the cell, leaving the door open behind him, Fen Game leaped from his bunk and struck Rose over the head with a brick. The blow forced Rose to his knees, almost knocking him unconscious. Fen Game made a second attempt to strike Rose, but was tripped by Rose, and went sprawling across the floor, losing the brick. Fen Game picked up the brick and tossed it at Rose, knocking him to the floor again. He then ran into the main hall of the prison where he was captured by Chief Warden Manning who was responding to Rose's call for help.

Rose had been saved from serious injury, or even death, by the uniform that he was wearing. There was a heavy wire running around the crown of the hat, and a thick band and peak, which cushioned the blow. The guard had a fully loaded revolver on him at the time, and it was felt that if the accused had managed to take it away, he would have attempted to shoot his way out of the prison. Rose was taken to the General Hospital and received several stitches to his head. The prisoner was returned to his cell where he was shackled in heavy irons and placed under strict watch. On Saturday, November 25th, the prisoner was brought to the courthouse for sentencing. Chief Justice Horwood read the death sentence to a hushed courtroom:

> The sentence of the Court is that you, Wo Fen Game, be taken from whence you came and from thence to the lawful place of execution, there to be hanged by the neck until you are dead, and after, let your body be buried within the precincts of the prison from which you were taken, and may the Lord have mercy upon your soul.

The sentence was set to be carried out at 8:00 a.m. on December 16th, at Her Majesty's Penitentiary. One of the privileges afforded the prisoner after being sentenced was to be given whatever food he requested. Fen Game took advantage of this right up until the day of his death. He ate all his meals, and frequently had fruit, and other delicacies brought to his cell.

The trial of Wo Fen Game and the triple slayings received wide publicity across Canada. It is interesting to note that covering the events for the *Globe* newspaper was a young journalist, later to change Newfoundland's destiny, Joseph R. Smallwood.

News items of the triple murder captured the attention of two professional executioners in Montreal: M.A. Doyle of 643 Verdun Avenue, Verdun, Quebec, and J. M. Holmes, whose given address was Box 385, Montreal.

Both vied for the job of executing Wo Fen Game. Doyle offered to do the job for $100 plus expenses; while Holmes offered to do it for $90 plus expenses. In addition, Holmes offered to supply references for efficient work from seven sheriffs across Canada. At the time, Holmes boasted eleven years' experience as an executioner.

Neither man was selected. Instead a totally inexperienced HMP prisoner was chosen for the task. Authorities made a deal with a prisoner from Bell Island, who was serving time for bestiality. In return for performing the execution his sentence was shortened.

While Fen Game lay in his cell awaiting his fate, Prison Superintendent Alexander Parsons and Sheriff Blandford worked out the details of the hanging. The execution was to be carried out in accordance with the regulations made under the Capital Punishment Act, 1868. The Superintendent of Public Works, Mr. Churchill, was ordered to construct the scaffold inside the penitentiary walls on December 1, 1922. That scaffold was built on the east side of the penitentiary, and was completed by the Wednesday prior to the date of execution.

At 5:00 a.m. on the day of execution, Wo Fen Game penned a letter to his wife living in China. The letter was given to the Minister of Justice who sent it to the Pinkerton Agency, New York, to be translated. He then screened it before forwarding it to Fen Game's wife. The condemned man did not rest well during the night, but he did eat a hearty breakfast in the morning. He had just finished breakfast when those involved in the execution procession began to arrive at his cell. By 7:30 a.m., the entire party had gathered. The masked executioner stepped forward, and began the process of pinioning the prisoner's arms. Fen Game remained calm during the process.

A few minutes before 8:00 a.m., the procession formed in the corridor in preparation for the death march to the gallows. The procession was led by Reverends Fairbairn and Joyce who recited the burial services according to Methodist Ritual. Next came Wo Fen Game, walking between Wardens Manning and Crotty, then Wardens Rose, Stone and Genge, followed by Sheriff Blandford and Superintendent Parsons. The executioner was last, but because he was an inmate of the prison, he was accompanied by a guard.

The press gathered in a room overlooking the scaffold. Also present in the room were the following members of the Chinese community: Kim Lee, Charlie Dean, Hong Yin and Fen Chat, the latter a cousin of the prisoner. The procession moved slowly along the corridor, and entered the prison yard where the gallows awaited its victim.

Three witnesses were required to attend the execution and to verify that the sentence of the court had been carried out. The witnesses were: Superintendent Parsons, Sheriff S.D. Blandford and the prison doctor, Lawrence Keegan. All persons taking part in the execution were required to report at the prison by 4:00 p.m. on the afternoon of December 15th, and to remain there until the execution was completed.

For a short period of time after being sentenced Fen Game deserted his Christian faith and returned to his Confucian beliefs. However, Reverend J.G. Joyce and Reverend Fairbarn of Wesley United Church succeeded in bringing Fen Game back into the Christian faith just days before the hanging. Reverend Joyce and Kim Lee developed a close relationship with the prisoner during his final days on earth. Fen Game's last night was spent chatting with Reverend Joyce and Kim Lee. His last thoughts were for his family. The condemned man asked Reverend Joyce if he could arrange for the refund on his head tax from the Newfoundland Government to go to his wife and daughter in China. Reverend Joyce promised he would do this, but he ran into a brick wall in dealing with the Newfoundland Government. While Sir Richard Squires was sympathetic to the request, he felt it could not be granted because of the high cost to government to conduct the trial. The total cost of the trail was $4,547.73.

A public notice of the hanging was placed on the prison gate the night before. At 7:45 a.m., Saturday, December 16, 1922, a large crowd gathered outside the prison. Inside prison walls, officials took their places in the execution procession to prepare for the morbid walk from the prisoner's cell to the hastily erected gallows outside.

When the procession was ready, the bell began to toll. What followed was a far cry from the outbreaks of rage and temper displayed in the days following the verdict at his trial. Fen Game now exhibited a fatalistic temperament and walked right up the gallows steps without faltering. He showed no emotion as he stood on the trap door for nearly ten minutes.

When he saw the six-foot-tall executioner approach him, dressed in an overcoat, and with a woolen hat pulled over his head, which revealed only his eyes and nose, the prisoner's whole body began to shake.

The hangman placed a black cap over Fen Game's head and fastened the rope around his neck. Fen Game did not speak or try to resist. Reverend Fairbairn of Wesley United Church stood on the corner of the scaffold reading the "Services for the Dead," while Reverend Joyce stood near the bottom of the structure praying.

Describing Fen Game's last moments, a *Daily News* journalist who witnessed the execution reported:

> While waiting for the final act in the terrible affair, Wo Fen Game trembled for a second or two as if he were feeling a chill morning air, and slowly turned his head towards the right where the hangman was preparing to spring the trap. Sheriff Blandford then gave the signal, and amidst a quietness that could be felt, the trap was sprung, and Wo Fen Game sent into eternity. Death was instantaneous, according to Dr. Keegan who viewed the body shortly after.

Despite Keegan's findings, many have claimed that the executioner had made the rope too short, and this caused Fen Game to strangle rather than dying instantly.

The prisoner died at 8:09 a.m. and a black flag was hoisted over the prison to signify that the sentence of the Supreme Court had been carried out. The body was cut down shortly after 9:00 a.m., and the required notices were posted on the prison gate.

At noon, Wo Fen Game was buried in a small enclosure adjoining the prison yard.

Almost twenty-five years later Penitentiary Guard Ed Durdle was searching prison grounds with a fellow guard looking for worms for a planned fishing trip. It was a misty night and the flashlight he carried could hardly penetrate the heavy fog that was rolling up from Quidi Vidi. Suddenly, the ground beneath him broke open and he found himself a reluctant visitor in the grave of Wo Fen Game.[4]

In recent years, his remains, along with two other executed men, Francis Canning and William Parnell, were transferred to a grave in the Holy Sepulcher Cemetery.

A Ceremonial Killing

Sixteen years after Wo Fen Game was hanged an even more bizarre murder took place within the Chinese community of St. John's.

On the morning of July 3, 1938, Kilbride farmer Gordon Stanley, found the body of Eng Wing Kit hanging from an iron bar in the kitchen of the Regal Café, located on Water Street west, St. John's. The finding set into motion an intensive investigation by the Criminal Investigation Division of the Newfoundland Constabulary, which saw every member of the

---

[4] Some years after I first wrote about this execution, I was given the trunk owned and used by Fen Game when he moved from China to Newfoundland. It had been stored in the attic of the laundry by its new owners and forgotten for decades.

Chinese community in St. John's interrogated, finally leading to the arrest of Quang John Shang of Duckworth Street.

The bizarre killing was referred to by some journalists as "The Tong Murder"[5] because of the ceremonial way in which the killing was carried out.

Wing Kit, known by friends and neighbours as 'Charlie,' was found strangled and hanging from a piece of iron pipe which had been laid from the kitchen table to the stove. A knife had penetrated the area behind his voice box and his throat had been slashed. A flour sack was folded and tied around his neck with twine, obviously to prevent bleeding. A circular piece of flesh had been cut from the chest and there were large bruises on the chest and upper left arm. The murderer had then tied three bands of rope around the neck, raising the victim's head about a foot from the floor and tied the rope tightly to the iron pipe. Several segments of the rope had carefully fashioned the figure eight.

The thirty-five-year-old victim was a native of Hi Ping, Canton, China. He came to Newfoundland on July 8, 1931, leaving behind his wife, two sons and two daughters. Upon arrival, he first settled on Bell Island where he operated a small restaurant until it was destroyed by fire in 1936. Moving to St. John's, he purchased the Regal Café from Tom Yet Soon. The Regal Café was located on Water Street west, the site now occupied by Edward's Drug Store.

The gruesome butchery was discovered by Kilbride farmer Gordon Stanley who delivered milk to the Regal Café daily. On the morning of July 3, 1938, Stanley entered the café, as he did regularly, through the unlocked front door and laid several bottles of milk on the table. He called out to Charlie, but his calls were greeted with a deadly silence. Sensing that something was wrong, he cautiously walked towards the kitchen. A

[5] The Tong referred to Chinese organized crime.

dimly-lit light bulb cast an eerie glow over the gruesome sight that greeted him.

The lifeless body of Charlie, dressed in pyjamas and apron and with his purple tongue extending from his mouth, was covered in blood. Stanley was horror-struck. Seized by sudden fear, he slowly backed away toward the main entrance of the café thinking that the madman who perpetrated the crime might still be hiding inside. Once outside the laundry, he encountered Jim Reddy who joined him in looking for the police officer on the beat. The two caught up with Constable Spracklin near Leslie Street just as Spracklin was jumping aboard a street car.

Led by Spracklin, the trio returned to the Regal Café and the police officer made a quick examination of the premises before reporting the incident to Sergeant James Manderson at police headquarters. Within an hour, the place was crawling with police.

Sergeant Michael Mahoney began gathering evidence. Directing several police constables, Mahoney removed five blood-stained sections of the floor and wrapped each section in cellophane. He also recovered the rope and twine used in the incident along with a knife, a piece of iron pipe, a flour sack, samples of blood from the victim and also the victim's shoes.

Sergeant Mahoney traveled to Halifax with the evidence where it was later examined by Dr. Ralph Smith, professor of pathology at Dalhousie University.

An intensive investigation by the Criminal Investigation Department was under way in St. John's. Inspector Edward Whelan conducted the investigation. He began by questioning the five occupants of the Chinese laundry who were next door to the Regal Café. This was followed by a painstaking and time-consuming interrogation of all members of the Chinese community of St. John's. The whole effort by police was useless because everyone questioned denied any knowledge of the incident.

Police suspected the laundrymen next door to the Regal Café knew something. They had determined that three of the five occupants at the laundry were at home on the night of the murder. The police surmised, after some experimentation, that it was easy for the laundry occupants next door to hear any conversation or quarreling happening at the Regal Café.

The police might have been stymied in their investigation if it had not been for the co-operation of some of the leaders of the Chinese community. Taking matters into their own hands, they set up a committee to encourage any of their countrymen with knowledge which could help the police to come forward. The Chinese community made sure that every member of their community was made aware of the seriousness of withholding evidence under Newfoundland law.

Next, they advised their countrymen not to fear reprisal from the murderer because they would band together to protect each other. They said, if necessary, the local police would provide protection to the witnesses. The committee's assistance to the police paid off. West end laundrymen, Tom Soon and Tom Loon, came forward with information which led to the arrest of Quang John Shang.

Soon told police that he saw and heard Shang inside the Regal Café on the night of the murder. Loon stated that he saw Shang walking up Leslie Street away from the Regal shortly after the time the murder was determined to have been committed.

On Tuesday night, July 12, 1938, Shang was arrested by the Criminal Investigation Department as he was leaving the Holland Café on New Gower Street. This was Shang's tenth anniversary in Newfoundland, having arrived here from China on July 12, 1928. The thirty-year old Shang hailed from Hi Ping, Canton, the same village of origin as the deceased Eng Wing Kit.

One week after Kit's death, the police were out in full force to control the crowds of curious people who lined the streets of St. John's to try and get a glimpse of the funeral procession. Funeral arrangements had been made by J.T. Martin and the victim was buried at the General Protestant Cemetery.

The preliminary enquiry into the murder of Eng Wing Kit resulted in Shang being committed to stand trial. The trial got underway on October 31, 1938. The jury consisted of: James Atkinson, William Taylor, Edward Ryan, Edward J. Russell, William Philips, Donald Whiteway, Captain Norman Herald, James Hickey, Gerald Kennedy, Ralph Maunder, William Woods and James Darcy. The Crown was represented by Hon. L.E. Emerson, Commissioner for Justice, and G.B. Summers, Assistant Secretary for Justice. Shang was represented by C.J. Fox and James Power. Gordon Yuen of the Canadian Department of Justice was sworn in as the interpreter for the trial.

Dr. Thomas Anderson, who conducted the post-mortem on Kit, told the court it was his opinion that Kit had been killed before he was hung from the iron bar. "The knife wound in the throat had been inflicted after the body had been suspended," Dr. Anderson said. He told the court he had reached this conclusion because there was so little blood on the floor, or on the side of the victim's neck.

In an effort to show that Kit was not killed until after midnight, the prosecution called as witness Mrs. Annie Byrne of 270 Water Street. Mrs. Byrne told the court she had gone to the Regal shortly after midnight and the victim was very much alive at that time. She told the court he put his hands under her chin and said, "I likee you. I have always likee you." She became frightened and ran out of the store.

The victim's body had been found displayed in a manner which did not immediately reveal how he died. Was death caused by his throat being slashed or was he strangled with the rope tied around his neck? That question was answered during the autopsy.

Dr. Ralph Smith, a pathologist, was then called to the stand. He testified that he had conducted four tests on the various blood stains and samples submitted to him by the police. Dr. Smith determined that all the blood samples were from the victim. The pathologist explained his procedures. He said the first two tests were chemical. The first was to show up the blood crystals while the second was by spectroscope to determine the various spectra given by the blood. This eliminated stains such as fruit juices. The third test was to identify the presence of round red blood corpuscles. This eliminated the possibility of the blood being that of birds, or of amphibian, as they all have a little nucleus in the cell centre whereas human blood does not. The fourth test was a biological test and was made using blood-serum. In this test, he used controls of human blood and blood other than human.

One of the two key witnesses for the prosecution was Tom Yet Soon, an occupant and part owner of the laundry adjacent to the Regal Café. Soon told the court that on the night of the murder he had returned home at about 11:30 p.m. He had caught the last street car for the night as he headed home, following a visit to the Imperial Café in the east end of the city. Because it was the last car for the night, it went only as far as the railway station, and Soon had to travel the remainder of the distance on foot.

It was raining, and Soon ran all the way home, stopping only a minute as he greeted Tom Loon who was walking east on Water Street. Once inside the house, Soon removed all his clothing except his pants, and went to bed. A few minutes later, he said he heard arguing coming from the Regal Café. Curious as to who was arguing, he got dressed and went out into the rear garden. While peeping through the kitchen window of the Regal, he saw the accused, Quang John Shang.

He explained he saw Shang getting off a barrel and heard him say, "I am going to have some bread." Having satisfied his curiosity, Soon claimed he went back to bed. Under cross-examination, he said that he did not see the victim Eng Wing Kit while he was peeping through the window.

According to his testimony, Soon was beginning to fall asleep when the sound of something being dragged across the floor next door startled him. Once more, he dressed and went to the rear garden to try and see what was happening. He said he saw Shang, but did not see the victim. Soon returned to bed and a short while later he recalled hearing footsteps walking around upstairs at the Regal Café followed by someone leaving and footsteps along the sidewalk.

He told the court he went to his front door to see if it was Eng Wing Kit because he wanted to talk to him. When he got there, the street was empty. He listened for a few minutes hoping to hear Kit inside the Regal, and hearing nothing, he returned to bed.

Soon testified that he first became aware of Kit's murder the following morning at 9:00 a.m. The witness testified that Tom Loon awakened him to tell of Kit's murder.

The second major witness for the prosecution was Tom Loon, who was also an employee of the West End Laundry. By the time of his testimony, Mr. Soon had placed the accused, Shang, inside the Regal Café around the time of the murder. The evidence of Tom Loon also placed Shang in the area of the café shortly after the murder. Mr. Loon told the court he had to deliver a parcel of shirts to the York Street area at approximately 11:30 p.m. A few minutes after leaving the laundry he met Tom Soon, the two exchanged greetings and Loon continued on towards the railway station, hoping to catch a late street car. When he arrived there, the street cars had ceased operations for the night. A night watchman called the ABC Cab

Company, and in a few minutes Loon was heading for York Street. Loon testified that it was near 1:00 a.m. when he returned home and saw Quang John Shang walking up Leslie Street.

To counteract this evidence, defence lawyer Fox called Ambrose Harris, a cab driver with the ABC Cab Company. Harris told the court he was the driver who picked up Tom Loon on the night of the murder. He denied having seen Shang or anyone else in the area to which Loon referred.

At 10:00 a.m. on November 3rd, the judge and jury visited the site of the gruesome murder and the laundry next door. Returning to the court an hour later, they continued the trial.

Fox felt the prosecution's case was weak. He had carefully analyzed the testimony given at the preliminary hearing and compared it, wherever possible, with the evidence given during the trial. He found a number of inconsistencies in the evidence of Loon and Soon and seriously considered asking the judge to throw out the case. After consultation with James Power, his partner in the defence of Shang, he decided to go to the jury instead. Shang was not called to testify during the trial. Fox, in addressing the court, said there was nothing but circumstantial evidence against Shang. "Because of its contradiction, and because of its suspiciousness, it is not evidence on which you would hang a dog," Fox said.

Skillfully, Fox began to devastate the prosecution's case. When he was finished, he had almost succeeded in shifting the suspicion of guilt from the accused to the witnesses.

Facing Tom Soon and Tom Loon, he commented, "I will prove to you that the only evidence we have is the two Chinese on the bench there." Pausing for effect, while all eyes in the courtroom focused on Soon and Loon, Fox continued, saying, "On the evidence of these two Chinese, do you not agree it is a mass of contradiction? There is an atmosphere of suspicion;

it is untrustworthy; it is improbable, and I am justified in asking you to disregard it altogether."

Injecting a point for the jury to ponder, Fox added, "We do not know the working of the Oriental mind, educated as we are, maybe, what do we know? What do we know of their thoughts, disagreements, their quarrels, their doubts and their diversions?"

Fox then began to discredit the evidence of Mr. Loon and Mr. Soon. He said:

> You saw and heard these two Chinese. They lived in the same house. Soon gave evidence here in court contradictory to what he gave during the preliminary hearing. On Saturday night, July 2, he went to a friend's café, and he returned home, on or about mid-night, and he very conveniently met Loon. It was a rainy night. They met on Water Street. He was wet and proposed to go home and go to bed. Then he tells the story of how he went home, took his shoes off down-stairs, goes upstairs and goes to bed. He took off his short coat and his collar and he gets in bed.

Pausing once more to give the jury the opportunity to visu-alize the scene of Tom Soon soaking wet and preparing for bed, Fox continued, "Would an ordinary man, no matter how low he is, get in bed with his wet overalls on? Then he does not go to sleep. He hears voices next door. He gets up and listens. Why?"

At this point, Fox began to twist the suspicion of the jury away from Shang and onto the Crown witnesses. In doing so Fox said:

> Gentlemen, he never intended on going to bed that night. He gets up and listens to voices. Not con-tent with listening to voices, he goes out the back door

and looks over the fence. Why?

He tells you he did not see the deceased. But he saw the accused! Strange thing, he never in all his evidence saw the deceased about, but he always saw the accused. Why? Because he wants you to concentrate your mind on John Shang.

Then he tells you the sublime story, that not like most of us when we go to bed we usually take up a detective story. No, he took up a Chinese songbook in order to lull himself to sleep. Next thing, he hears footsteps. Suppose he did. Immediately, he wants to know whose they were and concludes that Eng Wing Kit is going out. He gets out of bed. It was none of his business mind you. Why the tremendous interest? If any man hears his next door neighbor go out at night, he does not get up to see if he went or not. I am sure I would not.

Further attacking the credibility of the Crown's key witness, Fox argued, "In the enquiry Soon says he goes up to the back window again. He does not see Kit. He saw the accused bending over a table. Why did he not go inside?"

Fox pointed out that Kit and Soon were friends and visited each other regularly. He suggested to the court that if Soon was really curious, he could have gone to the front door of the café and entered. He continued, "It might have been Kit's steps he heard next door. Kit was dressed in pyjamas when found. His café was open until 12 o'clock. When did he go upstairs to take off his pants and put on the pyjamas?"

Referring to Soon's claim that he did not see Kit when he peeped in through the kitchen window, Fox said that it was an impossibility. He noted it would be impossible not to see everything inside the kitchen because it was only a little two-by-four room.

Fox continued his attack on the Crown witnesses, throwing suspicion on the witnesses whenever he could. Fox thought it was strange that when police went to the laundry the morning of the murder, they found a big fire in the kitchen.

The laundry was not opened and they had stopped working at 4:00 p.m. the day before. Turning to the jury, Fox asked, "Were they burning something?" He added that the same night, Soon and Loon were out in the garden behind the Regal Café cutting and removing weeds. "Why," he asked, "were they doing this?" He said, "The two men explained they were nervous and feared the spirit of the victim. Cutting the weeds, they claimed, would keep the spirit away." Continuing, he said, "Tom Yuen, an occupant of the laundry, was so nervous that night that he slept with two other Chinamen. Why was he so nervous?"

Turning his attention to Tom Loon, he repeated Loon's testimony that he had seen the accused walking up Leslie Street shortly after the estimated time of murder. Fox said that Ambrose Harris, the taxi driver, told the court there was nobody on the street. Fox said that Loon had claimed to have taken laundry worth $1.70 from the West End Laundry to York Street at around 11:30 p.m. and that he hired a taxi from the railway station to take him there and back to the laundry. Fox added, "Yet, he left the packages in the hallway and never saw any customers." Fox told the court that Dr. Thomas Anderson had erred in estimating the time of death because he did not take the temperature of the house or the body. Quoting Dr. Anderson, Fox stated, "There is even a possibility of Kit having been killed elsewhere."

He concluded, "The Crown had not produced one bit of substantiated evidence to convict the accused. God's greatest gift to man is life and the life of the accused is now in the hands of the jury. I am not appealing to your sympathies but to your sense of British Justice."

Following Fox, Hon. L.E. Emerson summed up the Crown's case against the accused. He told the court that the two witnesses had seen Shang inside and near the café at the estimated time of the murder. He said:

> It is not the Crown's duty to overstate the case against the accused. It is my duty to bring before you the direct evidence against the accused. You have heard the evidence. You have the final word.

Emerson tried to offset the effect of Fox's address to the jury by pointing out that the jury does not have the responsibility of life or death, only the responsibility of determining guilt. The judge decides on life or death for the accused. He emphasized that the Crown proved beyond any shadow of doubt that the accused was guilty of the offence. There is no evidence the victim tried to defend himself. He was struck suddenly by his assailant.

Referring to Fox's statement regarding the mysterious workings of the Oriental mind, Emerson argued, "We have been, in preparing this case for you, surrounded with difficulties and we now put it to you as good a case as if the accused had been a Newfoundlander. If the courts waited for complete evidence, there would be many criminals abroad today."

In his address to the jury, the judge asked, "There is no doubt a murder has been committed, but does the evidence in this case satisfy you that the accused committed that murder?"

The judge reviewed the evidence presented in the case and said:

> In dealing with malicious murder, the Crown must show it was caused with malicious intent by the accused. It is not for the accused to establish his

innocence, but for the Crown to establish his guilt. In civil cases the preponderance of probability may constitute sufficient grounds for a guilty verdict, but something more in the way of proof is required in criminal cases. In order to return a verdict against the prisoner, you must be satisfied beyond a reasonable doubt of his guilt. If you think the Crown's case is conclusive, it is your duty to pronounce the prisoner guilty. But if you feel the case has left you in doubt, so that you cannot safely convict, you will remember that it is better that many guilty men should escape than that one innocent man should be wrongly convicted.

After a four and a half hour deliberation, the jury returned its "Not Guilty" verdict to a crowded courtroom. The prisoner showed no emotion when the court interpreter told him he was a free man. Shang was escorted from the courthouse by friends, including Kim Lee, to a taxi waiting outside. As the taxi pulled away, there ended one of the most interesting sagas in the history of crime in Newfoundland.

Quang John Shang left Newfoundland soon after and never returned. He settled in Vancouver, British Columbia where he passed away during the late 1980s.

The 'ceremonial killing' of Eng Wing Kit as it was dubbed in the press has never been solved.

A prison cell in the old cell block at HMP where a prisoner awaiting execution was confined. *Panl*

A view of the original HMP prison. *Panl*

Wo Fen Game, mentioned in the Tong Story was hanged at HMP for the murder of three men. *Jack Fitzgerald collection*

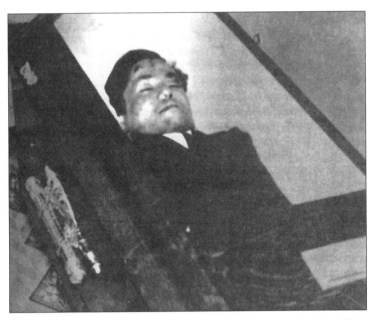

The victim of the 1938 killing inside a Water Street Laundry, Eng Wing Kit. *Jack Fitzgerald Collection*

Police standing outside the Chinese Laundry on what is known today as Carter's Hill where three men were murdered. *Panl*

97

The three Chinese victims of Wo Fen Game at a Carter's Hill Laundry (at the time Murray Street) were placed on the display in the front window of the Martin's Funeral Home on New Gower Street to satisfy public interest. *Jack Fitzgerald Collection*

Chapter 5: Tough Guys and Killers

Jim Robbins was known around St. John's in the 1950s as a 'tough guy.' It was a well-deserved title because his fists had gotten him barred from every tavern in St. John's at least once. Every cop on the beat knew him by first name and paid special attention when he was spotted in their areas. He not only had a police record in Newfoundland but also in the United States. In late 1955, he found himself a guest of Her Majesty's Penitentiary in a cell located in the west block along with one of his buddies, Gerald Hanlon.

It was winter, and while the Atlantic winds swept in through Quidi Vidi Gut and whistled through the cracks in the prison windows, Robbins and Hanlon debated whether Her Majesty would be offended or not if they suddenly declined her hospitality and broke out of prison. They chose to disregard Her Majesty's feelings and decided to break out. To carry out their escape the two agreed to make use of an abandoned door in the outside yard.

At 5:00 p.m. on January 10, 1956, the duo put their escape plan in effect. They succeeded in getting out into the yard where they propped the door up against the prison wall and used it as a ladder to make a successful getaway. Hanlon's freedom was short-lived. The police caught him on Murphy's Avenue in the north-west area of town, which was a fair distance from Her Majesty's Penitentiary.

Robbins had better luck, perhaps because he lived in the Battery, a short distance from the prison. There he had many friends whom he could turn to for help. In addition to being a tough guy, Robbins was also cunning and a decisive thinker, although this trait frequently led him into trouble with the law. Once freed from the confines of prison, Jim Robbins evaded police a lot longer than his partner and managed to arouse the kind of sentiment that had made Philip Brady a local folk-hero a half century before.

The thirty-six-year-old Robbins had a record of violence and city police were quick to advise the public through the media that he was considered dangerous. At the time, he was serving a thirty-month sentence for robbery and assault. His victim was Cyril Murphy, a Canadian Customs official.

Jim Robbins could be a great showman at times and one of his most memorable performances came at the end of that trial in March 1955. Throughout the hearing the prisoner displayed the arrogance and contempt for the justice system that was apparent throughout his criminal life. After being found guilty he engaged in an exchange with Magistrate Hugh O'Neill. He chastised the judge for what he described as making a very wrong decision and ordered him to, "Go to your chamber and look into your conscience and ask from the bottom of your heart whether I am innocent."

Unperturbed by the prisoner's histrionics, O'Neill replied, "You are not safe to be at large."

"I still maintain my innocence," the prisoner protested indignantly.

When O'Neill sentenced Robbins to thirty months in jail, Robbins was on his feet again and angrily questioning the judge, "Did Carter, (the prosecutor) influence your decision?"

Brushing him off, O'Neill, as he gathered his papers, replied casually, "No, he only brought out the facts." When the prisoner was taken downstairs to the lockup, a couple of inmates there, one named Murphy from Mundy Pond, taunted him with the words from a popular song of that period, "Poor little Robbins, walking, walking, walking to Missouri," to remind him of his return to jail and his prison time in the United States.

Inside prison Jim Robbins was every inch the tough guy he portrayed throughout the streets and taverns of St. John's. He was a constant source of problems for prison guards. Her Majesty's Penitentiary's Warden, Otto Kelland, was at wits end over how to deal with Robbins' contempt and disregard for any kind of prison authority, and chose an unorthodox way of trying.

In those days, the Warden carried a gun and on that day Kelland thought it could be effective in dealing with this prisoner. Leaving his administrative office, he walked firmly, gun in hand, to the solitary confinement cell, which so frequently was home to Robbins. Through the peek window in that cell, Kelland observed Robbins in the middle of one of his tantrums, a display of temper also referred to by fellow inmates as 'throwing a paddy.'

Kelland aimed the gun into the cell and pulled the trigger. Two loud shots rang out in succession hitting just where he had targeted – the cell floor. Any expectations the Warden had that gunfire would bring the prisoner under control evaporated when Robbins, in the memorable style of screen star Jimmy Cagney's bravado of tough guy, faced Kelland and pounding his index finger on the centre of his head while looking straight into his eyes, hollered, "If you want to stop me, the next time, you better shoot there."

This was not the reaction Kelland had hoped for. Yet it did get attention both public and political. The Warden got a suspension for firing his gun into a cell. John Q. Public sided with Kelland, who certainly earned their respect for his own 'enough is enough' decision.

Jim Robbins was not only a thorn in the side of the New-foundland justice system, but almost a decade earlier he had become a major irritant in the United States legal system, which he encountered after killing a man. That crime earned him a conviction of manslaughter and ten years in an American prison. In 1948, he was deported back to St. John's. Little is known about his life during those ten years but people who knew him in St. John's said it only made him more of a hard case when he returned home.

After his escape from Her Majesty's Penitentiary, Robbins evaded police for more than a year and attracted countrywide publicity. He hid out in a rented apartment in an area in downtown Toronto, which a year earlier was the hideout of Leonard Jackson, who was hanged for the murder of Detective Sergeant Edmond Tong of the Toronto Police Force.

Just a few weeks before his capture, Robbins gained nationwide notoriety when the nationally distributed weekly newspaper, *Star Weekly*, printed the feature, "Canada's Ten Most Wanted Criminals." Among the ten was Jim Robbins, picture included. In response to Robbins' notoriety, the London Theatre in St. John's resurrected the folk hero image of Philip Brady and tried to turn Robbins into a similar type of hero. The group put off a play showcasing many of the ideas used to depict Brady's escapades.

In Toronto, Robbins, using the alias James Parker, was keeping a low profile and had found a job as labourer with a pipe distributing firm. His tough guy image led to his downfall during a rowdy Christmas party in 1956, which brought police to his boarding house. Under the influence of liquor, the Newfoundlander was more abrasive than ever and got himself arrested by police. However, the police had no idea who he was until a fingerprint match identified him.

Elizabeth Tapp, his landlady, when told of her boarder's true identity, expressed surprise. She said, "He was a steady worker and was well-liked at the factory." Toronto police dropped the disorderly conduct charges against Robbins and shipped him back to St. John's. After completing his prison term, he moved to Montreal. In 1963, he was arrested again and charged with the non-capital murder of Constance Mary McGee, whom he had beaten to death.

Robbins enjoyed the limelight the trial gave him and took full advantage of it to keep the court in an almost continuous uproar. The court appointed Edwin Murphy, Q.C. and John Hannon as defence lawyers for Robbins. The Crown was represented by Kenneth MacKay.

On several occasions Robbins was ordered out of court because of his arrogant conduct. Throughout the trial Robbins refused to co-operate with his lawyers and even took the witness stand against their advice, demanding that the trial should be declared a mistrial. Before being removed from the witness stand, he hurled insults at his own lawyers and the presiding judge, Francois Caron. When he later returned to court, he was a model of good behaviour but still outspoken. He told the court, "I'm not asking for pity, only for justice." He claimed there had been numerous irregularities in his trial and the judge should have declared it a mistrial.

Some of the irregularities he referred to included, "... witnesses being coached by the police, and the failure of my lawyers to bring to court certain witnesses I wanted to have heard."

During his testimony Judge Caron showed great patience. He allowed Robbins to go on uninterrupted as he referred to 'kangaroo justice' in the Coroner's Court, and made references to such widely separated incidents as the assassination of President Kennedy and the Coffey murder case. He also said his lawyers had suggested he plead guilty to manslaughter, telling him he would serve about six years of what would probably be a ten-year sentence.

At this point Robbins' voice became louder and he faced the jury firmly insisting, "I refused to do this. There is no question of manslaughter in this case. You either find me guilty of non-capital murder or acquit me. And don't forget I am entitled to the full benefit of the doubt."

Robbins had spent enough time before courts to know that the Crown would bring up his past record at some point, so he beat them to the punch. In an attempt to influence the jury into thinking he was honest and straightforward in his testimony he stared directly at them as he provided the lengthy details of his court records. He followed this performance with the presentation of his 'alibi.'

Robbins boldly told the court that on the day of McGee's death, he had been drinking with some friends. The drinking was interrupted by a visit to a sick friend in hospital. Leaving the hospital, he went to a McGill Street club and continued to drink. He said, "I met Connie in the club. There was a fight there and that's all I remembered until I woke up."

He recalled that she was beside him in bed and was breathing heavily. He asked neighbours to call a doctor and ambulance. The woman died later that day in hospital.

During the lunch break while waiting for the jury's decision, he pulled another Cagney-style tough guy incident. As a fellow prisoner agitated him he used a small metal object held in his hand to swipe it across the prisoner's eyes. The prisoner instantly covered his eyes and fell back screaming in pain. Guards removed the man and brought him to hospital for medical attention. Meanwhile, Robbins had quietly returned to his seat as though nothing had happened.

When the judge read the verdict of guilty as charged and sentenced him to life in prison, he added that, "The jury's verdict is fully justified by the evidence." Before he could finish his thought Robbins loudly interjected, "This is a travesty of justice. I hope everyone sleeps well tonight."

But Judge Caron got in the last words. He said, "You were listened to as long as you wanted to talk. I have no alternative under the law but to impose a life sentence on you."

Robbins, the 'tough guy,' served his time at Dorchester Penitentiary.

The Five Dollar Hit Man

John James Rowe, a native of St. John's Newfoundland, survived the bloody battles of World War I only to be slain on a darkened Montreal street on May 19, 1921, for a five dollar bill. Just as sensational was the fact that the defence lawyer shocked the court by comparing the victim to a pig!

The final hours of John Rowe's life were spent at a restaurant at the corner of Vitre and St. Urbane Streets where he had a supper with the twenty-three-year-old Grace Morino. Morino and her husband, Giuseppe, were well-known to Montreal police. At that time Giuseppe was serving a two-year term at the St. Vincent de Paul Penitentiary for highway robbery. Giuseppe's victim was beaten and his money and watch stolen.

When Rowe removed a five dollar bill from his wallet to pay the restaurant bill, Grace grabbed the money from his hand and escaped out the door with John Rowe in close pursuit. It seemed like a simple theft. However, when Rowe caught up with her and demanded the return of his five dollars, Grace put her hand in her pocket and drew a penknife. Before Rowe could determine what was actually happening, Grace swiftly plunged the knife into his heart and ran. She tossed the knife away as she escaped.

John Rowe died instantly. Witnesses summoned the police and the murder weapon was easily recovered. A medical examination of the blood on the knife determined it belonged to the victim. The investigation at the scene led police to arrest Grace Morino.

When the trial got underway on November 11, 1921 it attracted newspaper headlines across Quebec. The prosecution presented a strong case, which included eye witnesses and blood-expert evidence, confirming the blood on Morino's knife belonged to the victim. The jury had no problem arriving at a verdict of guilty.

However, a comment made in low voice by the defence lawyer during the presentation of the expert medical evidence drew a strong condemnation by the judge and raised eyebrows of people inside the court when the judge stated what had been said. Judge P. Monet in his sentencing comments addressed himself to the defence lawyer. He told the court that he had heard the defence lawyer make a despicable comment in a 'sotto-voce' (undertone). He said that when Dr. J. Derome was telling the court that the blood found on the penknife was John Rowe's blood someone in the courtroom said, "... it could have been a pig's blood." In reply to this, according to the judge, the defence lawyer said in sotto-voce, "Yes, it was pig's blood ... the blood of an Englishman."

After condemning the lawyer's behaviour, the judge announced his verdict of life imprisonment for Grace Morino. In response to the sentence Grace exclaimed a sarcastic, "Thanks," and was escorted from the courtroom to begin serving her sentence.

Edward Jordan Hanged for Mutiny and Piracy

Edward Jordan took control of a small passenger ship by violence and murder. He then went on to several Newfoundland communities where he persuaded a magistrate to use his legal authority to force a Newfoundland seaman to join his crew.

Edward Jordan's pathway into the history of the gallows in Canada began on September 13, 1809, when he took his wife,

Margaret, and their four children on the schooner *Eliza* for a trip from Quebec to Halifax. Jordan, a passenger on the *Eliza,* was actually a fishing skipper who operated out of the tiny fishing settlement called Perce on thc Gaspe Peninsula.

After sharing a few drinks of grog with the ship's mate, John Kelly, Jordan, suggested that together they could dump the crew, take the ship and become rich men. Kelly agreed, and the two involved Margaret Jordan in their plot to overpower Captain John Stairs and his crew.

That night as the *Eliza* sailed peacefully in waters somewhere between White Head and Cape Canso, Nova Scotia, the trio cornered Captain Stairs alone, and beat him until he was almost unconscious. He would certainly have been killed if it had not been for the intercession of crewmen Ben Matthews and Tom Heath.

Matthews and Heath fought the three pirates long enough to divert their attack away from the captain. However, they were no match for Jordan and Kelly, who beat them senseless and tossed them overboard to drown. When they went for the captain to consign him to the same fate, they discovered he had escaped. While Jordan and Kelly were getting rid of Matthews and Heath, Captain Stairs threw a hatch overboard, then jumped in the waters, and pulled himself onto the hatch. Jordan saw the captain lying on the hatch, and he pulled his gun and began firing at him.

"Put away the gun, he's a dead man, anyway," shouted Kelly.

"Yes, he'll be dead by morning anyway." Jordan said as he put down his gun. This proved to be a fatal decision for Jordan. Captain Stairs drifted several hours on the hatch, and at dawn was rescued by a passing American schooner which was sailing to Boston. After receiving medical attention in Boston, Stairs told police of the piracy of the *Eliza*, and the murder of two crewmen by Jordan and Kelly. American and Canadian coast guards were alerted, and a massive effort was made to locate the *Eliza* and bring the pirates to justice.

Meanwhile, Jordan was sailing along the south coast of Newfoundland in the Fortune Bay area, trying to recruit crew members for a planned Atlantic crossing to Ireland. At Little Bay West near Harbour Breton, he tried to enlist Bill Carew and John Pigot for the *Eliza*. The two men went onboard the ship, and after sizing up the situation, choose not to join the crew. They had become suspicious after noticing the missing hatch, the fish not properly stowed, and only two men, a woman and four children on board.

Kelly then took a bold step in order to enlist a crew. He risked seeking out the magistrate in Harbour Breton for assistance. No doubt he was confident that he and Jordan had gotten away with their crimes. Kelly impressed the magistrate with his claim of dire need for a crew to help get their cargo to Ireland.

The magistrate summoned Pigot, who was unemployed, and ordered that he sign up as a crew member on the *Eliza* or face a public flogging. Reluctantly, Pigot gathered his belongings and went on board the schooner. This is the only known case in Newfoundland Justice where the court assisted pirates in getting a crew. Jordan then sailed for St. Mary's Bay and along the Southern Shore to recruit men to work on his ship.

A man named John Power heard the *Eliza* was getting ready for a trip to Ireland, and was looking for an experienced navigator. He applied for the job and was hired by Jordan at a monthly salary of twenty-five dollars. Jordan hired four more men along the Southern Shore then set out for Ireland.

Things did not go smoothly at sea. Jordan caught his wife sleeping with Kelly, and a fight broke out. Kelly got his gun and threatened to shoot Jordan. He may have done so, if Mrs. Jordan had not interceded and taken the gun from him. Kelly remained in fear of Jordan. That night, Kelly slipped over the side with one of the ship's rowboats, and rowed ashore. He was never heard from again. Some say he made it to Renews, where he married and settled down.

Not far behind the *Eliza* was the Canadian Coast Guard schooner *Cuttle*, which caught up with her on the Atlantic, a few hundred miles from the Newfoundland coast. Jordan remained calm, and was convinced that his murder and piracy had not been discovered. He told the coast guard officer that he was taking cargo to Halifax. The officers said they wanted to come aboard; Jordan agreed, but felt it was a routine boarding.

He was shocked when the boarding party presented him with a warrant for the arrest of the ship and all on board. The six Newfoundland crew members had no idea of why they were being arrested. Several coast guard sailors took control of the *Eliza* and brought her to Halifax. When told that Captain Stairs had survived, Jordan understood what was happening and he became sullen and depressed.

The investigation which followed cleared the Newfoundlanders, who were released, but kept in Halifax as witnesses for the trials of Margaret and Edward Jordan. Although there was overwhelming evidence sufficient to convict Margaret Jordan, the court acquitted her on the grounds that it would be shameful to leave her four children without a mother.

Edward Jordan, however, was found guilty of piracy and hanged at Halifax Harbour on November 20, 1809. His body was covered with pitch to preserve it, and left hanging on the British Naval gibbet, until it was eventually washed out to sea during a severe winter storm. Jordan's head was separated from the body and washed up on a beach. It ended up in the Nova Scotia museum, where it was on display until 1900.

Although some historians have claimed that Jordan was the last person hanged for piracy in Canada, a man named

Henry Dowsley holds that dubious honour. Dowsley went to the gallows for piracy in 1865. Dowsley, a black man, and a white man named James Douglas pirated the *Zero* and murdered the captain. Both were sentenced to hang, but Douglas had his sentence commuted to banishment for life.

Chapter 6: Four Women, Three Hangings

Four of the most infamous and disreputable women in the criminal history of Newfoundland were: Catherine Snow from Port de Grave, Conception Bay; Catherine Brown from Southside Road, St. John's; Eleanor Power from Freshwater Bay just south of St. John's; and Mary Power from Upper Path, St. John's.

Three of these four women were sentenced to hang and were executed at public hangings. The fourth, Mary Power, was shown mercy and spared the hangman's rope. Up until 1868, all hangings in Newfoundland were carried out in public; this practice was outlawed that year. From that point on, executions were held inside Her Majesty's Penitentiary in St. John's. No woman was ever hanged inside HMP.

The following pages reveal that blackened era in Newfoundland history.

Catherine Snow

The most tragic execution to take place in Newfoundland's criminal history was the hanging of a forty-year-old mother of seven children, from outside the window of the old courthouse on Duckworth Street in St. John's. Catherine Snow, Tobias Mandeville and Arthur Spring had been tried, found guilty and hanged for the murder of Catherine's husband, John Snow of Salmon Cove, Port de Grave. Although Catherine Snow was hanged about seven months after Mandeville and Spring, all three were publicly executed from the gallows outside the old courthouse window.[1] Mandeville and Spring were given the added penalty of dissection and gibbeting.

[1] The courthouse where these hangings took place was destroyed by fire. It was located behind the building which now houses the Newfoundland Supreme Court of Appeals.

A last minute petition circulated by members of the Roman Catholic clergy in St. John's, asking for a reprieve for Catherine Snow failed. Although the attorney general of Newfoundland told the court there was no direct evidence of Catherine Snow's guilt, but only a chain of circumstantial evidence, the jury delivered a verdict of guilty. The jury was convinced that Catherine Snow had instigated and plotted the murder of her husband for nearly two years, and that she had aided in his murder by sending her older children to a nearby wake so there would be no witnesses present when the deed was done.

Catherine's spouse, John Snow, a successful farmer and fisherman, disappeared on the night of August 31, 1833.

The next day, as the report of Snow's disappearance spread throughout the area, speculation on the possibility that he had been murdered, or had committed, suicide began to grow.

Rumors of foul play reached Magistrate Robert Pinsent through Mr. Jacobs of the coopering firm of Jacobs and Martin in Bareneed where Tobias Mandeville was employed as a cooper. It was known in Bareneed that twenty-eight-year-old Arthur Spring, who was employed as a helper by Snow, was having an affair with Snow's wife. He and twenty-four-year-old Tobias Mandeville were close friends. The magistrate sent a constable to the farm of John and Catherine Snow to investigate. The constable's report aroused further suspicion and the magistrate then personally undertook an investigation of the matter.

Three days after Snow's disappearance, Magistrate Pinsent, a police constable and two witnesses visited Snow's wharf, where he was reportedly last seen. What they found heightened the mystery over the fate of John Snow. The scene suggested that some sort of confrontation had taken place. Fish were strewn all over the wharf, rinds and trap lines were disturbed and dried blood was found spattered around.

The group of investigators then went to Snow's house in Port de Grave where they questioned Mrs. Snow. The missing man's wife recounted the happenings on the evening her husband disappeared. She told the magistrate that she had supper with her husband, Tobias Mandeville and three of her children.

Mandeville, in addition to his job as a cooper, also did some bookkeeping for Snow, and every Saturday he would go to the Snow residence to help John to make up his accounts for the week. Catherine Snow told investigators that during supper on the eve John disappeared, he had asked where the two eldest girls were. She told him they had gone to the wake of William Hele, about one mile down the road.

"John got awfully mad and started shouting at me. He grabbed the gun and went outside. He fired the gun into the air," Catherine added.

As John Snow entered the house, Mandeville said he was going over to the wake, and he got up from the table and left. Snow was very upset over the situation and insisted, in an angry manner that frightened Catherine, that she go over to the wake and bring the children home. When John left around midnight, she grabbed her youngest child and went to the home of her brother-in-law, Edward Snow.

The two girls returned home at 3:00 a.m. and, seeing there was no light coming from the house, got scared and went to their uncle's house where they found their mother. The next morning, upon returning home, they discovered John Snow was missing.

Mrs. Snow later told police that Mandeville and Spring had joined her and other relatives in a search for her missing husband. She claimed she did not suspect foul play was involved in his disappearance.

Spring and Mandeville told police they did not have any knowledge of Snow's whereabouts. Meanwhile, the police had their own suspicions and arrested Spring and Mandeville. This action seemed to irritate Catherine Snow. Mrs. Snow pleaded for their release. She told the magistrate that if Spring wasn't released to help harvest the hay and potatoes on the farm she would lose her crops.

The magistrate told her not to be concerned about the crops as she could easily hire a man to do the work for two shillings per day. Mandeville was given bail, but it was withdrawn within hours after the friend who had put it up became concerned that Mandeville would escape. Although police and residents had been searching the Port de Grave area for some trace of the missing fisherman, not one shred of evidence was uncovered.

Magistrate Pinsent then developed a scheme which he hoped would uncover information as to Snow's fate. He arranged for Mandeville and Spring to be locked up at his office in separate cells, divided only by a plank partition. A man was assigned to hide beneath the magistrate's desk and eavesdrop on any conversation the two suspects might have.

As suspected, when Spring and Mandeville thought they were alone they begun discussing the murder of John Snow. Spring suddenly interrupted Mandeville shouting, "There's a man listening under the table!" Then directing his comments to the stranger, he asked, "What did you hear? What did you hear?" The man denied hearing anything and quickly left the room. The move spooked Spring so much that he asked to speak to the magistrate. Later, at the magistrate's home, Spring broke down and confessed. His first words were, "We killed him, Mandeville, myself and Mrs. Snow."

Pinsent took the statement and had it signed by Spring and then witnessed. Spring claimed the murder was discussed and planned over a month before it happened. He revealed, "It was suggested by Mandeville. He said if we kill Snow, we'll have good times after." Spring told the magistrate that Snow was always rough on him, but he didn't want to kill him. He added, "I wanted to give him a good beating, but not kill him."

According to Spring, Mandeville thought the best way to get Snow out of their lives was to kill him. Catherine Snow was implicated when Spring declared that she became involved in the conspiracy to kill after telling Mandeville and Spring that she wished her husband was out of the way. According to the confession, Mandeville quoted Catherine Snow as saying "If he wasn't killed, he might kill me."

The first attempt to kill John Snow was with an axe. This ended in failure when Spring lost his nerve. He charged that Catherine Snow set the wheels in motion for the killing of her husband on Saturday evening, August 31st. John had gone to Bareneed, as he did every Saturday, to bring back Tobias Mandeville to do his bookkeeping. According to Spring, when Snow left, his wife sent the two eldest children off to William Hele's wake. She advised Spring that now was the time to kill her husband. She passed him the loaded rifle and told him to shoot him when he stepped out of the boat.

At 10:00 p.m. that night, the boat pulled in to Snow's wharf. Mandeville jumped out first and meeting Spring with the gun told him to shoot Snow as soon as he got up on the wharf. Spring lifted the gun, but told police his hands trembled, and he just couldn't do it. Spring said Mandeville grabbed the gun and fired at Snow, who was killed instantly. He said the bullet entered Snow's chest and he dropped suddenly without a word or a groan. They tied a rope around the victim's neck and fastened the other end around an iron grapnel. Mandeville and Spring towed the body out to deep water and tossed it, along with the iron grapnel, into the water.

With their cowardly, deceitful deed behind them, the two men, according to Spring, returned to Catherine and confirmed that the murder and the disposal of the body were successful. She then left the house and went to Edward Snow's, her brother-in-law's, for the night. Before leaving she instructed her companions in the nefarious plot to make sure that they upset things on the wharf so it would look like a robbery.

The police, armed with a signed confession from Spring, went to arrest Catherine Snow, but encountered a new twist in the case. After learning of the two men's arrest Catherine Snow fled the area. When Mandeville learned of Spring's confession, he fainted.

The next development in the case came while police were escorting the two prisoners across the bay to Portugal Cove for transfer by stagecoach to St. John's; Mandeville realized that the gallows at St. John's awaited their arrival and decided to confess his part in the slaying. He swore to the police officer, "I declare to you, as it were in the presence of God and as a man who has no hope of life and no inducement to tell an untruth, that I did not fire the gun, but this man (pointing to Spring) fired the gun!"

This comment upset Spring who shouted, "No! No! I did not do it. It was you who fired the gun."

When Spring's time came to appear before Chief Justice Boulton he was cautioned not to admit to anything. At this point he refused to speak about the incident.

While in St. John's people were excited about the sensational trial getting underway, fifty small boats were searching Port de Grave waters for the body of John Snow. By the time they finished, they were convinced that Snow had become shark meat, since the area was heavily infested with sharks during that time of year.

Catherine's attempt to flee the area was foiled by the police, who caught up with and arrested her. She was taken to

St. John's and charged, along with Mandeville and Spring, with the shooting death of her husband John Snow.

Catherine Snow's version of her husband's disappearance conflicted with her two co-defendants. First, she denied trying to get word to Spring, while inside his cell, to speak only Irish when talking with Mandeville so that the police would not understand their conversation. She added:

> Spring took a loaded gun to go shoot some dogs. The dogs were a problem because they ate his fish. I heard some gunshots and Spring came back with Mandeville, but he did not have the gun. I asked where the master was and Spring said he'll be here soon. Spring and Mandeville left and the master failed to show.

Mrs. Snow said she became frightened and took her youngest child to her brother-in-law's house. She told police that when Spring learned of the magistrate's visit he became angry and said, "Damn you, but I'll have your life if you say a word of what passed between your husband and me during the summer!"

Mrs. Snow replied, "My dear soul, I never said a word to anyone about you." She insisted she knew nothing of the plot to kill her husband.

There was tremendous interest in the Port de Grave murder case in St. John's, even though there were other murder cases to be tried by the Supreme Court that year. These cases included the famous Downing of Gibbet Hill murder trial, in which Peter Downing and Patrick Maloney were tried for the murder of Robert Crocker Bray, his child and servant girl in Harbour Grace. Also, Peter Fleming was tried for the murder of his wife in Harbour Grace. John Hennessey was tried for the murder of Timothy O'Rourke in Holyrood. Anne Morrissey was tried for the killing of her child in Trinity. Joseph Score was tried for the murder of John Ellvert in Labrador. Thomas Fitzgerald was tried for the murder of John Brady in Labrador and Joe Hackett was tried for the murder of Edward Power in Labrador.

The Port de Grave murder trial got underway on Friday, January 10, 1834, with the St. John's courtroom filled to capacity. The case was tried by Chief Justice Henry John Boulton, who had arrived in St. John's on the government yacht *Forte* from Upper Canada during November 1833. While waiting for the construction of his residence to be completed, he and his family stayed at Government House.

During the jury selection process, Mandeville was the only one of the three defendants to dispute the choice of jury members. He told the judge the jurors were all strangers to him and the other two prisoners. Despite his protests, the jury was sworn in and the murder charge read. The judge said that Catherine Snow was considered an accessory before the fact. City lawyer George Emerson represented Catherine Snow while Bryan Robinson, who later became a Supreme Court Justice, represented Spring.

In his opening address to the court the attorney general said:

> Arthur Spring's and Catherine Snow's offence was in a degree technically distinguished from Mandeville. His was simply murder. But owing to the relationship of wife and servant in which the woman and Spring stood towards the murdered party, their crime if proven against them would constitute a murder denominate "petit treason." The case is the most deeply atrocious and appalling that I have ever seen.

He said he intended to show the court that an illicit relationship existed between Spring and Mrs. Snow, that they got

rid of John Snow to get him out of the way, that they found
Mandeville a willing partner and that several of their plans to
kill Snow were bungled. On the day of the murder, Catherine
Snow went with her husband to deliver fish at Jacob's and Martin in Bareneed. While there, Catherine Snow planned her husband's murder with Mandeville. John Snow, after taking his
wife home, would as usual go alone in his boat on Saturday
evening and bring Mandeville back to Snow's house. As soon
as Snow left, his wife sent their servant, Catherine White, and
her two eldest daughters to the house of a deceased neighbour
to attend a wake. The younger children were put to bed. Spring
was then ready for the killing. Catherine Snow then gave her
husband's gun to Spring.

The prosecutor then outlined the murder plan and its execution, as he intended to prove it to the court:

> Mandeville was to leave Snow securing the boat
> and Spring would shoot him as he stepped onto the
> wharf. The two would then get rid of the body in the
> open sea. I can't prove which one fired the gun, but
> they were both present for the murder. As to Catherine
> Snow, there is no direct or positive evidence of her
> guilt. But I have a chain of circumstantial evidence to
> show her guilt.

The prosecutor then went on to trace Catherine Snow's
participation and co-operation in the plot. He described her
movements after the murder and pointed to her false accounts
of the fatal night, which she gave to a neighbour and a relative.
He drew attention to the fact that Catherine Snow had kept
her boyfriend in the house for the two nights after the murder.

"Catherine Snow," said the prosecutor, "made no efforts
to try and find her husband. She tried to influence the

statements of Mandeville and Spring after they were arrested and, finally, she tried to leave the area, deserting her children."

He explained to the court that the confessions of the two men were not admitted as evidence because they were not aware that the persons taking the statements were peace officers. However, he added, the statements implicated Catherine Snow.

The prosecutor said the jurors must decide, firstly, if John Snow was murdered; secondly, if the prisoners at the bar were his murderers; and thirdly, that she had premeditated the act.

A witness for the prosecution, Mark Henneberry, told the court that shortly after Spring's arrest, he met Catherine Snow on the road to Bareneed. He said she asked, "What news do you have?"

I replied, "Bad news."

"That's because whatever Spring told you to tell me, you did not tell me and you told Magistrate Pinsent of it," she said.

He testified that Catherine Snow asked him to go down and warn Spring, in Irish, not to tell anything.

Catherine Snow's statement was then read to the court, denying she was involved in the murder and claiming she did not have knowledge of the murder plot. Before the trial ended, Spring tried to clear Catherine. He said the statement he had made to implicate her in the murder plot was not true.

Catherine found some reason for hope in the judge's summation to the jury. He pointed out that:

> The evidence is conclusive against Mandevelle and Spring. But I ask you to pay close attention to the circumstantial evidence against Catherine Snow. If you do not consider it conclusive, then give her the benefit of the doubt. There is no choice of manslaughter; either you bring in a conviction or an acquittal.

The defence case was simply that Catherine Snow was not present when her husband was shot, she had no knowledge of the crime and did not participate in its planning. The defence for Spring and Mandevelle was that the body was never found and there was no evidence to say that the murder had been carried out.

The jury's quick decision came as a surprise to most of the spectators in court. In just thirty minutes, they returned with a guilty verdict against all three prisoners. The conviction of the two men was anticipated, but Snow, the mother of seven children, had gained the sympathy of the general public. Before sentencing, the judge asked the defendants if they had anything to say.

Mandeville and Spring asked to be given time to prepare for their fate and that their bodies be given to friends for burial. The judge's reply was harsh. He said:

> It is not in my power to comply with your request. The law gives me no discretion in the matter. They were both sentenced to be hanged, dissected and then gibbeted at Spectacle Hill in Port de Grave near where the murder occurred.

Defence lawyer Emerson asked the judge to consider that Catherine Snow was pregnant. In response, the judge appointed a jury of matrons who later confirmed the prisoner was indeed pregnant. In view of this, he then announced that he would allow Catherine Snow time to deliver her child. However, Mandeville and Spring would be hanged on schedule. Their execution took place on Monday, January 13, 1834. Bishop Fleming spent the entire two nights before the hanging with the prisoners and celebrated Mass in their cells on the morning of the execution. Their execution took place from a gallows erected outside the session's court window at the western end of the old courthouse building.

An hour prior to the execution, people began to gather at Gallows Gallery, an open area between Cathedral Street and Church Hill. This area was considered to be the best vantage point to view public executions outside the old courthouse. By the time of the execution, thousands had gathered to witness the event.

The two men walked to the gallows clad in the clothes in which they had chosen to be buried. When Mandeville stumbled and disrupted the death walk to the gallows, some gasped not knowing what was taking place. The delay was short. Mandeville's slipper had fallen off and he paused to put it back on. Each man wore a blue jacket, white trousers and white gloves.

The *Newfoundlander* reported, "They died bravely, and their execution was witnessed by thousands."

On July 21, 1834, after delivering her child, Catherine Snow was executed from the same gallows erected outside the session's courthouse window.

Catherine Snow's execution sparked a great deal of controversy because some people felt she was innocent. For years after, people who believed in Snow's innocence would point to the judge's comments to the jury as the basis for arguing the woman's innocence.

They would quote Judge Boulton's comments to the jury:

> You will observe that nothing said by any of the prisoners can be admitted to implicate her in the act. However, her affair of passion with her very much younger cousin was enough to condemn her. [It constituted Petit Treason]

In response to those who insisted Catherine Snow was innocent, Judge Boulton pointed out that although she did not pull the trigger, she initiated and participated in the plan and therefore, shared in the guilt and punishment.

Following her conviction, Catherine Snow was anything but repentant. Henry Winton, editor of the *Public Ledger*, described her behavior in prison:

> From the time of her conviction down to a very late period, she had exhibited a great deal of hardihood and recklessness, and when brought before the court last week and informed of the time when her execution would take place, she manifested anything but symptoms of contrition, and persisted in her innocence of the crime of which she had been found guilty.

During her final days on Earth, Catherine Snow became resigned to her fate. She never mentioned her children and tried to atone for her sins through prayer and fasting. At one point, she asked Father Waldron, "Oh, sir, is there no hope?"

He replied, "No, my good lady. It is my duty to entreat you to lay aside such thoughts. It is only in heaven your hopes are to rest."

The day before the hanging, Catherine was very weak. She had not slept or eaten in two days. Prison guards offered her all kinds of food, but she refused all, but only a mouthful of wine from Bishop Fleming on the night before her execution.

When asked why she refused to eat, she answered, "Oh, what is nourishment to me? God calls upon me to suffer death. That I cannot avoid, but let me add as much as possible to my sufferings so that I may try to make that death worthwhile."

At 3:00 a.m. the clergy celebrated Mass in her cell. At 5:00 a.m. the prisoner was dressed in burial garb. She didn't resist the move, but when it was finished, and she realized she was now dressed for her coffin, she let out a piercing scream and fell to her knees crying. Comforted by the clergy, she quickly regained her composure.

Before being hanged, Catherine Snow made one final declaration of her innocence. She proclaimed she had no knowledge of her husband's murder. Her final words before the rope was placed around her neck were, "I was a wretched woman, but as innocent of any participation in the crime of murder as an unborn child."

The hanging took place from the gallows constructed outside the northwest window of the old courthouse, which was located in a building just east of the present courthouse on Duckworth Street. The window sashes were removed and Catherine Snow stepped onto the platform connecting the window with the gallows.

Henry Winton, editor of the *Public Ledger*, described the scene:

> She proceeded to the gallows with a firm step and with a demeanor which indicated a resignation to her awful fate. She was conducted to the platform, attended by priests, shortly before the hour of nine o'clock, and the usual preliminaries having been arranged, the unhappy woman, after a few brief struggles, passed into another world. Her remains were interred last evening in the Catholic burial ground.

Her body was taken and laid to rest in the Catholic cemetery located where the Kirk now stands at the bottom of Long's Hill. The Catholic clergy allowed her burial there because they felt her guilt had not been proven.

In the century following the execution of Catherine Snow, the belief emerged that an innocent woman had gone to the gallows. Yet, popular feeling at the time of the execution was that justice was served. Trial evidence showed she had initiated the idea of murdering her husband and had participated and cooperated in the killing. Catherine Snow was the last person to be publicly hanged in Newfoundland.[2]

A petition circulated by members of the Roman Catholic clergy did not receive widespread support. Henry Winton said, that based on his knowledge of the petition, the wording of it was weak and lacked any strong legal argument to have the execution set aside. He explained that the petition asked for a commutation of the sentence because Catherine Snow had been improperly convicted.

He pointed out that the petition accused the jury of convicting Mrs. Snow without providing any, "... substantial evidence that their verdict was an improper one."

Soon after the death of Catherine Snow, reports began circulating throughout the city that her spirit was haunting the area of the scene of her execution. These claims were picked up and reported in local newspapers. As time went by, similar sightings were reported in the area of the old Catholic cemetery on Long's Hill. For more than a century, the sad story of Catherine Snow had been all but forgotten in Newfoundland. However, in the 1950s, two cleaning ladies, who worked at the present-day courthouse, reported seeing the ghost of a woman wandering through the building at night. It wasn't long before some of the old timers in the city were claiming that the courthouse was being haunted by the ghost of Catherine Snow.[3]

Catherine Brown
Catherine Brown, a young housewife from Southside Road, St. John's, and Richard Nickells, an agent with the firm of

[2] It has been claimed that John Flood, the highwayman, was the last person publicly executed. It has since been shown that Flood did not hang but was banished from Newfoundland.
[3] During the 1980s, I received a letter from an Edward Snow, living in Brooklyn, New York. He said he was a direct descendent of Catherine Snow and was in the process of tracing his relatives in Newfoundland.

Thomas Row, who operated a commercial establishment in St. John's, appeared before the same judge at the same time, and each was sentenced to be hanged for separate unrelated incidents.

Mrs. Brown's trip to the gallows resulted after she was found guilty of the shooting death of her husband, John Brown. Nickells was sentenced to take the ten steps to the gallows because of the forgery of a note valued at less than eighty dollars. Strangely enough, Catherine Brown and her husband were implicated in the alleged crime against Nickells.

In court, Nickells explained that he did not forge the note. He told the court that when he discovered it was a forgery and looked into the matter, he discovered that Catherine Brown and her husband had participated in the forgery. Aware of the serious penalty for such a criminal deed, Nickells gallantly took responsibility for the note, feeling that his employer would be sympathetic and allow him to repay the money.

"I'd rather pay the money myself than to see anyone hurt," he told the judge.

His boss, however, was not so chivalrous and he pressed charges against Nickells. This valiant effort by Nickells to save Brown was useless. The incident took a stranger twist when Mrs. Brown committed a deed that made her visit with the hangman unavoidable. Inside the Brown home on Southside Road, Catherine shot her husband, then set fire to the bedclothes and ran out onto the street screaming, "John has shot himself, my God help me!"

Catherine Brown was arrested, charged and found guilty of the shooting death of her spouse John Brown. The police investigation revealed that Catherine Brown had somehow obtained a pistol owned by her next door neighbour, George Whitten. Whitten told the police he discovered the weapon missing about three days before the murder. Further investigation determined that on the night of the murder, Mrs. Brown had asked Hannah Whitten, George's sister, if she could borrow a tablespoon of gunpowder. She explained her husband needed it to kill a dog. The police believed that Mrs. Brown stole Whitten's gun during that visit.

She may have gotten away with the murder if she had not confided her secret to George Whitten. On the morning of the crime, she told Whitten she had shot John and now she didn't know what to do. She said she was thinking of running away or drowning herself. Whitten responded, "If you do, there will be two dead instead of one." Whitten's evidence of this conversation, along with his sister's testimony concerning the gunpowder, was enough for the jury to bring in a guilty verdict.

As fate would have it, Nickells, who tried to save Mrs. Brown from the gallows by taking the rap on a forgery charge, now stood with her in court battling to avoid going to the gallows himself. Both had been pronounced guilty of their respective charges. The whole matter had gotten out of hand for Nickells and he took advantage of the judge's invitation to both of the accused to give the court any reasons as to why the death sentence should not be given them. Nickells repeated his claim of innocence, and stated he was only trying to save Brown from hanging. Brown remained silent, and did not respond to the judge's invitation.

On August 23, 1804, both Brown and Nickells were sentenced to hang. The hangings were to take place on Monday, August 27, 1804. However, due to the circumstances of Nickells' case, the governor commuted the death sentence to life in prison.[4]

Catherine Brown was hanged at the public gallows outside the session's room of the St. John's courthouse on September 1, 1804.

[4] James Brown from Trepassey who was also sentenced to hang for forging a note for less than fifty dollars had his sentence commuted to life imprisonment.

Eleanor Power

Eleanor Power was the most notorious of female criminals throughout the history of Newfoundland justice. She organized and led her own gang of criminals in a bold attack on a private residence of a Newfoundland magistrate in the community of Quidi Vidi.

The 'Power Gang,' as Eleanor's group became known, shocked the inhabitants of Newfoundland, when on the night of Monday, September 9, 1754, during a commando-type robbery attempt, they murdered prominent court magistrate, William Keen.

Eleanor Power, with the aid of her husband, Richard, put together the gang of ten members, including herself and her husband. Their aim was to steal the fortune they believed to be hidden inside the summer home of Judge Keen in Quidi Vidi, which at the time was outside the eastern end of St. John's.

The Power Gang included four soldiers from the Garrison in St. John's: Edmund McQuire, Dennis Hawkins, John Munhall and John Moody. The remaining members were from Freshwater Bay: Nicholas Tobin, Paul McDonald, Matthew Halleran and Lawrence Lamley.

In recruiting members for the group, Eleanor enticed them with a promise of over $3,000 each, which, at that time, represented a small fortune. One of the gang members, Edmund McQuire, had another reason for joining the gang. Apart from the enticement of a share of the loot, McQuire was motivated by revenge.

He had been unfortunate enough to appear before Judge Keen at one time and thereafter claimed the judge had wronged him. The thought of relieving Keen of his fortune appealed to McQuire almost as much as sharing in the take. Because of the seriousness of the planned attack upon Judge Keen's residence, Eleanor Power gathered the group together at Keen's Wharf, where the Fortis Building in St. John's now stands, and had each member swear on a prayer book to be true to each other.

The first attempt to pull off the caper failed when the group arrived at the scene only to find that Keen's son and some neighbours were working outside.

For the second attempt, Eleanor donned men's clothing and led the group aboard a skiff, which then took them from Freshwater Bay to the King's Wharf near where the War Memorial stands today. From there they went on foot to Keen's summer home. When they arrived at the scene, the house was in complete darkness. They forced entry into the home and removed a large chest which they believed to contain a treasure. Lamley and Halleran also pocketed some of Keen's silverware before leaving the house.

The group carted the chest into a nearby wooded area and broke it open, expecting to find it full of money, but to their dismay, the only contents of the chest were several bottles of liquor. Disappointed at not finding the money, and concerned over the consequences of their deed, Tobin and Hawkins expressed the wish to give up on the robbery and return to Freshwater Bay. Munhall, however, had other ideas and he raised his musket, pointing it at the two possible deserters, warning them that he would kill any man who walked out on the operation.

Because Tobin was getting nervous, Munhall ordered him to drink a dram of liquor. McGuire and Halleran said that this time they would wake and question old Keen, if necessary, and if he refused to tell them where the money was, they would punish him.

After some discussion, the gang agreed to make another try. Eleanor Power left no doubt as to who was in command. She initiated the plan by issuing the orders to her followers. She assigned Tobin and Hawkins the task of making sure that

Keen's neighbour, Edmund Wheland, did not interfere with the robbery. Tobin and Hawkins were stationed outside the Wheland home with orders to knock him out if he came outside.

Inside the house, Halleran and McGuire went upstairs to Keen's room. Richard Power and Moody guarded the servants in the kitchen. Eleanor and Lamley remained hiding in the woods. Halleran and McGuire removed a large box from beneath Keen's bed, but their movements caused Keen to wake up shouting, "Murder! Murder!"

Halleran put a quilt over Keen to muffle his shouting, but the tough old judge managed to free himself. He jumped up and used his fingers to douse the candle held in McGuire's hand and then grabbed Halleran by the leg. In the struggle that ensued, Halleran struck Keen with a scythe and McGuire hit the judge with the butt end of a musket, killing him.

When the body of Keen was discovered the next morning, news of the murder spread rapidly throughout St. John's. Citizens were outraged that such an atrocity had been committed against a court justice. The mood of the population was so intense that at least one of the perpetrators could not withstand the pressure. Nick Tobin went to the authorities and made a deal that lead to the arrest of the remaining nine gang members.

Their trial got underway in St. John's on October 8, 1754, with Judge Michael Gill presiding. All members of the Power Gang were given the chance to testify. The leader, Eleanor Power, and her husband had nothing to say except that they were not guilty. McGuire swore upon the Holy Evangelists that he had struck Keen with the scythe, but Halleran had also hit him with the gun. He testified that some members of the gang had held Keen's servants in the kitchen while the murder and robbery were being carried out.

John Moody asked the court to show mercy and sentence him to transportation[5] instead of hanging. He told the court he was not involved with the Power Gang until the night of the robbery and murder.

Moody said:

> I was a sentinel at the magazine, and between 6:00 and 7:00 p.m. Edmund McGuire came to me, and told me if I could keep a secret, he would tell me something of interest to me. When I said I would keep the secret, he pulled out a Holy Book, and asked me to swear upon the Holy Evangelists that I would not tell anyone what he was about to discuss with me. I knew nothing of the robbery until that time.

Other gang members incriminated Eleanor Power as the leader and the one who enticed them to participate in the robbery.

Doctors Thomas Allan and John Burton testified that they examined Keen's body on the night of the murder and determined that death was caused by the wounds inflicted with the gun butt and scythe.

It took the jury only thirty minutes to arrive at a verdict. All members of the gang except Tobin, who had co-operated with authorities, were found guilty and sentenced to be hanged. Hanging, however, was not a sufficient punishment for the murder of a judge. McGuire and Halleran, who directly carried out the deed of murder, were given the additional sentence of gibbeting. Their bodies were left hanging at Gibbet Hill on Signal Hill and remained on display for a week as a deterrent to others.

[5] Transportation was a form of punishment where the convicted person was sent out of the country on condition that he or she could not return.

The gang was then escorted from the courtroom. The military members were imprisoned at the Garrison in St. John's, while the civilian members were held on board the H.M.S. *Penzance*, which was harboured near Keen's Wharf at the foot of Prescott Street. The gang had been split up for security reasons.

The court decision was appealed to Governor Hugh Bonfoy, who showed mercy towards five of the condemned prisoners. He reprieved the execution of Lamley, McDonald, Moody, Munhall and Hawkins "... until the Royal will and pleasure be known." They were later pardoned.

Considering the fact that the Power Gang had met and taken their oath of secrecy at Keen's Wharf, the court felt it appropriate that the convicted murderers be executed from a gallows erected on that property.

At noon on October 10th, Halleran and McGuire were taken to the gallows on Keen's Wharf where the sentence of the court was carried out.

At noon the following day, Eleanor and Richard Power looked out over the harbour towards their home in Freshwater Bay for the last time. Crowds had gathered in the area, some in the area of the wharf, others on boats in the harbour, to witness the execution of the only man and wife team to be executed in Newfoundland history.

In accordance with the order of the court, Halleran and McGuire were placed in chains and gibbeted on Gibbet Hill overlooking St. John's Harbour. The bodies were left on public display for a week. The remains of all four were buried near the gallows on Keen's Wharf. Eleanor Power became the first woman to be hanged in Newfoundland.

Mary Power
The first woman sentenced to be hanged in Newfoundland was Mary Power of St. John's, who lived with her husband in

a shanty on the Upper Path (New Gower Street) not far from Fort William.

Mary was convicted of murder on October 14, 1772, and was given a pardon and immediately released on June 23, 1773. Power had been convicted of the murder of her husband, Maurice Power, and sentenced to be hanged. When it was brought to the court's attention that she was pregnant, the judge appointed two midwives, Elizabeth Fleming and Susanna Earles, to examine the girl and verify the pregnancy. They determined that she was five months pregnant.

Similar to the Catherine Snow case, an appeal was made to the governor for a reprieve of the sentence. The appeal argued that although Mary Power had been convicted of murder, there was nothing but circumstantial evidence to prove that she had committed the crime. The governor agreed that mercy should be shown, and Mary Power was given a full pardon.[6]

---

[6] McCarthy, Michael, *The Irish in Newfoundland*, Creative Publishers.

Chapter 7: Executed by Guillotine on St. Pierre

The discovery of sixty-one-year-old Francois Coupard's mutilated body at a cabin on Ile Aux Marins, St. Pierre, marked the beginning of one of the most bizarre murder cases and execution stories in the history of the St. Pierre and Miquelon, located off the south coast of Newfoundland. Coupard's murder was followed by an unsuccessful attempt by the murderers to sail to Newfoundland during a raging storm and a botched execution scene, which must have made Dr. Louis, the inventor of the guillotine, turn over in his grave.

Francois Coupard, a fisherman, lived in Ile Aux Marins in a small cabin with fellow fisherman Louis Ollivier. On the night of the murder there was a great deal of noise coming from Coupard's cabin. There was so much noise that the Juins, close neighbours of the victim, went to police early the next morning to report what they had heard.

Ile Aux Marins was a quiet community and murder was unheard of. Police officers Danglas and Bonnaux went to Coupard's cabin to check out the report. They did not feel anything serious was involved and consequently only conducted a minor investigation at the scene. They noted a broken window, and after glancing inside the house and not seeing any evidence of life, assumed the occupants had gone hunting sea birds. The police officers left Coupard's cabin and returned to their station for what they expected to be an uneventful day.

On the afternoon of New Year's Day 1888, two of Coupard's friends, Mr. Poirier and Mr. Fourre, went to Coupard's cabin hoping to borrow a pair of boots. The two men were not concerned. Other than the broken window, there was nothing disturbed nothing that indicated anyone was there. Both men's attention quickly settled on a discarded sail, which was covering something in the corner of the kitchen.

Poirier edged his way towards the object to remove its covering but quickly stepped backward, horrified by the scene that greeted him. His gaze did not leave the view of a man, who was in a sitting position with his head resting upon his chest and his knees bent towards his stomach. Poirier recognized the blood-drenched body of his friend, Francois Coupard.

The two men reported their finding to the police. The same two officers who earlier that day had responded to complaints from neighbours were now accompanied by the local physician, Dr. Caniail, and inspecting a murder scene. Dr. Caniail's first act was to stretch the victim's body out on the floor to facilitate a more thorough examination. The grizzly mutilation that had been inflicted upon Coupard was plain to see. His chest had been ripped across from left to right with a knife. His throat was slashed and there was evidence of a knife penetration into the chest, which the doctor surmised had penetrated directly into the victim's heart.

Continuing his examination, Dr. Caniail determined that the sternum had been broken in two and the stomach was ripped apart with the intestines visibly hanging outside. There were many knife wounds inflicted all over the body. One report among the court records noted, "Other things were also done to the body which were too sickening to mention."

It did not take long for police to come up with a suspect. Suspicion immediately focused on Louis Ollivier. Police discovered that Coupard's boat was missing and suspected that Ollivier was using it to escape. In response they initiated an island-wide search for their man.

Meanwhile, police learned that Ollivier had been seen over the previous few days with another young fisherman,

Augustus Neel. This tip led them to Neel's boarding house, where they were informed that the two suspects had persuaded several others to join with them in sailing their boat to New-foundland. By now the police were close on their trail. They received unexpected help by a sudden storm that struck along the coast.

The men were still close to the coast when the windstorm surprised them, forcing them to head back to the nearest port, which was a little place called Henri's Cove. They secured their boat and then found an abandoned cabin where they planned on sitting out the hammering, gale-force winds. The storm lasted longer than expected.

After the men awoke the next morning, they were frustrated to witness that not only had the storm not abated but it was intensifying. The winds had grown more powerful overnight and the seas were more treacherous. In desperation they abandoned their shelter and started walking back to St. Pierre. Another surprise awaited them there.

Word of the murder and the identities of the two suspects had already spread throughout the French island. No sooner had they entered a residential area when the police took them by surprise and arrested them. Getting a confession to the killing was easy when both men broke down and agreed to co-operate with the police.

The information contained in the police statement suggests the men were hungry and were contemplating cannibalism. They confessed that there had been a verbal conflict at first, which led to Ollivier striking the first blow. Neel joined in the attack on Coupard. He explained, "We were both dead drunk then." Neel followed this with the nauseating comment, "We cut up Coupard to see if he had any fat."

The trial got underway on February 8, 1889, and lasted only two days. It provided the kind of sensational attention that had the population of the little islands alive with rumours about what some called the "slaughter of Coupard."

The talk of cannibalism that was associated with Coupard's murder was reinforced when the accused told the court the only reason they went to Coupard's was to seek food because they were hungry. It was certainly not a social call because when they arrived at the cabin the door was locked. Their response was not to knock on the door or peek through a window; instead Ollivier kicked it wide open while Neel smashed open the window.

Coupard seized a fishing knife when he heard the uproar and faced the two assailants as they entered his home. Ollivier wrestled with Coupard in an effort to take the knife away from him. Neel raised the level of the attack when he shouted to his partner, "It's better to kill the devil than have the devil kill you!" He then stepped in and knocked the knife from Coupard's hand.

Neel bent to pick up the knife, and, while moving to an upright position, without warning, he plunged the steel blade deeply into Coupard's stomach. This murderous attack brought an immediate end to the struggle as Coupard, profusely bleeding, doubled over to the floor.

According to trial records, the two attackers lit a candle and attempted to determine if Coupard was still alive. The fact that he was still breathing did not bring an end to his attackers' viciousness. Neel passed the knife to his partner and instructed him to, "…take your turn at cutting." Ollivier hesitated but Neel did not. Neel ripped open Coupard's chest and with blood pouring out in all directions proceeded to cut the still alive victim's heart out of his body. After completing his barbaric act, he seized the heart in his two hands and stood up to proclaim, "What a big heart."

Ollivier claimed he had not intended to harm Coupard and did not participate in any of the mutilation carried out by

Neel. Even after removing the heart, Neel was still unsatisfied. He began hacking, slicing, cutting and ripping away flesh like a rabid animal. The arrival of the first rays of the morning sun brought an end to Neel's madness. Ollivier helped Neel move the body into the kitchen corner and covered it with a sail.

According to Ollivier, he was too drunk to comprehend what was happening. He claimed he bore no grudge against Coupard and said he was a good man and that he liked him. The accused explained he had blindly followed Neel's orders. Other witnesses in the case testified that when they had seen the two men earlier that day it was Ollivier who was sober and Neel who was drunk. This testimony had little effect on the prosecutor, who argued that Neel had a sort of hypnotic hold over Ollivier, "… a sort of incomprehensible fascination."

While the prosecutor asked for the death sentence, Neel remained silent and showed no emotion. Both men were found guilty but only Neel was sentenced to be guillotined. The early suspicions of cannibalism were discredited and never became part of the trial.

While awaiting his execution Neel was very pleasant, displayed a good sense of humour and got along well with the jailers. However, Neel was not destined to leave this world without a last reminder of how vicious the cut of a butcher's knife could be.

Since there was no guillotine on the islands and French law specified the guillotine as the instrument of execution, the death machine had to be imported from France.

The guillotine sent over by France had a remarkable connection with French history. According to many accounts written about the execution of Neel over the past century, the instrument operated was the same guillotine used to sever the head of Marie Antoinette and Robespierre plus twenty-one of his loyal followers. This would have likely added greatly to public interest in the gruesome enforcement of the court's order.

French records show that this, the most famous of all guillotines in French history, was designed by Dr. Louis, the life-secretary of the Academy of Surgeons, and constructed by a man with the very un-French name of Schmidt. One of the identifying markers of the original guillotine was its color. It had been painted, not surprisingly, a dull blood red.

Adding to the intrigue of the 'Antoinette Guillotine' was the fact that in 1789 Nicholas Jacques, the first criminal guillotined, lost his head beneath that same blade.

The same guillotine is also associated with France's most famous family of executioners, the Sanson family. The Sansons' reign as France's official executioners began in 1699 and ended in 1847. The end of their hereditary claim was ironic.

The guillotine itself caused the downfall. This was not brought about by dropping the blade on the head of any Sanson. The historic guillotine was in the possession of the Sanson who held the executioner's post in 1847, until he sought to enhance his savings by pawning this piece of French history.

The guillotine's impressive background was of no concern to Neel, who awaited his day of execution. Authorities in St. Pierre had no problem assembling and erecting the instrument. Their problem arose when trying to find a person willing to assume the post of executioner. This did not bother Neel, who was less than anxious to make French history through the guillotine.

Eventually, authorities found a man willing to become Monsieur Guillotine for one day. Jean Legent was certainly no Sanson. Court records straightforwardly described the island's pending executioner for a day as, "A lazy bum fisherman." Legent had just begun serving a three-month prison term for theft.

Justice officials offered Legent a deal he was only too enthusiastic to accept some cash in his pocket and his freedom. The deal gave him 500 francs with an added inducement to free his brother. In return, he would act as an assistant to Legent. Both gentlemen accepted the offer.

The brothers took their assignment seriously and set out to examine the efficiency of the aged machine. The one thing that always concerned justice officials was a botched execution. This was told to the inexperienced executioners and they promised to carry out their assignment as "professionally as possible." In this, they bit off more than they could chew.

Calamity faced the two during their first attempt to use the machine. They easily subdued a young calf and strapped it in place, where the neck of Marie Antoinette once rested. On signal from his brother, Jean Legent released the blade which quickly descended but only partially severed the calf's head. Jean was ready to end the executioner's act; borrowing a sharp knife from a guard, he successfully completed the butchering of the animal.

The brothers then sliced meat from the bones of the calf and offered it to the government workers supervising their activity. Each and every one of them refused to accept the offering, perhaps due to the suspicion that such a blunder was a bad omen. However, authorities learned from the incident and on the day of Neel's execution provided Jean with a sharp fisherman's knife just in case the guillotine failed again.

Unlike the traditional thunder and lightning storms that accompanied most executions in Newfoundland, in St. Pierre the sun was radiant without any clouds in sight on the day Neel knelt to place his head on the guillotine. Neel's last day on Earth began very early. He was awakened by guards at 3:30 a.m. to prepare to meet the Legent brothers. After washing and dressing, he was given a glass of wine and a hot cup of tea. There is no mention among the records that he shaved. After finishing his tea he turned to his guard and commented, "Who would have believed that the land would have me after the sea could have had me a hundred times?"

In the days leading up to his execution, Neel was visited daily by a priest. The priest urged him to turn his thoughts from this world and to prepare for the next. On the eve of his execution the priest heard Neel's confession. Before the priest left the cell, Neel asked him for one final favour. He asked him to bring his body to the cemetery after the execution stating, "I don't want to be buried like a dog!"

Neel's sessions with the priest were not wasted. Just before taking his place at the guillotine he addressed the crowd. People suddenly ceased their conversations and paid close attention to Neel, straining to hear every word. His comments were short and to the point. Where earlier he had blamed Ollivier for the butchery of Coupard, now he said, "Let my example serve as a lesson. I killed and now I am going to be killed. Don't do like me."

Jean Legent appeared to be more nervous than the condemned man. When Neel took his position with his head on the chopping block, Legent froze in hesitation. This was the real thing, quite different than executing a calf. Neel provided him with the encouragement he needed to proceed with the lethal ceremony. He said firmly, "Come on then, and don't miss me."

The guards who had been present at the practice run with the calf felt the omen of that event was now unfolding. Jean Marie Legent released the rope and the blade fell swiftly to Neel's neck. To the horror of all, the blade failed to do its job. Neel's head was not severed and he was still alive. Jean Legent was more in control of his feelings at this stage and quickly took over the completion of the execution using a butcher's knife.

The reaction to the failure of the guillotine was one of disgust and repulsion. The doctor, who was to take the body for a medical study, changed his mind and refused to accept it.

The state honoured its agreement with the Legent brothers. Both were released and Jean was given his executioner's wage. He returned to his wife and two children, but the population shunned him. Shopkeepers refused to accept his money, which they described with contempt as, "blood money." This factor, combined with an employers' boycott against hiring him, forced the authorities to step in help the Legent family.

They were aided with food and personal needs and were given transportation to France on September 17, 1889, aboard the fishing vessel *Le Drac*. That was the last anyone in St. Pierre heard of the Legent family. It is assumed that Jean's brother had accompanied them. Neel, however, had a street named after him in St. Pierre called *Place Neel*.

There were many superstitions associated with executions. The laws and punishments which prevailed throughout Britain and its colonies during the eighteenth and nineteenth centuries appear to be harsh and cruel. However, in earlier times there were also some extraordinary methods of force used by the clergy to determine a person's guilt.

The *Daily News* of July 1886 published a special feature article on ancient justice practices which outlined these unusual trials:

> The power to demand that a man be found guilty of a crime unless he was cleared by a miracle was given to the clergy in the time of the rule of King John when bishops and clergy were permitted to use the *Trial by Iron, Fire and Water.*[1]

Although the bishops and clergy presided at these trials which were performed only in churches or on consecrated

---

[1] The ordeals used to determine guilt, were referred to in writings as the practice of *Trial by Iron, Fire and Water.*

ground, the Canon Law very clearly declared against "trial by ordeal" as the fabric of Satan and it was abolished in England by an order of the King in Council in the reign of Henry the Third.

The "ordeal of fire" was performed either by picking up a piece of red-hot iron, one or two pounds weight, or else by walking blindfold and barefoot over nine red-hot ploughshares, laid lengthwise at unequal distances. If the prisoner escaped unharmed, he was deemed to be innocent. However, if it turned out otherwise, as without collusion it often did, he was declared to be guilty.

"Water ordeal" involved by plunging the bare arm up to the elbow in boiling water and removing it unharmed, or by casting the prisoner into a river or pond and, if he floated without swimming, he was found guilty. However, if he sank, he was acquitted.

Some people in the era of these punishments possessed secrets as to how to pass the trials unharmed. For example, in the "ordeal of boiling water" they used to rub the arm a long time with the spirit of vitriol and alum, together with juice from an onion.

The "trial by bread" involved using a piece of bread or cheese that was consecrated with a prayer asking the Almighty that it might cause convulsions and paleness and find no passage, if the man was guilty but might turn to health and nourishment if he was innocent. This piece of bread, called the coarsened or "morsel of cursing," was then given to the suspected person. The bread had to be made in a special way. It had to be of unleavened barley and the cheese of ewes' milk and made in the month of May. There was no special power in any of the remaining eleven months. For centuries after this practice was abandoned, people would say, "May this piece of bread choke me, if I am guilty, or may this morsel be my last!'

Perhaps the most extraordinary method of trial was that of "the bleeding of a corpse." If a person was murdered, it was said, that at the touch or at the approach of the murderer, the blood would gush out of the body at various parts.

These "trials of ordeals" were mostly of Saxon origin. The "trial by battle or single combat" was derived from the Normans.

Chap 8: Unlikely Criminals

A bizarre episode in Newfoundland criminal history took place during the summer of 1957. Its surprise ending marked the beginning of a mystery that has remained unsolved for almost forty years. Many around St. John's remember it as the perfect crime.

The mystery first came to light when three boys playing in the sand pits, located off of Elizabeth Avenue, discovered a bundle with the charred remains of a baby. The police were called to the scene and began gathering evidence. Sergeant Ron Evans recalled, "The baby was burned considerably and covered with charred papers, tissues and bits of clothing." The investigation was turned over to the RCMP because Elizabeth Avenue was outside the city at the time.

During the autopsy at the city morgue, police made another gruesome discovery. A second bundled taken from the scene was opened by Corporal Pat Noonan and the charred remains of a second baby was found. Noonan described the condition; "It was in a decomposed state and dead for some time. It was in a mummified condition, flattened to a thickness of about three inches and dried and hard like a piece of board."

Who were the children? Were they alive before being burned? Who did it? Were there any witnesses? Why? These were some questions confronting the RCMP as they took charge of the investigation that night. Their investigation took off the next morning after news reports of the mystery hit the airways. Al Downey, a city taxi driver, recalled taking a woman from 92 Queen's Road to the sand pits several nights before. She brought with her a carton of what she described as old clothes. He told police she asked him to wait as she set fire to the box and left only after the fire had burned out.

Based on the driver's information police arrested thirty-seven-year old Louise Dunn of 92 Queen's Rd. They searched her apartment and gathered evidence including papers from the fireplace and some old clothing. Although two bodies were recovered, she was only charged with dumping the body of one child and attempting to burn it.

City lawyer Sam Hawkins was hired to defend Dunn. After hearing her story he expressed doubts regarding the legality of the charge. He explained that the charge was related to a mother disposing of her child's body. Dunn had been examined by a doctor and it was determined she had not recently given birth. She told Hawkins she had not been pregnant since 1953.

Louise Dunn denied having any knowledge of the affair. She explained that the blood evidence police took from her bed was from a pregnancy in 1953. Hawkins questioned the police line-up and asked what description the police had prior to arresting his client. Sergeant Hugh Coady answered that he was told the address of the woman and that she was from the mainland. Dunn was the only mainlander in that house. Neighbours described her as a friendly, intelligent lady whom they felt was unlikely to be involved in the murder of infants. However, as details of her private life were revealed at trial the same people were shocked.

When police mentioned that they took a large sum of money from the accused at the time of the arrest the defence objected claiming, "... it is irrelevant and could prejudice some of the issues for the defence." Magistrate Hugh O'Neill agreed.

The pathologist, Dr. Joseph Josephson, caused a stir in the courtroom when he suggested the babies had been murdered before being dumped at the sand pits. Both babies had been carried full-term and were alive at birth. He could not find any blood traces to base a conclusion of relationship. Dr. Josephson noted that death by natural causes was possible but it was likely that the children had been smothered.

The Crown relied on the evidence of Al Downey for its case. They argued that he had credibility because he was able to take them to the exact site and he identified Louise Dunn in the police line-up. When asked if the accused had explained what she was doing, the cab driver answered, "She said she was burning some soiled clothes which she didn't want to throw in the garbage." The next day the *Daily News* headline read, "Fingered by – Body Burning Trial Starts."

There was public speculation that the babies had been killed to cover up some prominent people's involvement with prostitutes. However, no evidence surfaced at trial to support that belief.

Near the end of the trial Hawkins called a surprise witness and drew the ire of the prosecution for not giving proper notice. The witness, John Mahoney, a contractor with offices in Argentia and St. John's, provided the accused with an alibi for the night it was claimed she disposed of the bodies. He testified Louise Dunn was with him from 10:30 p.m. to 1:00 a.m. on June 25th. The defence concluded she was innocent because this was proof she was not at the sand pits that night.

Although Dunn testified in court that she was with Maloney at the Pioneer Restaurant on the night of the crime, she had given two separate statements to police that she went home at 11:45 p.m. that night and had not seen anyone she knew.

When the prosecution questioned the discrepancies between her evidence in court and the police statements, she answered that she had not read the statements and felt no obligation to tell them anything about Maloney.

Louise Dunn told the court she had known Maloney for three years, but when cross-examined testified she did not know his address or telephone number. She said she had been meeting with him about every ten days and that he would initiate the contact.

When asked if she knew the cab driver who identified her she stated she did, adding that he tried to set her up with servicemen on occasions before, but she ignored him. She said she had never been in his taxi. Dunn stuck to her story that she was at the Pioneer Restaurant with Maloney on June 25th. She denied any knowledge of the dead children. When pressed by the Crown to disclose her source of income, she said she received support from her ex-husband and operated a small business modelling and selling clothes.

In his summary at the end of the trial, Hawkins argued that the Crown made no attempt to prove the child belonged to Louise Dunn. He claimed the entire case revolved around the identity issue and that the taxi driver was not a credible witness. Hawkins contended that the evidence of Maloney was sufficient to acquit his client. He added that medical evidence showed that Louise had not given birth during the four week period prior to the discovery of the charred bodies.

He concluded saying, "It is dangerous to convict when there is an indication that the witness is an accomplice."

The Crown's summary argued that there was sufficient evidence to convict. The prosecutor told the judge that Al Downey was credible and he was present when the bodies were burned. He said the defence alibi should not be believed because the accused made no effort to present this evidence to the police. He said, "The defence of alibi ought to be introduced at the earliest point as a rule of expediency. She made no attempt to tell anyone of her alibi."

After reviewing the evidence Magistrate Hugh O'Neill said he was left with no choice but to acquit. Linda Dunn thanked her lawyer, tossed her hair back and smiled at police officers as she left the courtroom. The trial was over but the crime was not solved. Two murders had been committed and despite efforts by *The Evening Telegram* through its editorial pages, the case was not reopened and nobody has ever been charged with the murder of the two infants.

Pindikowski

Two things stand out in the life of Alexander Pindikowski. First, he was a very talented Polish artist and second, he was a convict at Her Majesty's Penitentiary in St. John's. Unlike other criminals, Pindikowski is not remembered for the crime he committed, but for the beautiful art work he left behind.

The artist's Newfoundland criminal experience started following his arrival in Newfoundland in 1879. The Anglo-American Telegraph Company operated a cable office at Heart's Content. The company was civic-minded and treated its employees and the community very well. It was the Telegraph Company's effort to help its employees that resulted in Pindikowski coming to Newfoundland in the first place.

The company hired the Polish artist to give art instructions to interested members of its staff in Heart's Content. He enjoyed instant popularity among the residents of the community. During 1873, the old Anglo-American Telegraph office, which had been constructed in 1867, was converted into a theatre by the company. Pindikowski was commissioned to paint six twenty-five-foot-long backdrops for the stage.

Things went well for Pindikowski. He was doing work he liked. He made many new friends and he was admired and respected by all. Then his luck began to falter.

In early 1880, Pindikowski found himself in St. John's and short of money. He thought he could solve his financial problem by forging a cheque in the name of Ezra Weedon, Esquire, chief of the Anglo-American Telegraph company's staff at

Heart's Content. The artist took the cheque to the commercial bank and handed it to a teller named Cooke. The cheque was made out for £232, which in those days was a considerable sum. For some reason, Cooke became suspicious and refused to cash the cheque. Pindikowski returned a second time, but with a lesser amount. He now submitted a cheque for sixty-five pounds. This time Cooke wired Mr. Weedon enquiring about the cheque and received a quick reply, stating that Weedon had not issued any cheques to Pindikowski. Cooke contacted Inspector Carty and reported the incident.

Inspector Carty, accompanied by Sergeant Sullivan, began a search of the city to locate the artist. In those days, the Total Abstinence Society of St. John's operated a coffeehouse in the downtown area. At this house, non-alcoholic refreshments were served during and after business hours. Recreational activities were available and the house had a reading room for patrons. It was at this coffeehouse the search ended. On the night of March 9, 1880, the police arrested the Polish artist and escorted him to the lock-up. He was charged with attempting to pass a forged cheque. On June 8th, he was sentenced to fifteen months of hard labour at Her Majesty's Penitentiary. Included in the sentencing was an order that Pindikowski leave Newfoundland within five days after his release, with the stipulation that if he ever returned he would be jailed again for two years. He was then escorted to HMP to start serving his time. However, his reputation as an artist and fresco painter resulted in the opportunity for him to do work on the 'outside.' He was assigned to paint and decorate the ceilings in the state rooms of Government House. His work delighted Governor Glover so much that he suggested to Prime Minister Whiteway that the artist be assigned to decorate the ceilings of the two legislative chambers in the Colonial Building. This job was followed by the paintings of the ceilings at Presentation Convent.

The artistic work of Alexander Pindikowski earned him five weeks remission from his sentence and gained him many supporters and friends in St. John's. These friends collected an amount of money equal to the amount forged and succeeded in having him released from prison. For a short while after his release, he set up a business in the city. The business was a failure and Pindikowski left Newfoundland and never returned. His work in St. John's continues to draw much praise.

Chapter 9: The Arsonist Calls

On December 14, 1942, a St. John's resident had an interesting story which he told police regarding the night of the Knights of Columbus (K of C) Fire on Harvey Road. Fred Molloy was an accountant with the Newfoundland Railway and resided at 4 Bradbury Place. He was deemed a credible witness. The story he told fuelled the German saboteur theory and to this day it is firmly believed by many.

There was actually nothing at all unusual about claims that enemy agents were behind the arson at the Knights of Columbus hostel; after all, World War II was in its third year and the K of C, a hostel for the military, would have been a likely target.

However, within a week after the fire, a rumour that German agents had set it had taken root and was being fueled by a claim that a mysterious telephone call from a man "speaking broken English" had originated from the K of C just after the fire broke out. This theory prevailed despite the fact that Sir Brian Dunfield, chairman of the enquiry into the fire, concluded it had been the work of a pyromaniac. One of the sources for the German saboteur theory is based on the story that Fred Molloy gave to police two days after the fire.

Molloy experienced something on the night of the tragedy which captured his curiosity. He took time to investigate the puzzle before going to police. By 3:44 p.m. on December 14, 1942, Molloy had gathered some alarming evidence and was in the process of giving a written statement to Constable Rudolph Nash. The incident that sparked his interest occurred between 11:00 p.m. and 11:30 p.m. on December 12th. The K of C fire broke out at 11:10 p.m. that night.

Molloy said in his police statement:

> I was in the kitchen. My wife was present also. My telephone rang. I answered it; a party on the line asked if the telephone number was 3113 or 3311 or some number similar to these. I informed the party making the enquiries that they had the wrong number. My telephone number is 3312W. The party asking for the number was speaking in broken English. I am quite sure on that. It was also a man's voice. In the background I could hear voices. I thought it was laughter at the time and shuffling. I thought it to be dancing.

Molloy's statement was given two days after the fire; by this time most of the general population who had never visited the facility firmly believed that the *Uncle Tim's Barn Dance* was an actual dance. The fact is there was no dance at the K of C Hall that night.

This is a truth known by any of the witnesses inside the building. The public's misconception of this reality resulted from the name used to advertise the weekly Saturday night live radio broadcast from the building of the *Uncle Tim's Barn Dance Show*. Three hundred and fifty collapsible chairs had been set up in the auditorium to accommodate spectators for this onstage performance. The enquiry determined that there was no dancing going on anywhere else in the building.

Mr. Molloy believed the man on the phone had been drinking and instead of hanging up the phone, he laid it down to prevent any recalling, which could possibly awake his children. The caller remained on the line and continued talking. What he was saying only made sense to Molloy the next morning after learning of the fire.

Molloy recalled that "over and over again" the caller had repeated, "The house is afire." Molloy told police, "I thought he was trying to get me off the line, in order that he could get his message through, and make the right connection. My telephone number was different from the one he was calling." Originally, Molloy was not sure whether the caller asked, "If this was 3113 or 3311."

In those days a party-line system was being used. Telephone numbers in homes using this system had a letter at the end of a four digit number. Molloy's number was 3312W. Private lines used four digit numbers without a letter at the end.

Because of the role this incident had on the birth of the German agent theory of the fire, it should be noted that Molloy's on the spot interpretation of the call changed next day when he learned of the tragedy. A part of his statement, ignored on the few occasions this was written about, included, "At the time I thought this man to be under the influence of liquor but since, and on hearing of the K of C disaster, it made me think different, and at the time the man may be excited or nervous."

One has to consider just how much Molloy's impression and memory of the call was being influenced by the rapidly unfolding story.

Molloy told police:

> At first when I answered the telephone in my home I could hear this shuffling or dancing in the background plain, then it was after this man kept repeating the shout of 'fire!' In fact it died away when the man shouted this over the telephone. When he was repeating this, everything was quiet. After a while the telephone went dead. In my opinion he did not hang up the receiver, if he did I would hear the receiver click at the other end.

Although Molloy had originally been uncertain about the telephone number the caller had mentioned, he informed police that he felt certain the number was 3113. That confirmation came about after his investigation of possible variations of the number and checking the ownership of each telephone number. The number 3113 caught his interest above all others.

He was startled to discover that the number 3113 belonged to the Bavarian Brewery Co. Ltd. on Leslie Street, where the brewmaster was a German American. This was just the sort of information to cause excitement among investigators. However, this information was later thoroughly investigated by police, who ruled out the brewmaster after learning that he was out of town the week of the fire. Yet this was not enough to satisfy public suspicions.

Another variation of the numbers Molloy toyed with included 3111, which was the telephone number of Marshall Studios on the corner of King's Road and Military Road. It was Marshall who took the famous photos of the fire in progress which appeared in local newspapers.

Hanged

Three men were hanged in 1791. One of these was hanged for murder, while the other two went to the gallows for the crime of forgery. Justice was swift and the three were tried on Monday and hanged on Saturday. On Monday, September 26, 1791, Cornelius Bryan was convicted of the murder of Henry Brooks. Patrick Murphy and John Noddy were convicted of forgery. All three were sentenced by Governor Mark Millbanke to be hanged on Saturday, October 29, 1791.

The bodies of Noddy and Murphy were to be buried immediately after their executions, while Cornelius Bryan had the sentence of gibbeting added to his punishment.

The records show that after the executions, Bryan was gibbeted in chains as a "salutary lesson and a deterrent to criminals." The penalty of hanging for the crime of forgery seems harsh, but elsewhere in the eighteenth century men were being sent to the gallows for stealing a loaf of bread.

Governor Millbanke may have feared some rescue attempt could be made on behalf of the prisoners before the execution date. He had issued an order to increase the prison guards to seven until Saturday evening, the day of the executions. To assure justice was done, a detachment consisting of fifteen men from the Royal Regiment of Artillery, and forty-five men from the King's Own Regiment, under Lieutenant Hornden and Ensign Lefarque, were marched from the garrison to the town jail off Duckworth Street at 11:00 a.m. to witness the execution. It is also likely that they were assigned the task of carrying out the order to gibbet Bryan on Gibbet Hill overlooking St. John's Harbour.

Most Hideous Crime Committed

In 1805, the outport village of Harbour Grace was not the kind of place one would expect a hideous crime, such as the killing of an infant child, to take place. To say the population was shocked when such a deed was uncovered would be an understatement. Even more repulsive is the fact that the killer was the child's father.

James Conway of Harbour Grace was sentenced to be hanged on August 3, 1805, for the murder of his ten-month-old daughter Jane Deay. The child had been found dead in the woods a couple of weeks after her mother reported her missing. The child's head had been kicked and there was evidence she had been beaten.

The child had been born out of wedlock to thirty-five-year-old Elizabeth Deay. Although Conway admitted that he was the father, he never married the girl and showed little affection for the child.

Elizabeth Deay continued to see Conway, and the child was the source of bitter arguments. In July 1805, Elizabeth walked into the kitchen of Conway's home as he was eating breakfast. She laid the child on the floor and announced that, since he was the father, he should look after her. Conway became angry and ordered her to take the child out of the house. Elizabeth became frightened and did as he commanded.

About an hour later, while she was sitting on a grassy bank near George Hefford's garden opposite of Conway's home, Conway suddenly appeared and forcibly took the child from her. She later told the court that he did not hit her, but when he disappeared into the woods with the child, she heard the infant scream.

Elizabeth ran home and sought the help of relatives and friends in searching for her infant daughter. The search ended without success and without anyone questioning Conway. She could not imagine that he would have harmed the child and believed he had hidden the child at the home of one of his relatives.

Two weeks later, Elizabeth confronted Conway and demanded to know what he had done with the child. He told her he had taken the baby to the nurse in Bay Roberts and left it there. Deay refused to believe Conway and told him that she feared the child was dead. Around the same time, rumours were circulating around the community that little Jane was at the home of Mark Delaney in Bay Roberts. Elizabeth went to Delaney's, but he told her he had never seen the child, nor had he spoke to Conway.

Shortly after Elizabeth left Delaney's, Conway arrived and was informed of the mother's visit. Delaney suggested that Conway let the mother know where the child was because she was terribly upset. Conway insisted that he would not give her that satisfaction, but warned that if she continued to ask questions he would kill her and the child.

Within days the child's body was found in a wooded area near Harbour Grace. Conway was arrested and charged with murder.

In court Conway testified, "The screams of the child when I took her were usual for an infant just taken away from its mother." He added that after he took the child, he was "confused and upset."

Conway said he was in a hurry to return to his employer, so he laid the child down in the woods intending to return for her later. He insisted that he did not beat the child, and said he didn't go back because he was scared by the people in the woods who were looking for the child.

The trial lasted only a day and the jury took only a half hour to arrive at a verdict of guilty. The court showed no mercy for Conway and he was sentenced to hang in August 1805.

Burial Sites for Hanging Victims

A part of Newfoundland folklore passed down throughout the years has been the stories surrounding the disposal of the bodies of those hanged. While it is impossible to determine the burial places of all those executed, we can solve the mystery surrounding the burial of most of the condemned victims.

For example, the famous Peter Downing, who was hanged at St. John's and gibbeted in Harbour Grace, is buried inside the prison yard at the Harbour Grace prison.

Catherine Snow, contrary to the practice of the Roman Catholic church not to bury those found guilty of murder in consecrated grounds, was buried at the Roman Catholic cemetery on Long's Hill.[1] The hierarchy of the church did not accept the court's guilty verdict, therefore allowing Mrs. Snow's

[1] Long's Hill was known as Freshwater Road when the Roman Catholic Cemetery was opened there. It was commonly referred to as the Queen's Road Cemetery. After the cemetery was closed the part of Freshwater Road from Harvey Road to Queen's Road was renamed Long's Hill.

burial inside their cemetery. However, Long's Hill Cemetery may not be the final resting place of Mrs. Snow. During the 1890s, most bodies were removed from this cemetery and re-buried in Belvedere Cemetery on Newtown Road and Mount Carmel Cemetery on The Boulevard. It is not known for certain whether Catherine Snow was among those reburied. New plots were not added at the Long's Hill Cemetery after the Belvedere Cemetery and Mount Carmel Cemetery were opened.[2]

During the removal process, old coffins, and some newly constructed to replace those that had decayed were piled up on Livingstone Street. Several children playing in the area contracted a disease which spread throughout the neighbourhood, claiming the lives of thirteen children.

Similarly, about a decade earlier bodies buried at the Church of England Cemetery on Church Hill were transferred to other cemeteries in the city.

By 1906, the grounds at the Long's Hill Cemetery had deteriorated, which prompted one citizen to write the following letter to the *Daily News*, October 24, 1906:

> Editor *Daily News:*
> Dear Sir, – I thank Councilor Carew, and the other members of the Council for the interest they are taking in the Long's Hill neglected cemetery grounds. Plant the place with some of our Newfoundland juniper and fir trees, and make some mounds for receiving flower trees and seeds which many persons having old friends and relatives buried there, will gladly contribute to beautify the sacred ground.
>
> Sgd. CITIZEN

[2] The Belvedere Cemetery was consecrated on July 1, 1855, and the extension to it was consecrated on July 4, 1881. Mount Carmel Cemetery was consecrated June 26, 1855. Graves in both places transferred from the Long's Hill Cemetery have tombstones with earlier dates.

The Roman Catholic Church leased part of the old graveyard to the Presbyterian Kirk for the token sum of one dollar per year to allow greater access to it from Queen's Road. Eventually, the property was signed over to the Kirk.

Patrick Geehan, William Parnell, Francis Canning and Wo Fen Game were originally buried inside the grounds of Her Majesty's Penitentiary. During the early 1990s, Parnell, Canning and Wo Fen Game were removed from the penitentiary grounds and buried at the Holy Sepulcher Cemetery on Topsail Road. This action was taken after a period of time, because workmen kept accidentally digging up the old graves. Geehan was the only person hanged at Her Majesty's Penitentiary whose body remains inside the confines of the prison. He was buried in a different area than the other three, and there is no record of his grave ever being interfered with.

There is an interesting anecdote regarding the graves of the hanging victims at Her Majesty's Penitentiary. During 1944, inmate Stephen Janes was working on an excavation project to make way for construction of the west wing of the penitentiary. Janes, who was wearing leg irons at his own request, because he couldn't resist the temptation to try to go over the prison fence, discovered a larger than usual coffin. Upon opening it, he discovered it contained more than one body. The contents were sent to the General Hospital where it was determined that there were actually three bodies. The common coffin contained the bodies of Parnell, Canning and Wo Fen Game. The three graves had been disturbed several times before, and in 1939 all three were placed into one coffin. The graves were disturbed in 1859, when construction began to replace the wooden walls with new concrete walls. The following item appeared in *The Evening Telegram*, September 14, 1940:

The front section of a new fourteen-foot wall to re-place the old wooden one surrounding the penitentiary was completed yesterday afternoon. The main entrance also has a new sliding gate, and wicket. The wall, which is a substantial one, was started last spring by the Department of Public Works under the foremanship of Mr. Tobias Matthews. The prisoners of the penitentiary broke all the rock for the new wall, and all the mixing was done by hand. The new wall which is eight inches thick is re-enforced with sixteen-inch columns set nine feet apart. Iron lighting standards have been built on top of the wall to which is attached barbed wire entanglements. About forty feet of the new wall on the western side of the penitentiary has been completed. It is proposed to continue the work on this section until the cold weather sets in.

Ducking from the Yard-Arm

Ducking was a form of punishment sometimes used in the Newfoundland justice system. Ducking from the yard-arm was an ancient naval punishment used up until the end of the nineteenth century. The culprit was hoisted to the yard-arm, suddenly dropped into the water, and hauled up again from one to seven times. The following court extract is from a case involving the punishment of ducking:

Whereas Francis Knapman, John Wallis, William Couch, Samuel Wood, four of the six persons who did the damage at Colinet last winter to the Frenchmen, have been taken and confined aboard this ship. We, the undersigned, have seriously considered having ye above duck at ye maine yarde of this ship for a public example to all this Island; and they shall be liable for the said damage legally proved, and the damage shall be made good by Pollard and Rolson who fitted them out for that fishing voyage. The damage is said to be more than £50 or £60. – H.M.S. *Assistance*, Bay Bulls, September 29, 1680, Robert Robinson, Captain, R.N., Stephen Akarman of Bay Bulls, John Beverly, Aaron Browning.

The Role of Banishment in Old Time Newfoundland

Banishment was a legal penalty for many crimes in old time Newfoundland. The penalty of banishment or transportation was part of the criminal justice system of the nineteenth century. It resulted in the criminal being deported and banned from returning to Newfoundland for a period determined by the court. It was applied in the following cases:

On October 9, 1822, Jim Wade was sentenced to seven years banishment for stealing two sheep from J.B. Garland, Trinity; at the same time, James Lanigan, for stealing about fifty dollars from Slade and Kelson and forty-five dollars from Slade and Sons was sentenced to fourteen years banishment.

On July 4, 1834, Michael Aylward was found guilty of aiding and abetting the escape of three prisoners from the Harbour Grace jail. He was sentenced to perpetual banishment from the country.

On November 30, 1837, the sentence of seven years banishment from this country was passed on John Sheehan, Philip Monaghan, Joseph Hudson, William Delahunty, Joseph Bonan, Thomas Dwyer and James Meagher for larceny.

On December 28, 1837, George Avery of Bonavista was convicted of manslaughter and was sentenced to perpetual banishment.

On November 11, 1850, Thomas Martin of Twillingate was sentenced to fourteen years banishment for stealing from the shop of Slade, Cox and Co.

On December 3, 1867, John Wadden was found guilty of manslaughter of a man named Fahey and sentenced to two years imprisonment with hard labour and then banished.

On December 11, 1869, Mrs. Garland, who stabbed her husband to death with an awl, was sentenced to twelve months imprisonment and then banished.

His Punishment was Branding Irons

Laurence Kneeves of Harbour Main ordered his friend, John Kelly, to drink a mug of flip. The suggestion resulted in an argument between the two that ended in a gruesome death for Kelly and a most unusual punishment for Kneeves. The term 'mug of flip' has long disappeared from usage in Newfoundland, but during the mid-eighteenth century it was quite common. Flip was a concoction of liquor, eggs and sugar, which was used as a pep drink to give energy to the consumer. To suggest or order someone to drink flip was to accuse them of being lazy, certainly an insult to any man priding himself on being a hard worker.

The tragic story of John Kelly took place in Harbour Main on Thursday, June 26, 1748. Kelly and a friend, John Cuddy, were paying a social visit to the home of James Moores, a merchant. Kneeves, an employee of Moores, was at the house which was located nearby. As they were leaving, Kneeves called to Kelly, "Go drink a mug of flip." This sparked an argument, and before anyone knew what was happening punches were being thrown.

The fight moved outdoors where Cuddy made a move to part the antagonists. Derby Callahan, a heavy-set rowdy Irishman, stepped in and warned that he would "knock to the ground" any man who tried to stop the fight. Cuddy realized he could not handle Callahan, so he left to seek help. When he returned the fight was over and Kelly was stretched out on his back.

"Is he dead?" Cuddy asked.

Kneeves, who was standing nearby with his hands covered in blood, replied, "No, he's just drunk. I'll throw some water in his face."

There was no response. Kneeves then realized that Kelly was dead.

There were very few doctors in those days. In fact, in these situations, a panel of private citizens were picked and authorized to examine the body and submit a sworn account of their findings to the Justice of the Peace in Harbour Grace, George Garland. The panel included: John Moore, Roger Benlite, John Woodford, Thomas Balaine, William Brown, Pearce Butler and Philip Renough.

Their statement read:

> By all first circumstances and appearances found, John Kelly was barbarously murdered and abused, his head being battered severely and his handkerchief so tight around his neck that it was impossible to put a knife between the flesh and handkerchief.

Kneeve's trial took place at the old wooden courthouse in St. John's. When all of the evidence had been presented, the judge gave the jury an opportunity to ask questions. After giving them instructions, they were sent out of the courtroom to deliberate and arrive at a decision. To make sure that the jury was seriously focused on its responsibility, the judge directed the bailiff to deny the jury meat, drink, fire, candle, lodging, or suffering any person to speak to them until they agreed on a verdict. The jury was back with its verdict in ninety minutes. They found Kneeves guilty of manslaughter.

In this case, the judge ordered that on the following day at noon, Kneeves be brought back into the courtroom and burnt on the right hand with a red hot iron marked with the letter 'R.' In addition he was ordered to forfeit all his goods and chattels, and then he was banished from the country.

It was a customary practice for person sentenced to banishment to leave on the first available boat leaving the country. Because of this there was no mention of the place of banishment. The branding of 'R,' standing for "rogue," was used to mark the convict who had committed murder or was a repeat offender for life.

Mutiny and Murder Near St. Pierre

A bungled mutiny, murder and robbery on the sea near St. Pierre led to the arrest and hanging of a small band of men. The story begins in October 1828, when the *Fulwood* set sail from Canada to England to purchase provisions. As was the custom in those days, the ship carried a supply of Spanish gold and other coin to make the necessary purchases. When the ship left port, the gold and coin had been locked in several large chests and stored below the deck.

The crew members did not become aware of the treasure on board until they had been at sea for several days. They banded together, mutinied, stabbed the captain and officers to death and took control of the ship. In their haste to steal the treasure, the gang neglected to consider one essential aspect of the mutiny; there was no one among them who could navigate a ship.

Between St. Pierre and Miquelon there is a stretch of sand sometimes covered by water and known as the Dunes. Many vessels have been shipwrecked at this place. Without anyone to navigate, the *Fulwood* sailed straight into the Dunes and became wrecked. The ship was sinking faster than the men could work to unload the gold. In desperation they tied together some lifeboat oars to make a raft to carry the last of the gold chests. The raft broke apart and the chests sank beneath the waves.

French authorities in St. Pierre investigated the sinking of the *Fulwood* and discovered the murder, mutiny and robbery that had led to its demise. The men were rounded up by the French police, and sent to military authorities in St. John's, Newfoundland. From there they were taken to London, England, under guard, where they were tried and executed at a hanging place near the old Bailey courthouse. Many unsuccessful attempts were made to find the gold. During the early twentieth century, the uncle of Emilienne Parrot of St. Pierre, while on a trouting trip, found a birch wall protruding from a sandy embankment.

He dug at the site and found a quantity of gold. According to Emilienne, her uncle told no one of his discovery. He took the gold to the Canadian mainland, changed it to French money and returned home. He built himself an expensive home on the island and furnished it lavishly. Emilienne, up to the time of her death, had two of her uncle's valuable paintings in her own home.

May 2, 1861: Politician Murdered

There was a time in Newfoundland history when it took a great deal of courage to enter the political arena, or even to accept a post as an Election Day official. The General Election of 1861 was such a period. Intimidation was rampant; there were beatings, shootings, destruction of property and riots. May 2nd was polling day and in Harbour Main, George Furey, cousin of the government party candidate Charles Furey, was shot and killed. The returning officer was so intimidated by threats of violence that when the vote count was completed he refused to make the results known. His fear was not alleviated by the presence of fifty members of the Royal Newfoundland

Regiment, who were sent to the district to keep the peace on Election Day.

The decision on the outcome of the election was left to the House of Assembly to announce. The count in this dual riding was Nowlan, 325; Byrne, 322; Hogsett, 316; Furey, 310. Hogsett, a lawyer and former attorney general, insisted on taking a seat in the legislature even though he had lost and the outcome of the election had not been properly proclaimed. *The Times*, a local newspaper, warned Hogsett that, "A forcible entry may propel the perpetration into quite a different atmosphere to answer for the violence. No outrage, my good Sir! Or else. You understand?"

The violence in Harbour Main and Harbour Grace forced the *Harbour Grace Standard* to suspend publication for several days. When the paper resumed printing, no mention was made of the Furey shooting or other Election Day violence. Meanwhile, Furey and Hogsett, the losers, went to the legislature in St. John's and took the Harbour Main seats in the House. Furey left when the Speaker insisted that they had no right being there, but Hogsett had to be forcefully removed.

The ladies of St. John's boycotted the legislature because of the violence expected to take place at the official opening. A member of the House, Kenneth MacLean, was attacked by a mob as he walked to the House, but he managed to break away and outrun his attackers. Another MHA, P.G. Tessier, was followed by the mob but managed to gain entrance to the House before they could catch up with him.

The crowds then turned their energies to property destruction. They demolished the premises of Nowlan and Kitchen. Judge Robson's stables were burned, as was the nearby building of the Theological Institute. The mob also burned to the ground the cottage and outhouses of prominent citizen, Hugh Hoyles. An effort to burn the house of the Anglican Bishop failed.

In response, the Prime Minister ordered out the troops. Reporting on this action, *The Times* stated:

> It is melancholy to record that such was the rebellious disposition and conduct of the mob that neither the presence of the magistrate, accompanied by Lieutenant Colonel Grant, officers and men, nor the utmost and unceasing entreaties of the Roman Catholic clergy, could prevail upon the crowd to retire peaceably to their homes. They kept their ground applying the most insulting language to the colonel and his troops.

It was not until they had pelted the soldiers and struck the colonel that the riot act was read. When the crowds refused to move, the colonel ordered the troops to open fire. Several people were wounded and Father O'Donnell, a Roman Catholic priest was shot in the foot. When word of the confrontation reached Bishop Mullock he ordered the ringing of the Cathedral Bells to summon all Catholics to the church grounds. The crowds were quick to respond and in no time the church yard was crowded. Bishop Mullock pleaded for common sense to prevail and asked his followers to observe the peace. Bishop Mullock was effective and the crowd dispersed and returned to their homes as the Bishop had requested.

Who Was Jacques R. Millere?

One of the longest unsolved mysteries in Newfoundland history involves the discovery of the body of a French man on the west coast of the province almost ninety years ago.

At 4:00 p.m. on March 15, 1909, Frank Penney found the body of Jaques R. Millere on the grounds of the Humber River Pulp and Lumber Co. near Deer Lake. When the police arrived they searched the man's clothing and found some very intriguing documents.

The papers featured every conceivable kind of astronomical drawings and plans, as well as sketches of aircraft designs. In addition, police found writings which were highly imaginative descriptions of the planets and unusual philosophical dissertations on the relationship between humanity and the heavenly bodies.

The most amazing aspect of the discovered material was the post office receipt issued in Summerside, Prince Edward Island, showing that Millere had recently sent a registered letter to the Duke of Orleans in Paris.

Who was Jaques Millere? One newspaper suggested he might have been some visionary royalist dreaming of the restoration of the French Monarchy, or some scientific crackpot.

Despite police efforts to shed light on the Millere mystery, his secrets died with him. He was buried at the Catholic cemetery in Birchy Cove.

Chapter 10: The Solving of Two Criminal Mysteries

Among the criminal mysteries that once baffled Newfound-landers are the cases of murder victim, Alfreda Pike, and Michael Whelan, a convicted killer, who escaped from Her Majesty's Penitentiary and disappeared into history.

Both cases remained a mystery for almost a century, despite the fact that deathbed confessions were made in both cases, but were not made public. In Pike's case, the killer confessed a half century after the crime, but this fact escaped the attention of writers and historians, resulting in the case being mistakenly recorded in history as an unsolved murder.[1]

Thomas Pike and Alfreda Pike were not related, but they were in love with each other. The attractive seventeen-year-old Alfreda left Harbour Grace one cold winter's evening to walk to her home in Bristol's Hope. According to Thomas, that was the last time he saw her alive.

Thomas Pike awoke the next morning to discover that his sweetheart had been sexually attacked and murdered. The mutilated body of Alfreda Pike was found in a pool of blood off the road near Harbour Grace. A lengthy police investigation failed to identify the sadistic killer and the incident was remembered in history as an unsolved murder. Yet, the killer, who was among those visiting the murder scene after her body was discovered, made a death bed confession that offered one of the most surprising solutions to any murder case in Newfoundland's criminal history. But it came far too late for Thomas

---

[1] Michael Whelan made his deathbed confession in New York but that went unnoticed in Newfoundland until I came across it while researching criminal cases for one of my earlier books. In the following pages I record both stories including the discovery of both confessions.

Pike, who carried the weight of public suspicion on his shoulders for a lifetime.

Unfortunately, suspicion fell on Pike from the beginning, although there was no evidence connecting him with the deed. In spite of this, the townspeople made it so difficult for the boy that one day he left Newfoundland for the United States and never returned.[2]

The tragic story began on Wednesday, January 5, 1870. Alfreda had been visiting her grandmother all day in Harbour Grace. Her home was in a nearby community, then called Mosquito, but has since been renamed Bristol's Hope. Shortly after 6:00 p.m., she left Harbour Grace to walk home. Witnesses who last saw her alive recalled that a man was walking with her when she left the town. However, they were too far away to identify him.

Early the following morning a boy named Flannery was proceeding along the road in a wagon and noticed a trail of blood in the snow. It did not take long for him to discover the body of a young girl lying in a pool of blood a short distance from the road. He wasted no time rushing to Harbour Grace to notify Constable Furey.

Word of the discovery spread like wildfire throughout Harbour Grace. By the time police arrived at the murder scene, a large crowd had gathered. The next day, an article in *The Harbour Grace Standard* stated, "There indeed was seen the body of a girl-dead-murdered-slaughtered by the hand of some miscreant a devil incarnate, a monster of blood, reeking his savage butchery on this defenceless victim."

---

[2] While researching material for my book, *Too Many Parties, Too Many Pals*, I uncovered the existence of a long forgotten confession to the murder. Despite the fact the deathbed confession was sent to authorities, it was not made public. Paul O'Neill's *History of St. John's*, published in the 1970s, records the crime as unsolved.

What was not known at the time was that the sadistic killer was standing there among the crowd that day, expressing his horror over the murder. He was one of the most respected residents of the community and the least likely of all possible murder suspects. He attended the victim's funeral and offered sympathy and support to the family.

The newspaper article described the condition of the victim. The horror of the scene obviously touched the writer who wrote:

> What mind can grasp the intensity of agony which the poor victim must have undergone – the struggle for life, the cry for mercy, the fearful death wounds, the pool of blood, and the melancholy tragedy – a human being mangled and butchered by another human being? Ten thousand times worse than the beast that perishes.

The body of the victim was wrapped and taken to a nearby hospital where she was identified by her brother as Alfreda Pike of Mosquito. The police investigation that followed heightened fear among citizens throughout Conception Bay. *The Standard* tried to encourage public cooperation in its editorial which stated:

> We are sure that the feeling of our people is such that everything will be done to help even in the most trifling way towards its solution; particularly too, when a very solemn, moral and legal obligation rests on every person to communicate to the proper authorities any and every information which may tend, even in the slightest degree, to throw light on the question and towards the detention of the guilty. Any person failing

to do this will render themselves liable to heavy punishment, in fact, they will be considered as accessories to the murder for such neglect of their duty, and when it becomes known, as it undoubtedly will, they will be dealt with as such. Therefore, we would advise them to take warning before it is too late.

The warning was in vain. No witness came forward and the murderer continued to live in Harbour Grace, remaining beyond suspicion for several years. Throughout those years he never gave any indication of the burden of guilt, which must have rested on his shoulders. The coroner's jury conducted an investigation, which concluded with a verdict of, "Willful murder by person or persons unknown."

Over fifty years later, around 1924-1925, the real killer lay on his deathbed in Grand Falls. His own record remained unblemished and he was still a man respected by the public. His conscience weighed so heavily that he decided to rid himself of his burden before meeting his maker. Not only had he taken the life of an innocent young woman, but also allowed an innocent man to be labelled a murderer by the public. Just how much he had been burdened with the knowledge and memories of what he had done is not known. However, he was remorseful on his deathbed and wanted to ease his conscience with a confession before death.

Who the killer was turned out to be as much a shocker as the murder itself. He was the same man who was called to the scene next day, a man who took part in the police investigation; in fact, he was a police officer! The man was an ex-Harbour Grace Constable named Furey. Unfortunately for the descendants of Thomas Pike, authorities decided to let sleeping dogs lie because more than a half century had passed. That would have left the slaying of Alfreda Pike to remain as unsolved. However, not all those who had knowledge of the confession were content with the decision.

The telegraph operator in Harbour Grace when the confession was received there was J.C. Crocker. He was stunned when the telegraph came through from Grand Falls with the sensational news that the killer of Alfreda Pike, a policeman who investigated the murder, had confessed the crime and the full notarized confession was included. This revelation may have gone unrecorded if it had not been for a letter written by an employee of the Harbour Grace Post Office who had read the confession when it came through. Crocker was bothered by the fact that the suspicion of guilt still lay on the shoulders of Thomas Pike.

On September 13, 1924 or 1925, Crocker shared his knowledge of the deathbed confession with *The Barrelman*, a nightly radio show hosted by Joe Smallwood. He stated, "I feel an injustice is being done to the descendants of Thomas Pike. I feel the stigma of supposed guilt for so dastardly a deed may still be on his children and grandchildren."

It would have been a great criminal mystery for Smallwood to have provided the solution, despite the fact that seventy-five years had passed since the killing. Many descendants of those involved were still around and Smallwood asked himself how this might impact on them.

The former premier considered the matter for days and finally concluded he would respect the decision made by authorities to "let sleeping dogs lie." He chose not to broadcast the story. In a letter to Crocker, Smallwood explained he did this, "... in consideration of the peace of mind of those who may possibly have some relationship with the dying confessor."

Discovery of Another Deathbed Confession

One of the most successful escapes from Her Majesty's Penitentiary in St. John's was carried out by a Horse Cove fisherman named Michael Whelan. At the time of the escape, Whelan had served four years of a life sentence for the murder of Levi King.

The incident which resulted in King's death and Whelan's imprisonment started on Saturday afternoon, October 8, 1883. It was an argument over religion. Whelan had stopped at a beer shop located at the foot of Kenna's Hill for a few drinks of spruce beer and rum. While there, he met his neighbour George Squires. The two sat and drank for almost an hour. Squires was returning from the banks fishery and was anxious to get home to his family. When Whelan and his wife got up to leave, Squires was kind enough to offer them a ride to their home in St. Phillips.

The trio boarded the horse-drawn carriage and headed up Portugal Cove Road towards St. Phillips. Squires later told the police, "At that time, Whelan was rowing and jawing with me all the time. But he didn't touch me. I got off his cart at Kenny's Farm and walked ahead. But he overtook me and passed me on Lawlor's Hill."

Squires said that when Whelan challenged him to a fight, he ran ahead and jumped on a cart driven by Henry Jones. When Whelan followed behind shouting insults, Squires jumped from the cart to seek security and protection on another cart driven by Richard Tucker and Levi King. In a matter of minutes, the two carts were racing in over Portugal Cove Road with Whelan gaining the lead and finally forcing Tucker to bring his horse to a halt. Whelan jumped off his cart and asked Squires if he still had a bottle of rum, which he displayed earlier at the beer shop. Whelan then became verbally abusive towards Squires. The two walked side by side arguing over the rum. When they got to a place known as Brigg's Bridge,

Whelan challenged Squires to a fight. Squires prudently refused to tangle with the six-foot-tall, 200-pound Whelan. Squires ran ahead and again joined Tucker and King.

Whelan began cursing the Orange Lodge and all Orangemen. Richard Tucker asked, "Mick, what need you bother about Orangemen?" Whelan answered, "It's what they done to our fathers. They got a lodge built now at the Cross Roads without a window or anything else in it. Why are they so secret?"

Tucker chided Whelan saying, "You're on the wrong side, Mick boy." That was too much for the rowdy Irishman. He jumped from the cart and ran to the side of Tucker's shouting, "I'm on the right side now. Get down off that cart and I'll fight you all." Seeing his challenge was going unanswered, Whelan stepped back and roared, "There's not the principle of a man among ya! Get off the cart. Get off and kill me. I'm not afraid to die!"

Undaunted by Whelan's threats, Levi King said calmly, "We have better principles than to do the like."

Whelan moved closer to the cart and asked King, "Do you think you can do it? Get off the cart and we'll see."

King replied, "I wouldn't want to be able to do it, Mick."

Whelan quipped, "Is there anything you fellows can do?" to which King replied, "Yes, we can haul down yer Chapel." All three aboard King's cart burst out laughing which only added fuel to Whelan's burning temper.

When Whelan attempted to pull King down from the cart, Tucker whipped the horse and they dashed away, leaving Whelan shouting obscenities and cursing all Orangemen.

The trio arrived at King's house and went inside. Levi King picked up a hatchet helve and said, "If Whelan comes here he won't bother us." No sooner had the words been spoken when Whelan could be heard outside, challenging anyone and everyone in the house to come outside and fight.

King was the first to go out and face Whelan. Tucker, Squires and King's wife followed. After a brief exchange of insults between Whelan and King, Whelan stooped and ran towards King, grasping King's legs and throwing him to the ground. Whelan then pulled a knife and stabbed King in the groin. King got to his feet and attempted to run back to the house, but Whelan stabbed him again in the back.

Whelan then turned and attacked Squires. However, Squires stepped aside and delivered a forceful blow to Whelan's temple, driving him head over heels to the ground. Not waiting for the hot-tempered Whelan to regain his senses, Squires followed his friends into King's house and locked the door. As Whelan got back on his feet, his wife grabbed him by the arm and coaxed him aboard the cart. The two then drove off down the road. King, who had been sitting on a kitchen chair, moaned, then keeled over onto the floor. It was only then that the others noticed he had been stabbed. When Squires saw the knife wound in the victim's left groin area, he covered it with a half stick of tobacco.

Squires sent for a doctor and as he moved around to help his dying friend, he noticed that he too had been stabbed. His wound was a minor one. It seemed that during his brief scuffle with Whelan, the knife nicked his left side between the hip and the ribs. By the time the doctor arrived, King was dead. The incident was then reported to the police.

Constable Alfred Rees led two other constables to Whelan's home to make the arrest. Whelan and his wife locked themselves inside and refused to open the door. Rees tried to persuade Mrs. Whelan to allow them in, but she held firm in support of her husband. Finally, the police forced entry into the house.

On October 6, 1883, Michael Whelan was brought before Justices Carter, Pinsent and Little, and charged with the wilful murder of Levi King. The trial lasted one day and the jury took only one hour to reach its verdict. The jury reduced the charge and found Whelan guilty of manslaughter. They did not recommend mercy and Whelan was sentenced to life imprisonment.

Four years later, Whelan's good behaviour had earned him the trust of the prison officials. On the morning of November 25, 1887, he was permitted outside prison walls to work with other trusted prisoners on a drainage system they were constructing for the General Hospital.

A fight broke out among the prisoners and when the guards moved in to break it up Whelan seized the chance to make his dash for liberty. He ran down alongside Quidi Vidi Lake with a prison guard in pursuit close behind. He outdistanced the guard and soon disappeared into the White Hills.

McCowan, a superintendent of the prison, ordered a search for the fugitive and a $200 reward was offered by the colonial secretary's office for Whelan's recapture. He was never found. Many thought he had drowned while trying to swim across the harbour. Others suspected he escaped and was living in the United States. Adding fuel to the claim he had made it to the U.S. was the fact that soon after the escape his wife left Newfoundland and moved to New York.

Whelan's escape remained one of Newfoundland's unsolved mysteries until the mid-1980s when researching one of my books on crime I discovered evidence which verified that Whelan had succeeded in making it to the U.S. His wife joined him and they reared a family there. However, on his deathbed he confided to a priest of his past crime and escape from a Newfoundland prison. This revelation was published in New York newspapers in the 1930s.

Notes

More than forty-five years after Smallwood declined to reveal this piece of our criminal history, I was researching the same Alfreda Pike murder among old records stored in the offices of the Newfoundland Historical Society in the basement of Colonial Building. I located several file folders with pages of information relating to the Pike case and gathered the material I needed to write the story for a book I was planning.

After finishing writing the story and reading it over, I thought that I should return to the Historical Society files and make one last effort to determine if I had missed any relevant information. It was no skill on my part that brought the secret to light, but rather one of those unexpected and unexplainable things that often happen in life. I picked up a collection of multiple papers that were already stapled together and browsed through them.

"Nothing new here," I thought. I then closed the attachments and was in the process of laying them on top of the pile I had finished reviewing when several papers separated and floated to the floor. While picking up these papers, I noticed they were separate documents to the one I had just finished reading but had been stuck to them.

As I examined it, I experienced the type of enthusiasm common to researchers and writers when discovering something new and significant. These papers which Crocker had written decades earlier had not been destroyed. They had been in the file so long that they stuck to the document next to them. Very few people had bothered to even look through these files up to that time.

For a while I considered not releasing the information. At that time the case had long faded from public memory, few even remembered the name of the victim and fewer remembered the name of her boyfriend who some believed was responsible for the killing.

However, when faced with the, perhaps unavoidable, likelihood that some writer would later resurrect the case and, not being aware of the confession, identify unjustly Thomas Pike as the killer, I decided to reveal it. I did that in the mid-1980s. Only now, I am including the background to how the disclosure came about.

Some public hangings were held from a scaffold erected outside the windows of the old courthouse, which was built on the vacant site, east of the present courthouse, around 1829 and destroyed by fire in 1848.
Jack Fitzgerald Collection

The old horse drawn paddy wagon was a familiar site around town in oldtime St. John's. *City of St. John's Archives*

A prisoners cell in the original cell block at Her Majesty's Penitentary, St. John's. *Panl*

K. of C. LEAVE CENTRE

PRESENTS

Uncle Tim's Barn Dance

THIS PASS entitles you to this Radio Broadcast on Saturday night, ... at K. of C. Leave Centre, Harvey Road, from 10.30 to 11.30 o'clock.

COMPLIMENTS OF

....

IMPORTANT—All guests must be in their seats not later than 10.15 No admission after this time.

A photograph of one of the actual tickets sold to the public for the Uncle Tim's Barn Dance, Saturday night broadcast from the Knights of Columbus on December 12, 1942. *Panl*

The Uncle Tim's Barn Dance group on stage at the Knights of Columbus in 1942. *Panl*

Despite a thorough search for murder victim John Snow, his body was never found. *Panl*

Journalist and author Bren Walsh solved the K of C fire mystery and while preparing to publish a book on the fire passed away. Walsh obtained long hidden information through personal visits to an adjutant general at the Pentagon in Washington. Walsh is shown on the right of this photo sitting next to Jack White, a journalist and later a judge. He passed the true story onto Jack Fitzgerald and it is included in *Newfoundland Disasters. Panl*

Chapter 11: A Glimpse of Hell

At 11:00 p.m. on August 8, 1945, the air-raid sirens sounded over Nagasaki. It had no effect on those POWs at Camp Fukuoka who heard it and, like most people in Nagasaki, had become desensitized to its frequent sounding. For months, American B-29s had flown over Nagasaki on their way to bomb military targets in other cities. Each time they approached Nagasaki, the sirens sounded and, by August 8th, people responded in a routine manner. Sometimes, people even ignored the warning.

Newfoundland-born Jack Ford slept undisturbed by the commotion taking place in the city across the harbour. The hardships of prison life had taken their toll and Ford, who weighed 174 pounds when taken prisoner, was now down to a skeletal weight of ninety-six pounds. Disease and malnutrition were rampant in the POW camp, and it was unlikely that Ford would have survived another six months. The all-clear sounded over the city as Ford tossed and turned trying to find escape and comfort from the fleas that infested the beds and attacked his body each night.

How Nagasaki Became a Target

The concentration of Mitsubishi Industries, major suppliers to the Japanese military, made Nagasaki a legitimate target for the atomic bomb in the eyes of American military strategists. The city faced the East China Sea and was located at the head of a long bay, which gave it the best natural harbour in southwestern Kyushu.[1] It was surrounded by hills, which were

---

[1] Kyushu is an island in southern Japan where Nagasaki is located. Kyogi is the island, at the mouth of the harbour entering Nagasaki, where Camp Fukuoka #2 was located.

divided by fertile valleys that spread upwards from the harbour's industrial area. Nagasaki was the setting for Giacomo Puccini's immortal opera, *Madame Butterfly*.

In 1945, Nagasaki had a population of 280,000. Ninety percent of the city's work force was employed with the Mitsubishi Industries, which included shipyards, electrical equipment works, steel mills and an arms plant. Nagasaki was a peculiar Japanese city because it was the most Christian and Western-influenced city in all Japan. There were many Catholic schools and churches throughout the city. Nagasaki also had a Catholic hospital and a Catholic seminary.

Portuguese missionaries and European merchants brought western culture and Christianity to Japan in the sixteenth century. Christianity was not accepted by the Japanese and in 1639 all Portuguese had been expelled from Japan. A tiny and scattered band of 'hidden Christians' kept the light of faith burning.

In response to the efforts of missionaries to introduce Christianity to Japan, a ritual developed at Nagasaki that lasted for more than 200 years. It was called *Fumi*. The practice of *Fumi* demanded that every citizen of Nagasaki had to submit to an annual ritual of stepping on a Christian image. These were engravings of saints and martyrs on a small square of wood.[2]

It was through Nagasaki that the first missionaries and merchants came to Japan and by the outbreak of war on December 7, 1941, there was a strong foundation for both in the city. Japan was never happy with those outside influences and for four centuries tried to suppress both. Nevertheless, in 1925, permission was given to the Roman Catholic Church to build the Urakami Cathedral which at the time became the largest church in the Orient. It was destroyed by the atomic bomb in 1945, and not rebuilt until fourteen years later.

[2] City of Nagasaki brochure entitled *Nagasaki, Where East Meets West*.

When war broke out in 1941, all the European members of the clergy were arrested and imprisoned in concentration camps. Those of Japanese nationality were permitted to continue to practice their religion and serve in the Catholic clergy.[3]

1945: Japan Was Losing the War

By 1945, the Japanese Air Force and Navy had been decimated. Japan's people were starving and more than sixty of its cities had been almost entirely wiped out by B-29 fire-bombing attacks. With so many of its young men dying in battle, every able-bodied man was conscripted.

To fill the tens of thousands of vacancies the conscription left in its work force, Japan turned to POWs, old people, high school students and the thousands of Koreans who had been uprooted after their country was conquered by the Japanese.[4] Concerns like Mitsubishi Industries were crying out for workers and their needs had to be filled. In his book *Nagasaki 1945*, Dr. Tatsuichiro Akizuki pointed out that government censors had succeeded in keeping the truth about Japan's deterioration from the public, who were led to believe Japan was winning the war. By the time the first atomic bomb was dropped on Japan, 500,000 civilians had already been killed and millions were homeless. With so many B-29 bombers flying over Nagasaki almost daily on their way to other targeted cities, many people of Nagasaki believed they were being spared by the Americans because of the widespread existence of western culture and religion in their city.

Jack Ford slept through the night, unaware of developments taking place in the war that would, in a matter of days, bring an answer to his longtime prayer for freedom. At midnight on August 8th, Russia fulfilled a commitment to the

---

[3] Akizuki, Tatsuichiro, *Nagasaki 1945*. Quartet Books, London, Melbourne, New York. 1981.

[4] Kirby, Major General S. Woodburn. *The War Against Japan (Official History of the Second World War)*. H.M.SO. 1957.

Allied Forces and declared war on Japan, then invaded Manchuria, China which was occupied by the Japanese.[5]

Nagasaki Was a Secondary Target

At 1:56 a.m. Tokyo Standard time on August 9th, the B-29 bomber nicknamed *Bock's Car* taxied down the runway at Tinian Island in the Marianas[6] on the start of its 2,000-mile journey to drop a second atomic bomb on Japan, a plutonium bomb, more powerful than the uranium bomb dropped on Hiroshima on August 6th.

The second atomic attack on Japan was scheduled for August 11th and the target city was Kokura. This date was moved ahead to August 9th, after the American military received reports showing that the weather in the target area would not be favourable.

It must be stated here that following the bombing of Hiroshima, the American forces prepared six million pamphlets to be dropped over Japanese cities warning civilians to prepare themselves for more atomic attacks.

The bomb on its way to Japan was dubbed by the world's first atomic strike crew *The Fat Man*, which was a reference to its comparison to Sir Winston Churchill. It was 3.5 metres long and weighed 4.5 tons. This bomb had the explosive potential of twenty-two kilotons of TNT, compared to the twelve and a half kiloton force of the Hiroshima bomb.

The mission to drop the second atomic bomb on Japan was assigned to Major Charles (Chuck) Sweeney and involved three B-29 Super fortress bombers. It was almost cancelled

---

[5] Just as Japan attacked Pearl Harbour before informing the United States that it had declared war, Russia attacked Manchuria and then informed the Japanese that it had declared war. Stalin did this by first informing the Japanese Ambassador to Russia, then preventing the Ambassador's letters from leaving Russia until after Manchuria had been attacked.

[6] The Marianas Islands were located in the Pacific, 1,300 miles from Japan and 2,000 miles from Kokura. They had been occupied by the Japanese, but retaken by the United States Marines.

when Major Sweeney discovered that the fuel-pump of his plane was malfunctioning and preventing access to 600 gallons of fuel. After some quick calculations, Sweeney decided to move forward on schedule, knowing that the amount of fuel he could access would be adequate to reach his target and return. Two other B-29s were part of the mission. Their assignment was to act as observer planes. One carried cameras to photograph the bombing and the second was loaded with scientific instruments for measuring the effects of the explosion.

Sweeney's B-29 had a small winged boxcar painted on it. It was named in honour of its regular pilot, Fred Bock. On this mission, Bock was flying Sweeney's plane *The Great Artiste*, which was the observer plane carrying the scientific instruments. Twenty-five-year-old Captain Don Albury was the second pilot on *Bock's Car*. This B-29 had a crew of twelve men. The planes participating in the mission were scheduled to rendezvous over Yakoshima, a small island south of Kyushu. Their target was an armaments plant in the city of Kokura on the north coast of Kyushu.

B-29s were near impossible targets for the Japanese Zeros because they could fly higher than any fighter planes at the time. Those that had been shot down were planes that either developed mechanical problems and dropped to lower altitudes, or changed to a lower altitude due to the weather. Squadrons of Zeros often trailed the B-29s hoping that one would break formation and change its altitude.

On the morning of August 9th, *Bock's Car* had passed into Japanese airspace and was approaching Kokura without any resistance from the enemy. Weather reports from Kokura indicated that conditions there were favourable for the mission.[7]

---

[7] Because of the violent jet streams crisscrossing the more than 1,200 miles of sky between the Marianas and Japan, the Americans welcomed help from an unexpected source. Mao Tse-tung, a Chinese guerilla leader who became leader of China after the war, radioed regular forecasts from northern China. His help enabled many B-29 attacks upon Japan.

As Sweeney approached his target, he faced another problem. At 31,000 feet over Kokura, the bomb doors opened and Captain Kermit Beahan, the bombardier sitting in the Plexiglas nose of the B-29, gazed down through the rubber eyepiece of the bombsight. He scanned the terrain below with his crosssights, looking for the military arsenal which was his specific target. A heavy industrial haze and smoke from a large fire obstructed the view of the arsenal. "No drop!" he shouted, and Sweeney turned the plane to circle and make a second approach. Beahan could see a river and buildings, but the arsenal was still not in sight.

If it were not for this problem, the bomb would have been dropped and Sweeney would be on his way back to base. By this time people below had seen the silver plane far above them, and were scrambling to take refuge in the city's air raid shelters. Anti-aircraft batteries quickly responded and began firing at the plane. Sweeney, out of reach of the flak and undeterred, made a third attempt to line-up the target. The smoky haze still covered the target and for the third time Beahan shouted, "No drop!"

The decision to drop the bomb on Kokura, or turn to the mission's alternate target, was now in the hands of Major Chuck Sweeney. Sweeney was facing serious problems. By now the Japanese Zeros were in the air, and with the firepower coming from the batteries below, *Bock's Car* was running out of fuel. Sweeney decided to abandon the primary target, and he advised the crew that they were heading for the secondary target – Nagasaki.

The Atomic Bomb was Dropped

As *Bock's Car* passed over Japanese villages and cities on its way to Nagasaki, Captain Sweeney had reason to be concerned about the plane's ability to survive the mission. With the worsening fuel situation, he realized they could not make it back to Tinian Island, and might not make it to the closer U.S. base at Okinawa. To make matters worse, there was only enough gas for one attempt at the target and clouds were moving in from the China Sea towards Nagasaki.

The target was the Mitsubishi Ordinance Plant near the head of the harbour, just a short distance from the harbour island of Kyogi, where Camp Fukuoka was located. Sweeney was flying at 29,000 feet as he approached Nagasaki Harbour. Near the mouth of the harbour and a very short distance from the target was the shipyard where Jack Ford was working. *Bock's Car* had moved up to 31,000 feet as it flew inward over Nagasaki Harbour. Once more bombardier Beahan saw that clouds were obstructing his view of the target.

Just as the plane passed over the target, the clouds opened enough for him to see the oval outline of a stadium below. This was his final chance to release the bomb. If he chose to pass, the plane would have had to make an uncertain flight to Okinawa carrying the atomic bomb. Beahan quickly adjusted his sights and aligned the crossbars of the bombsight on the stadium. As he pressed the button, he shouted, "Bombs away! "Bombs away!"

The atomic bomb fell silently and then exploded 1,890 feet above Nagasaki, one and a half miles off its target. A minute after the bomb was dropped, *Bock's Car* was hit with five separate shocks caused by the explosion. One crew member described it, "... as if the B-29 were beaten by a telephone pole."

The bomb had missed the stadium, and exploded over the home and tennis court of the manager of the Mitsubishi Ordnance Factory.

Earlier the Morning at the POW Camp

At 6:00 a.m. that morning, things were still quiet at Camp

Fukuoka. Reveille sounded just as it had for each and every day Jack Ford was a prisoner there. The most brutal guard in the camp, Bokugo, was already stomping down the corridors of the prison followed by his minions and shouting rude remarks to the POWs ordering them to get out of bed.

The first thought to flash through Ford's mind was, "Will I survive today?" This was a question he asked himself every morning for three and a half years, since the day in 1942 when he was captured. As he pushed his aching body to get up out of bed and to prepare for the daily challenge of surviving, Ford recalls:

> I thought this was going to be another long day of hunger and boredom. The day started as routinely as it had since I first arrived there. When the guards were ready, they began to march us to the shipyard. Nobody wanted to start the day by getting the guards angry because we knew only too well what would follow. By this time, we were walking skeletons; the horrible conditions at the camp had brought us to that. Sometimes on the way to and from the shipyard, Japanese civilians living on the island would stare at us as we passed, but at no time did they bother us. We knew they were having a hard time too, and we thought that most of them didn't want the war any more than we did. On that day, we were not even considering that there could be a bomb attack on Nagasaki, and as for an atomic bomb attack, well that was not even in our vocabulary.

Ford recalled the events of that day with clarity, as though it had happened yesterday:

> August 9, 1945, was to become a cruel awakening

for the prisoners at Camp Fukuoka. We went to work in the dockyard, just the same as we did any other day. It was hot with blue skies and not a cloud in sight. Near eleven o'clock some clouds were moving over the city in the harbour area. The sun occasionally broke through the clouds. We had no reason to expect that there would be an attack of any kind. We did not hear any air raid warning, no siren sounded on our island, nothing to suggest that there was any enemy aircraft in the area. We had not heard the sound of anything until 11:02 when we were startled by a tremendous blast and immense heat, followed by complete turmoil in the dockyard with pieces of glass, stones, wood, and asbestos flying in all directions, and the employees, who were Koreans as well as Japanese women and children, were screaming, cowering, and running in all directions because they didn't know what had happened across the harbour at Nagasaki. When the bomb exploded, I had just stepped away from the guillotine where I was cutting sheet metal. Thoughts of some hot, green tea to break the monotony of a ten hour shift at the shipyard came abruptly to an end when I was knocked flat by a terrific blast. I lost consciousness for a few moments, but I recovered and quickly got to my feet. When I got to my feet, I looked up at the sky away from the mushroom cloud that was rapidly spreading out and moving upwards. I could see a reflection of light on a plane flying away from the city. I remember thinking how high it was. I estimated it was about 33,000 feet. At that time, we didn't know if the explosion was a dropped bomb, or something else.

The bomb's explosion was accompanied by very intense heat and balls of fire exploded everywhere. The roof of the shipyard building was no longer there. We later learned that the bomb had exploded 500 metres above the city and caused disturbances in the air that ripped the roofs from some of the strongest buildings in Nagasaki. It quickly got so dark that it seemed as though night had suddenly descended upon us. The boom was followed by a rapidly moving vertical cloud that burst into a magnificent sized mushroom cloud, the likes of which none of us had seen before, and it was moving upwards very fast and at the same time blotting out the sun. I learned later the cloud had risen to over 40,000 feet and could be seen twelve miles away.[8]

Some of us wondered what it might have been. We had not heard a bomb since we left Singapore, and basically we got the fright of our lives. We thought it may be the end of the world. It was that bad and, of course, some thought that it might have been an ammunition ship in Nagasaki Harbour, or an ammunition dump explosion. Who knew?

When the dust cleared off, the Japanese rounded us up and put us in a shelter dug out in the side of a cliff which had steel doors on it. They left us there for about an hour. The shelters were located near the shipyard. These were the same shelters where Bokugo warned they would gas us if the Americans invaded. Of course, we were curious and would look out through whatever cracks and openings we could find to try and see what was happening. Nagasaki was in flames. Nobody could come up with a satisfactory explanation as to what had caused the explosion. The

[8] The crew of *Bock's Car* reported seeing the mushroom cloud at a distance of twelve miles from Nagasaki as they were returning to base following their mission.

guards did not tell us anything about the bombing of Hiroshima because they had not been told.

Some days later, I learned that a B-29 had dropped an atomic bomb on Nagasaki. It was then that I realized the plane I had seen turning away from the city was *Bock's Car*, the plane that had carried out the mission.[9]

It was a blessing for Jack Ford that he turned away to get tea; otherwise he might have been blinded by the atomic flash. The instant the bomb exploded, a fireball appeared in the air. The estimated heat released by the fireball was several million degrees at the moment of the explosion and was about 300,000 degrees a ten-thousandth of a second after. A second later, when the diameter of the ball had reached the maximum of 280 meters, the surface heat of the fireball was 5,000 degrees. The deep red fireball was blazing furiously like a small sun for about ten seconds. Ford did feel the force of the blast and its heat, but fortunately missed the flash of super-bright light.[10] The pilot and crew of *Bock's Car* had a very different view of the explosion of the nuclear bomb. It was stunning, spectacular and absolutely unforgettable.

Incomprehensible Forces Released

Charles Sweeney viewed the atomic explosion from the skies above Nagasaki. The bomb was dropped at 11:01 a.m., after which Sweeney took *Bock's Car* into a descent, making a 155-degree turn to get away from the blast. At 11:02 a.m. the

[9] The crews of the B-29s that dropped the atomic weapons on Japan had trained long hours to drop the bomb, make an abrupt turn and get away from the target as far as possible before the explosion. Jack Ford had witnessed this important maneuver on August 9, 1945.

[10] *Days to Remember, an Account of the Bombings of Hiroshima and Nagasaki.* Published at Tokyo, Japan in 1981.

atomic bomb exploded. Sweeney described the magnificent view he witnessed:

> As I completed my turn, I could see a brownish horizontal cloud enveloping the city below. The bomb had detonated at 1890 feet, and in a millionth of a second compressed its core into a critical mass, releasing forces that were still incomprehensible. From the center of the brownish bile sprung a vertical column, boiling and bubbling up in those rainbow hues – purples, oranges, reds – colors whose brilliance I had seen only once before and would never see again. The cloud was rising faster than at Hiroshima. It seemed more intense, angrier. It was a mesmerizing sight, at once breathtaking and ominous.

Although we were twelve miles away, it appeared to some crew members that the cloud was heading straight for us. At about 25,000 feet, an expanding mushroom cloud broke off, white and puffy, and continued to burst upward at accelerating speed, passing us at 30,000 feet and shooting up to at least 45,000 feet.[11]

According to the *Report of the Committee of Japanese Citizens*, which was made up of Japanese research scientists:

> The intense heat rays released by the fireball burned a tremendous number of persons and houses. Those who had no shelters around and were directly exposed to the heat rays in the area within one point two kilometres from the hypocentre[12] were fatally

---

[11] *War's End, An Eyewitness Account of America's Last Atomic Mission.* Major Gen. Charles w. Sweeney, U.S.A.F. with James A. Ntonucci and Marion K. Antonucci.
[12] The hypocentre refers to the point where the Atomic bomb exploded. In Nagasaki that was 500 meters above Number 171 Marsuyama Street in the northern end of Nagasaki.

burned. People got their bare skin burned within four kilometres from the hypocentre in Nagasaki and within three point-five kilometres from the hypocentre in Hiroshima.

Japanese Doctor Said Japan was Warned
From the shell that was once Urakami Hospital, Dr. Tatsuichiro Akizuki looked down over Nagasaki – the city which was devastated before his eyes – and suggested, "Only thousands of B-29s carpet-bombing the city could have caused such destruction." In August 1945, the Japanese people knew little or nothing about the atomic bomb. Dr. Akizuki explained:

> Preoccupied as we were in getting food and seeking shelter in air raids, we had little or no opportunity for study. All advances in foreign knowledge had been prevented from coming into our country. As I heard later, the American authorities had, however, warned the Japanese government that the A-bomb was a terrible new weapon, that when it exploded something dreadful would happen, and that it would be dropped on Japan before long. But this information was suppressed by some department or other in Japan and never made known. Why were we never informed? Because certain of our leaders were afraid that if we knew about the A-bomb, our people would lose their fighting spirit. Japan was rushing blindly towards disaster.

Ground Zero As Seen By Ford
Ford could see the evidence of that disaster across the harbour in Nagasaki from the shelter where the POWs were temporarily imprisoned. The city had been turned into a gigantic inferno that extended beyond an observer's vision. Entire

blocks of concrete city buildings were reduced to rubble almost instantly. Fire erupted in neighbourhoods of wooden structures 1,500 metres from the epicenter, and at 1,000 metres from the same point, iron structures melted. Less obvious from Ford's vantage point were the sights and sounds of tens of thousands of the dead and near-dead. Like zombies they moved slowly in all directions begging for help. Strips of flesh were hanging from their bodies, and they walked with arms extended to avoid touching their own bodies. Their condition was caused by the thermal flash and the heat that together caused severe blistering and tearing of the skin.[13] Added to this ghastly spectacle taking place were the sounds coming from the victims. Dr. Akizuki said, "These were the horrible sounds of groaning as if they had traveled from the depths of hell."

According to the *Nagasaki Prefectural Report*:[14]

Within a radius of one mile from ground zero, everybody died, and within two to four, some died while almost all suffered injury. Many who survived the blast died later from radiation sickness, anemia, leukemia and purpura. Only the Mitsubishi Dockyards were far enough from the explosion to escape serious damage.

One of the several military targets destroyed in the blast was the "Torpedo Plant." Ironically this was the same factory which had made the torpedoes used to attack Pearl Harbour on December 7, 1941.

---

[13] Walker, J. Samuel, *Prompt and Utter Destruction: Truman and the use of the atomic bomb against Japan.* The University of North Carolina Press. 1997.
[14] This report is contained in the *Record of the Atomic bombing in Nagasaki*, published by the Museum in Nagasaki.

Horror Spreads Among The Population

While the POWs pondered their fate inside the shelter, some of the horror that had taken place was becoming evident throughout Nagasaki. At about 10:40 a.m., *Bock's Car* was sighted heading towards Nagasaki. The air raid siren was activated in the city, but it was ignored by the majority as many people had become accustomed to its frequent sounding. The alarm was not heard at the shipyard where Jack Ford was working. At 11:00 a.m. the 'all clear' sounded and those in shelters began to emerge. The on-duty soldier at Nagasaki Fortress Headquarters, just four and a half kilometers from the epicenter of the blast, came down a ladder from the roof and was vaporized when the bomb exploded.

According to *The Records of the Atomic Bombing in Nagasaki*:

> He took off his sword-belt, hung it from a peg on the tar-covered wall, and unbuttoned his coat. At that instant, he was showered by the flash of the atomic explosion. The tar exposed to a direct flash burned and disappeared, that which was in the shadows remained. The shadows were of the watchman, his sword on the peg, and the ladder.

At the time the atomic bomb was dropped, 200 Roman Catholics were lined up to attend confession inside the Church of St. Francis in the Urakami district of Nagasaki. The Catholic community in Nagasaki was getting ready for its annual festival, the Ascension of the Virgin Mary, which was celebrated on August 15th each year. The bomb instantly destroyed the church, which was just 500 metres east of the epicentre, killing all 200 parishioners and twenty priests who were inside.

At the Roman Catholic school on Motohara Hill, not far from the epicentre of the bomb, the Franciscan Sisters had taken the students into a nearby graveyard to participate in a special outdoor project. This involved the draining and collecting of turpentine from the roots of trees. According to one of the nuns, she had heard the sound of a plane and just as she looked upward there was a blinding flash of light and an explosion that shook the earth where she stood. The first plutonium bomb in history had just exploded 500 metres above. In an instant, all the children and most of the nuns were dead. The explosion had ripped tombstones from the ground, some of which landed on top of the children, crushing them to death. The nun who looked up at the time the bomb exploded was blinded, and critically burned. She died several days later.

In another incident, evidence of what had instantly taken place was found in a lump of glass at the epicenter of the explosion, which had the bones of a hand imbedded into it.

Three hours after the attack, a relief train began operating on tracks that ran through Nagasaki. Most of the destruction and deaths occurred in the north end of the city where the bomb had exploded. The train operated throughout the day, picking up hundreds of victims at each station and bringing them to hospitals in and near Nagasaki.

Thirty thousand people died in the first few minutes following the explosion, and that amount more than tripled over the next few days.[15]

Ford Had New Reason to Fear Captors

Jack Ford had reason to be concerned over what might happen to him and his fellow prisoners in the hours following the dropping of the bomb. During March 1945, a bone-chilling communication was sent by the Imperial Japanese War Ministry to all POW Camp commanders regarding the fate of

[15] Akizuki, Dr. Tatsuichiro. *Nagasaki-1945. The first eyewitness account.* New York. 1981

Japanese-held POWs in the event that an invasion of Japan was attempted. The bottom line of the order was that POWs be exterminated rather than allowed to be rescued by any of the Allied Forces. It read:

> Prisoners of war must be prevented by all means available from falling into enemy hands. They should be either relocated away from the front or collected, at suitable points and time, with an eye to enemy air raids, shore bombardments, etc. They should be kept alive to the last whenever their labour is needed.

Ford looked around the shelter where he and other prisoners were confined and wondered if this place was about to become a gas chamber as Bokugo had predicted. He described the shelter:

> It had two steel doors and was built into a rock cliff with the doors facing across the harbour towards Nagasaki. There were enough cracks and openings around the steel doors for prisoners to see through. There were no other doors, and no windows. We took turns looking out. Those peering outside would describe to the rest what was happening.

Through a crack in the door, Ford could see the fires breaking out all over Nagasaki. The fireball created by the bomb was 100 m. in diameter with a surface temperature of 7,000 to 9,000 degrees. Witnesses said it looked like a miniature sun.

The Records of the Atomic Bombing in Nagasaki reported:

> The heat rays from this fireball burned human bodies and houses, melted the surface of roofing tiles,

and even changed the quality of stones. In addition, direct heat caused fires to break out in various places, and these merged into a great conflagration that spread and reduced one third of Nagasaki City to ashes.

While Ford was looking across the harbour at Nagasaki, Dr. Akizuki was examining it from inside the city on a hill in an area of much death and destruction. Akizuki was thankful that his hospital, although damaged, had not been destroyed. Looking out over the city from what had been a window in his consulting room, Akizuki recalled, "A huge force had been released above our heads. What it was, nobody knew. Had it been several tons of bombs, or the suicidal destruction of a plane carrying a heavy-bomb load?" As the dust and smoke in his area lifted, he could see the southwest section of the city. He continued, "Gradually, the veiled ground became visible and the view rooted me to the spot with horror." In addition to the destruction throughout the city, there was a very strange appearance over Nagasaki.

Ford was not the only person to think the world was coming to an end. Akizuki had the same feeling:

> To say that everything burned is not enough. It seemed as if the earth itself emitted fire and smoke, flames that writhed up and erupted from underground. The sky was dark, the ground was scarlet, and in between hung clouds of yellowish smoke. Three kinds of colour, black, yellow and scarlet loomed ominously over the people who ran about like so many ants seeking escape. What had happened? That ocean of fire, that sky of smoke! It seemed like the end of the world.[16]

[16] Akizuki, T. Dr. *Nagasaki-1945.*

Ford's Thoughts Amid The Terror

Ford experienced conflicting feelings while being held inside the shelter. He had prayed every day throughout his internment that the Americans would arrive and set the prisoners free, and during 1945 he expected that an American invasion of Japan was imminent. With Nagasaki covered in smoke and flames, and destruction and death everywhere, the warnings of Bokugo echoed in his head, "You will never leave here alive! If the Americans ever invade Japan, we will kill all our prisoners."

Another factor that had Ford questioning whether he would survive long enough to be set free was his physical condition. The question on Jack's mind as August 1945 approached was, "How many more months can I survive?" It was a question he would answer himself, "No longer than Christmas, unless the war ends first."

Soon after the attack on Nagasaki, the smoke spread out over the harbour and onto the island of Kyogi where it temporarily covered the shipyard. The view from the shelter was blocked for several minutes by the tremendous amount of smoke. Flames occasionally gave a glowing affect to the smoke and then disappeared. The rapidly changing scene briefly obstructed the prisoners' view of the city at times. The prisoners eventually abandoned their observation of the outside and some began speculating among themselves about what had happened.

Anxiety and uncertainty overwhelmed the POWs in the shelter on the island in Nagasaki Harbour. Ford recalled wondering if what was happening was the start of the American invasion. If so, would they be rescued in time to be saved from the certain execution planned for them by their captors? "The Japanese could have killed us all and not have to answer for it," said Ford.

Suddenly, the sound of keys opening the steel locks on the door caused an eerie silence inside the shelter. All eyes focused on the doors and all ears on the creaking sound of them opening. The POWs could now see and hear Japanese soldiers taking up positions outside as an officer shouted orders for them to exit the shelter and line up. Ford thought, "This could be our end or it could be good news for us." Apprehensively, the prisoners obeyed the orders given by their captors. There was a quick roll call and a sigh of relief among the prisoners as they learned that they were being taken back to camp. Ford reasoned that they would not be going back to camp if the Japanese intended to execute them. As the prisoners were being marched from the shelter to the camp, Ford thought about what effect the attack on Nagasaki had on the civilians working with them. He explained:

> There were quite a few civilians living on the island, and there were ferries running every day from Nagasaki, bringing over civilians to go to work and taking them back in the afternoon when they completed work. As a matter of fact, there was quite a civilian settlement right on the back of us, and these civilians had to pass our camp every day on the way to and from work in the shipyard. Civilians never bothered us, not one iota. As we marched, we could see that the impact of the bomb had been powerful enough to damage buildings on and near the docks. We passed many civilians, but they paid little attention to us, because obviously, they now had some horrible problems of their own. Many of the guards and workers rushed back to their homes in Nagasaki to see if they had survived and to help in any way they could.

Despite supporting historical evidence, many writers and commentators ignored the fact that Japan had previous warnings.

Americans Warned Japan of Atomic Bomb

On July 27th, less than two weeks before the nuclear attacks upon Japan, the Americans dropped pamphlets over Japan's major cities warning the people about the forthcoming atomic bomb attacks, but not mentioning potential targets. Japanese war leaders made no efforts to either evacuate its main cities or even encourage its people to prepare for the attacks.

Before it became known that atomic weapons that had been used on Hiroshima and Nagasaki, survivors referred to what had taken place as the day of the 'Pikadon.'

The people of Hiroshima and Nagasaki had no idea of what had destroyed their cities for days and weeks after the atomic bombs were dropped. Dr. Michihiko Hachiya, Director of the Hiroshima Communications Hospital, was as puzzled as anyone, and he began keeping a daily diary of what was taking place. He noticed that the survivors had different words for describing the event depending on how close they were to the centre of the explosion. Those survivors closest to the atomic blast referred to the incident as 'Pika,' which means a glitter, sparkle or bright flash of light, like a flash of lightning. Survivors a little farther away from the epicentre used the word Pikadon to describe the rapid flash-boom. In time most people referred to it as the Pikadon.

Dr. Hachiya was amazed that those closest to the explosion did not hear the blast. After consulting with some colleagues, he concluded that those at the centre of the attack only saw the flash, but heard no boom because of the disturbance in air pressure around them which made them temporarily deaf. Among those was POW Jack Ford.

Jack Ford was seven kilometres from the epicenter of the atomic bomb explosion in Nagasaki. Just as in Hiroshima, some people in Nagasaki saw only the flash, but heard no boom, while others heard the boom, but saw no flash. Jack

Ford heard the bomb explode and felt its heat, but he saw no flash. He will never forget the sound caused by the explosion of the world's first plutonium bomb. He stated:

> It sounded like nothing on earth. It was a sound I had never heard before. There was a terrific explosion that instantly spread intense heat and a mushroom cloud. There was fire breaking out everywhere. What we experienced and saw, really reinforced what most of us thought was happening. The extraordinary roar and sound would have been unbearable had it lasted a moment longer than it did. I later heard much about the atomic flash when the bomb exploded, but I did not see it.[17] I saw the amazing mushroom cloud that quickly formed and shot high into the sky, then in a short while disappeared. The only light I remember seeing was from the numerous fires all around Nagasaki. I saw only one plane over Nagasaki and it would have taken hundreds of B-29s, or even more, to cause the death and destruction that had taken place in an instant.

Ford continued to describe the terror caused by the atomic explosion:

> It happened so fast, in a split second, there was no time to think about what you should do. When I recovered, in a matter of seconds from the impact of that horrendous explosion, self-preservation kicked in like an instant reflex, and I wanted to find a shelter. My work station was not down in the dockyard, but up on

[17] Scientists who assessed the atomic attack said that the flash some people reported seeing was not the instant flash caused at the moment of explosion. The flash occurred so fast that what people saw was the reflection of the flash from the hills around the city.

the top level of the place, where I was unprotected and exposed. There was no shelter for us to take. I got to my feet with everything swirling around me. There was falling and flying asbestos and pieces of glass, pieces of wood and everything that could move, all caught up in the hurricane-force wind resulting from the explosion. I thought I wouldn't survive what was happening. Then I looked all around me and saw men, women and children running and screeching and the flashes of fire were all over the place. We didn't know what it was except that it was a horrible turmoil unlike anything we had witnessed before. I was fortunate to survive it all with a few cuts and bruises. Other POWs were injured, but none were killed. Across the harbour, in Nagasaki itself, it was far worse. In the days to follow we got a glimpse of the hell suffered by civilians.

The New Horror That Followed

Days after the atomic attack on Nagasaki, when people were recovering from the terror of it and were trying to deal with the tremendous loss of life and widespread destruction of their city, a new horror began spreading among them. It was the silent, unnoticed killer which they soon came to know as 'fallout.'

When the atomic bomb exploded, it scattered a great deal of radioactive material over the land and over the rubble that once stood as the buildings and homes of Nagasaki. The fallout was highest in the area of the epicentre. Survivors roaming aimlessly among the ruins in search of help or seeking loved ones often exposed themselves to this hidden source of radioactivity.

Dr. Tatsuichira Akizuki, who worked round the clock with great risk to his own health to provide medical care for survivors, explained the new phenomena of fallout:

209

The source of this radioactivity was the swarm of various corpuscular, metallic elements produced by nuclear fission. They were comparatively large in atomic weight, but minute in terms of size, and the time it took for them to fall to the ground varied considerably. Some fell on the ground like rain directly after the explosion; others drifted down like a mist. People thought this was some kind of poison gas. In fact, there was radioactive barium and strontium in those microscopic particles that floated down like snow and gathered in tiny radioactive heaps on the earth. Initially, we had no reason to be afraid of these fatal ashes. We were simply glad to have survived. It was not until the concentric circle of death expanded, until our neighbours began to die of radiation sickness that we became stricken with fear for the future.

A twelve-year-old girl who had been walking aimlessly around the ashes of Nagasaki came upon what she thought was a puddle of water. She cried, "Water!" "Water!" She rushed over to the blue liquid, but was stopped by others who told her it was poison and could not be consumed. The girl disregarded the warnings and helped herself to the fallout. Many people, feeling the mist of the fallout and believing it was rain, drank the liquid. This led to radiation sickness and eventual death.

Glimpse of Hell
The mystery over what had caused the sudden and enormous devastation in Nagasaki with its population of 280,000 was still very much on the minds of the POWs as they marched back to Camp Fukuoka. Ford recalled:

We were all worried and concerned about what we had witnessed on that day. The explosion spread smoke so fast

in all directions, the mushroom cloud moved rapidly upward and the flames that rose all over Nagasaki had
changed our world immensely. It was like having a glimpse
of hell.

As the horror of the morning's event began to settle in,
POWs were feeling that whatever had happened, it might have
beneficial results for them. They had long anticipated an American invasion and were speculating that this could be its beginning. The mood of the Imperial Japanese Army guards
escorting them back to Camp Fukuoka had changed notice-
ably. They were very subdued. There was no visible evidence
that the Japanese were considering any special measures against
the POWs at the prison camp. Ford observed, "No extra forces
were added to the island or to Camp Fukuoka. The military
were too busy dealing with the disaster that had taken place
over in the city."

Jack Ford described the march back to the prison camp on
the day of the Pikadon:

> We were talking among ourselves because we were
> feeling some optimism about our own survival. Earlier
> that day, before the bomb dropped, our future seemed
> so bleak. We were suffering from malnutrition and
> hunger and it was getting more difficult to summon
> enough strength for the daily routine of walking to and
> from the shipyard and working a ten-hour-day. Al-
> though I had no doubt that the Japanese would lose
> the war, I was beginning to wonder if I would survive
> to see it. Just about every day at the camp, someone
> was dying from the abuses of prison-camp life. On that
> day we were finding a new hope from what had hap-
> pened. We were fortunate to escape the kind of death

and destruction that was taking place across the harbour, but on our march back we could see that some buildings on the island had been hit by the blast. In many cases roofs were gone, or windows were broken, and fences were blown away.

The civilians we passed on the road were in a daze, and they paid no attention to us. This was a big difference from what had taken place over in Hiroshima three days before. American prisoners who were being escorted through the city by the IJA after the bombing were attacked and killed by mobs of civilians who blamed them for the bombing of Hiroshima. I guess our guards had too much on their minds, worrying about friends and relatives over in the city. I am pretty sure that none of the civilians on our island had been killed or seriously injured that day. But, with the destruction and the death and injuries all over Nagasaki, survivors were being rescued and brought to hospitals for treatment. In most cases, this meant bringing them to small hospitals in the villages surrounding Nagasaki. As we marched down the road, boats were coming to our island with injured people to be treated at a small hospital, similar to our cottage hospitals in Newfoundland. They were being carried on stretchers along the road and some of the bodies we saw were burnt like pieces of raw beef. We had gone through such a terrible time ourselves as prisoners of the Japanese that we were not too concerned immediately over what had happened to them. Yet, the suffering we witnessed that day was awful. You had to have some pity. Being human, you had to say, "You poor son of a gun." I knew by the look of many of them that they couldn't possibly survive because they were burned so severely.

Camp Fukuoka was several kilometres farther away from the blast than the dockyards, yet it didn't escape the destruction caused by the explosion of the atomic bomb. The end of the building where Ford's dormitory was located had been devastated. Ford thought, "What a terrific blast it must have been to destroy our building which was so far away! The entire section was flat on the ground."

Confusion Reigned at POW Camp

The daily routine which the IJA had so rigidly followed was now replaced with confusion and uncertainty. Ford described the mood:

The guards were not certain as to what they should be doing. They confined us to camp for the rest of the day and got us to work in sorting out the debris and getting ready to rebuild the section of the prison that had been destroyed. Those of us who had lost our sleeping quarters were moved into other rooms in the prison. We could sense that the guards were alarmed and frightened to death after the attack. When you consider the horror of that day, it was only common sense that anyone would be scared. The Japanese leaders had been telling their people that they were winning the war, and now something devastating had happened that made them question what they were told. The prisoners, on the other hand, took hope from what had happened. We felt that, whatever it was, it was a big setback for the Japanese and probably good for us.

Although the shipyard had been badly damaged, and most of the civilian workers had gone over to Nagasaki to help their families, the IJA went through the daily routine they knew so well. For a few days, Reveille sounded at the usual time, and we responded as we always had. We went through the delousing, the massaging of limbs, the rice rations, the roll-call and the march to and from the dockyard. Despite all the destruction and death around them, the IJA tried to carry on business as usual.

However, there was a change in the mood of the guards, although they had not been told that an atomic bomb had been dropped on Hiroshima, and they still had no explanation for what had happened in Nagasaki. Nevertheless, news of the destruction of Hiroshima was being brought to the civilians of Nagasaki from relatives and friends who had survived and escaped from Hiroshima. Regardless, if they had heard the rumors or not, they obviously knew that a very major development in the war had taken place. Up to the bombings of Hiroshima and Nagasaki, the Japanese people were told by their leaders that they were winning the war.

Bokugo, the terror of Camp Fukuoka, also had a mood change, but not for the better. Ford remembered:

> Bokugo was worse than ever. Who knows, perhaps, he may have had family lost in the bombing, but whatever the reason, he was more irritated, angry and aggressive than ever before. This was all the more reason for prisoners to keep their distance from him and not do anything that would spark his temper. During this period, he did more shouting than usual, and we couldn't understand much of what he was saying. Meanwhile, we still did not know what had happened, and there was always the thought that at any moment, Bokugo and his thugs would follow through on what

he had so often threatened, and that was to annihilate all the POWs.

The change in mood was even more evident when the POWs returned to the shipyard after the attack on Nagasaki. For a few days, the POWs were marched to the shipyard to work, but there was very little work carried out. Most of the place was still in ruins. The majority of civilian workers did not return from Nagasaki. The POWs, some Japanese civilians and some Korean women prisoners made up the entire work force. Ford explained:

> The Japanese were in turmoil for days, and it showed at the shipyard. Nobody seemed to know what the POWs should be doing. Some of the equipment was okay to use, but I can assure you, there was not much work done. In the area where I was stationed, I got a glimpse of what the civilians over in Nagasaki were dealing with. The Japanese civilians working near me were constructing little coffins for the ashes from the cremations that were set up all over the city. Family members were taking on the responsibility themselves, and they were gathering wood and anything that was flammable to cremate their dead. We learned later that people were dying from radiation by the hour over in Nagasaki, and burying the dead became a big problem.

Japan's Leaders in turmoil

Japan's leaders were in a state of turmoil after the nuclear attack on Hiroshima, and the pressure intensified when another atomic bomb was dropped on Nagasaki. Following the attack on Hiroshima, when the Japanese leaders were speculating on what type of new weapon had been used against them, they received news that U.S President Truman had issued a statement. Truman's statement revealed that the world's first atomic bomb had been successfully used on Hiroshima, along with a warning to the Japanese leaders:

> We have spent more than two billion dollars on the greatest scientific gamble in history and won. We are now prepared to obliterate rapidly and completely every productive enterprise the Japanese have above ground in any city. We shall destroy their docks, their factories and their communications. Let there be no mistake, we shall completely destroy Japan's power to make war.[18]

Some members of the Japanese Supreme Council doubted the President's claim and expressed doubt that the bomb used on Hiroshima was an atomic weapon. Two scientists were immediately sent to Hiroshima to determine the truth of Truman's claim. Within twenty-four hours the scientists confirmed that the weapon used on Hiroshima was an atomic bomb. Despite this finding, the War Cabinet remained evenly split on whether or not to surrender. Those opposing surrender argued that an atomic bomb was simply another war weapon and was not reason enough to surrender.

The Americans appealed directly to the Japanese people to pressure their leaders to surrender. In the days that followed, six million pamphlets were dropped on Japanese cities. The pamphlet stated:

> We advise the Japanese people to read this leaflet carefully. The United States now possesses the most powerful explosive that has ever been invented. A single atomic bomb has as great an explosive power as

---

[18] Rees, David, *The Defeat and Occupation of Japan*, London, 1997.

all the bombs that would be carried by two thousand B-29s. You should carefully consider this fearful fact, and we assure you, in the name of God, that it is absolutely true. We have now begun to use this weapon against Japan. If you still have any doubts about its destructive capabilities, consider what happened when only one atomic bomb was dropped on Hiroshima. We advise you to beg His Majesty the Emperor to bring the war to an end, before we use this bomb to destroy every military installation that is prolonging this senseless war. We advise you to take the necessary steps to establish a new, peace-loving Japan by accepting the thirteen items relating to an honourable surrender, of which the President of the United States has recently given you an outline. You should at once take all the necessary steps to end all armed resistance or we shall be forced to bring an immediate end to this war by unhesitatingly using this bomb as well as every other powerful weapon we have.[19]

Truman noted that Japan had not availed of the opportunity given in the ultimatum issued at Potsdam, Germany, on July 26, 1945, that would have spared the destruction that had taken place. The Potsdam Declaration had called upon Japan to surrender unconditionally. Truman said, "Japan's leaders promptly rejected that ultimatum. If they do not accept our terms, they may expect a rain of ruin from the air, the like of which has never been seen on this earth."

Inside the Emperor's Palace
On the night of August 9th, while the POWs slept at Camp Fukuoka, the Japanese War Cabinet was holding an emergency

---

[19] Dr. Tatsuichiro Akizuki, *Nagasaki 1945*.

meeting with Emperor Hirohito several hundred miles north, in the basement of the Emperor's Palace in Tokyo, to discuss the rapid changes taking place in the war. The six-member War Cabinet included Premier Suzuki, Foreign Minister Togo, Navy Minister Admiral Yonai, War Minister General Anami, Army Chief of Staff General Umezu and Navy Chief of Staff Toyada. Hirohito presided over the meeting.

United States President Truman had hoped that after Hiroshima was destroyed by the atomic bomb the Japanese would surrender. This had not happened. The War Cabinet was split, with three favoring ending the war and three opposed.

Now that a second atomic bomb, more powerful than the first, had been dropped on Nagasaki, and the Russians had declared war on Japan only hours later, Emperor Hirohito was feeling the pressure. At the meeting inside the palace that night, the War Cabinet remained divided on the question of surrender. Suzuki, Togo and Yonai favoured surrender. At this point, they had no knowledge of the extent of the casualties and knew nothing about radiation sickness and the effects of fallout. The meeting focused on the great amount of destruction caused by the March B-29 bombings of Tokyo, the attacks on Nagasaki and Hiroshima and the destruction of Japan's top sixty-six cities.

The Emperor was shaken by Truman's statement that he would use the new weapon to destroy Japan. The emergency meeting went on into the early morning hours of August 10th, and ended when the Emperor sided with those who favoured surrender. There were tears in the eyes of the generals in the room when the meeting ended. This was the first time in history that Japan had been defeated. The decision to surrender was communicated to Washington, and took several days to work out. It was not until August 15th that the Emperor notified his people in a carefully worded announcement that did not mention the word surrender, but stated the war had ended. On the eve of the announcement, an unsuccessful coup attempt took place outside the palace while the War Cabinet met inside. An officer in the palace guard was killed, and the next day General Anami, a member of the War Cabinet, committed suicide.[20]

The entire story of Jack Ford's amazing experience can be found in Jack Fitzgerald's *The Jack Ford Story*.

---

[20] Note: *The Jack Ford Story* (Creative Publishers, 2007), page 120, reads, "Yamamoto was killed in 1943 when his plane was shot down by American fighters attacking Hiroshima." Correction: "Yamamoto was shot down in the Solomons on his way to Bourgainville."

Jack Ford as a Royal Air Force mechanic just before his capture by the Japanese in 1942.
Jack Fitzgerald Collection

The Japanese Consul General of Japan, Atushi Nishioka is shown here with POW Jack Ford and Jack Fitzgerald, author of *The Jack Ford Story,* **at a private dinner in downtown St. John's. Mr. Nishioka noted that he was impressed by the knowledge of Japan's history contained in the book. He praised Ford's resilience in rebuilding his life after the war. Ford left the meeting with deep respect for the Consul General.** *Maurice Fitzgerald Photography*

Author Jack Fitzgerald speaking at the launch of The Jack Ford Story at the Royal Canadian Legion Hall, Blackmarsh Road, St. John s.
Maurice Fitzgerald Photography

While sailing to England to begin his training with the R.A.F Ford witnessed allied ships being attacked and survivors being rescued. *Panl*

Chapter 12: Horrid Gulch

When the schooner *Water Witch* set sail from St. John's for Cupid's, Conception Bay, on the evening of November 29, 1875, none of the twenty-five people on board knew Alfred Moores, a fisherman from Pouch Cove. Within eighteen hours of leaving St. John's, the lives of eight passengers would be dependent on his courage and skill.

Within a week, all Newfoundland would know Alfred Moores and within a year his name and heroic deed would be described in newspapers throughout Europe and North America. Moore's notoriety came from his role in one of the most dangerous and adventurous rescues in Newfoundland's history.

The *Water Witch* was a British built schooner constructed at Trinity Bay in 1869 and owned by Charles Bowring, a St. John's merchant. The vessel had one deck, two masts and measured sixty-nine feet from stem to stern. She was nineteen feet, two inches wide at the beam and had a gross tonnage of 62.30.

On the evening of November 29, 1875, the vessel left Bowring's Wharf and slowly headed for the Narrows of St. John's Harbour. Captain Sam Spracklin hardly noticed the change taking place in the weather. The skies had darkened considerably since the last of the ship's cargo was loaded on board just hours before. A trickling of snow lightly fell over the city, and winds which had earlier caused a slight swell on the harbour waters were now intensifying.

The four ladies standing on the deck, all wrapped snugly in winter clothing, were there to enjoy a final view of Newfoundland's quaint and charming capital, St. John's, which was blanketed in glistening white snow. As the *Water Witch* cleared the Narrows, the bitter cold, caused by the increasingly cold and heavy winds from the ocean, forced everyone on deck to take refuge in the warmth of the cabin below.

The light snowfall and winds quickly developed into a raging winter's storm. Captain Spracklin and his crew struggled to keep the vessel on course, but the situation continued to worsen until finally the captain and his crew found themselves fighting to keep the vessel from being smashed against the jagged rocky coastline north of St. John's.

A deep sense of danger permeated every inch of the *Water Witch*. The women sought comfort in each other and prayed to be delivered safely from the storm raging around them. The men struggled bravely against the elements. At about 8:30 p.m. the vessel was being violently tossed around in high seas near Pouch Cove.

The powerful waves repeatedly carried the *Water Witch* almost into the rocks, and just when it seemed it would strike, there was a reprieve. The taunting waves would reverse and carry the vessel back to sea only to repeat the cruel process over again and again.

During this helpless tug-of-war with nature, just off Horrid Gulch, an appropriate name for the location, Captain Spracklin's years of experience at sea kicked in and convinced him his ship was doomed. He knew what had to be done and wasted no time in moving into action. He shared his conclusion with all on board and instructed them that they had only a brief time to act. He stressed that the next time the seas tossed the ship near land they had to jump for shore.

Nature was cruel in more ways than one that fatal night. Of all the possible places along the coast to make such a life-saving attempt, Horrid Gulch was by far the worst. The gulch is located about a mile and a half to the north of Pouch Cove and the waters are deep up to the foot of the shore, which runs along the bottom of a very high and rocky incline.

On the north side of the bight, the rocks run straight up to about 600 feet. In comparison, Signal Hill in St. John's is 500 feet above sea level. The sea strikes with tremendous force in this area.

The other side of the gulch, however, is not as steep and a narrow ledge runs close to the water's edge. Spracklin saw this as their best chance for survival. When the *Water Witch* was tossed near this ledge, the captain, his son and two crewmen successfully made the jump to land. The others did not act fast enough and were left trapped on the ill-fated ship.

Watching the receding waves carry the vessel away from shore and minutes later watching her rapid return, riding a gushing wave towards a jagged rock side of the gulch, was agonizing for those still trapped on the *Water Witch*, as well as those who had made it to land.

On this run, George Noseworthy made a daring jump and landed safely on a ledge, opposite to the side where the others had landed successfully. Helplessly, they watched again as the ship washed out and was tossed back towards them twenty minutes later. This roll turned out to be more successful, as five men made the courageous jump to safety. They were: William Wells, Thomas Ivany, Sam Rowe, William Spracklin and Thomas Spracklin.

Exposed on a high cliff to savage winter winds, intensified by a blinding snowstorm and high waves threatening to drag them back into the uncontrollably rolling waters, the group linked arms and huddled together for dear life.

George Noseworthy, who was among those still in danger, later recalled, "The spray dashed over us constantly, and every twenty minutes or so a large sea would come and dash right over us."

They remained trapped and repeatedly shouted for help. They encouraged the captain and his group to bring back assistance as soon as possible. Although in a perilous situation, the captain and his group were able to climb to safety and make their way into the nearby community of Pouch Cove to look for help. By this time they were near exhaustion, extremely cold and soaking wet to the skin.

Jim Langmead of Pouch Cove had just gone to bed and pulled the blankets over himself. He could hear the wind howling and the rain battering against his house and windows. Although he was half asleep, Langmead heard the distant sound of human voices, which alarmed him and brought him up to a sitting position on the bed. As the voices came nearer, he clearly heard their shouts for help!

Langmead jumped out of bed, partially dressed, lit his lantern and went to the door. He urged the group to come inside and did his best to make them comfortable as they told their horrific story of being wrecked at Horrid Gulch and of those still trapped there. Langmead put on his raingear and went throughout the community gathering volunteers to go to the rescue of those still fighting for their lives.

Several groups were organized and set out in short intervals on the rescue mission to Horrid Gulch. The first rescue party left Pouch Cove at around 11:00 p.m. and included Bob Moulton and Thomas and Aiden Noseworthy. Captain Spracklin had left his son in charge of those still trapped at the gulch. When he heard the rescue party approaching, he left the others and climbed the cliff so he could guide them to the survivors trapped a couple of hundred feet below them. Beyond the trapped men were eighty fathoms of water and high, rolling seas. All thoughts of a rescue effort by water were abandoned.

At this point the team led by Reverend Reg Johnson arrived on the scene. Included in this party were: Alfred Moores, James Langmead, Bill Ryan, Bill Gould, Bill Langmead, Eli Langmead, David Baldwin, Christopher Mundy, Uriah Langmead, William Noseworthy, Nat Williams, James Langmead Jr. and Thomas Bassett.

Following a discussion among the men about the best way to proceed with the rescue, they decided to lower some men down the cliff by rope to bring up those trapped. Alfred Moores volunteered for the dangerous task. A strong rope was fastened around him and the others slowly lowered him over the high cliffs at Horrid Gulch.

Along with darkness, Moores had to contend with the heavy winds, snow and sea spray during his rescue efforts. Although he could not see the men below, he could hear their shouts for help. He began swinging back and forth like a pendulum as he looked for a suitable place to descend. Eventually the Pouch Cove fisherman slid along a steep chute or crevice in the rock, and succeeded in reaching a ledge immediately over the spot where he determined the men were located.

Other rescuers soon followed and each took up positions between Moores and the top of the cliffs as part of their rescue plan. These included: David Baldwin, Eli Langmead, William Noseworthy and Christopher Mundy. William Langmead controlled the rope at the top of the cliff which had been tied firmly around a nearby tree.

When Moores got near enough to the stranded men, he was able to see them clinging tightly to each other. Twice Moores dropped a hand-line to the victims and each time it missed its mark. On the third attempt one of them caught hold of it. A stronger rope was then dropped from above and was fastened around one of the men. Slowly he was pulled up to the level controlled by Alfred Moores. From there, he was lifted step by step to the other positioned rescuers until he reached safety.

This risky procedure was repeated again and again as the storm raged until finally all those who had been trapped on the ledge were brought to safety. They were given some brandy, wrapped in warm clothing and blankets and escorted to homes in Pouch Cove where people waited to welcome them and provide shelter.

News of the tragedy and heroism at Horrid Gulch was sent to St. John's by Reverend Johnson. The Newfoundland Government responded immediately by sending Mr. Lilly, clerk of the peace, and Mr. Dunphy, an official of the poor office, to assist the survivors. Captain Sam Spracklin of the *Water Witch* left the recovery of bodies and personal belongings to Reverend Johnson to organize. The reverend secured the Wesleyan school room in the community for use as a temporary morgue. The first corpse recovered was Elizabeth Spracklin, Captain Spracklin's daughter-in-law. Within a few days all the bodies had been retrieved. Coffins and clothing for the dead were gathered and delivered to the temporary morgue by John Sullivan and a group of volunteers.

Constable Spracklin, not a relative of the captain, played an important role in recovering bodies from the wreck. All property retrieved was handled by the Episcopal and Methodist ministers and the Roman Catholic school masters. All items were recorded in a ledger and then turned over to relatives of the deceased and to the rescued passengers.

In recognition of the outstanding heroism demonstrated during the rescue operation, Governor Sir Stephan Hill sent a recommendation to the Royal Humane Society in London that the men of Pouch Cove be awarded the Society's Silver Medals. A silver medal was awarded to Alfred Moores and bronze medals were awarded to: David Baldwin, Eli and William Langmead, William Noseworthy, and Christopher Mundy. Governor Hill responded by pointing out that the honours bestowed on "our brave countrymen" reflected on all Newfoundlanders. The medals were presented at a special ceremony held at Government House. Decades after the tragedy an unidentified person recorded the tragedy and heroism in the song, "Ballad of the *Water Witch*."

More Sea Adventures: Two Amazing Races

The speed of Newfoundland sealing vessels was put to the test many times, but none were on par with the two competitions described in the following pages. The first involved a trans-Atlantic race between the *Fanny Bloomer* and the *Sally Ann;* the second competition saw the sealing ship *Sagonia* racing for time against the *Newfie Bullet*. These events, held about fifty years apart, were often told by the many "tellers-of-tales," travelling on the *Kyle*.

The Newfoundland-built *Fanny Bloomer* was one of the most successful sealing ships of the nineteenth century. During that era, she was closely identified with the famous Southern Shore seafaring family, the Jackmans of Renews. When Captain Thomas Jackman was injured on the *Fanny Bloomer* by a swinging tiller, his son, William, took command. It was his first command and he was a natural. When the Bowring Brothers made him a lucrative offer to take command of the *Sally Ann*, he accepted and his brother, Captain Arthur Jackman, took command of the *Fanny Bloomer*. Captain Jackman became one of the most successful sealing captains in Newfoundland history.

The *Fanny Bloomer* and another Newfoundland vessel, the *Mary Belle*, earned notoriety not only as great sealing ships, but for an impromptu race across the North Atlantic during the winter of 1856-1857. This remarkable story began mid-December 1856. The *Fanny Bloomer* was under the command of Captain John Flynn and the *Mary Belle* was under the command of Captain James Day, a former member of the Newfoundland legislature for St. John's west.

The two ships were being towed down the Mersey in England by the same tug boat when Captain Day shouted to Captain Flynn, "I'll bet you £25 I'll be in St. John's before you!"

"I can't bet you that much, because I have no money to pay you only out of my wages, but I'll bet £10," answered Captain Flynn.

The race was on. Both crews felt it would add excitement to the long and often treacherous return trip across the Atlantic. Side by side, the *Fanny Bloomer* and *Mary Belle* sailed down Saint George's Channel, England, keeping each other in sight for several days. It wasn't smooth sailing and wind and rainstorms quickly separated the two rivals. Although they were out of each other's sight, each captain never forgot he was in a race. By mid-way, they were again in sight of each other and signals were sent back and forth between the ships. Once again, the ocean tossed and they lost sight of each other until they neared land, at which time they were about three-quarters of a mile apart.

At this point, the ships were between Bay Bulls and Petty Harbour. When they caught sight of each other, the competitiveness of the crews showed. On went studding sails and every inch of canvas was hoisted and respective house flags

(Bowring's and Tessier's) were posted to the foremast head, as signals to Cape Spear. The ships passed the Cape as they had started in England with less than 100 yards separating them. Finally, after a thirty-eight-day crossing, they passed through the Narrows of St. John's Harbour. The harbour pilot boarded Captain Day's vessel first because she was to the windward of the *Fanny Bloomer*. He then boarded the *Fanny Bloomer*. The ships had entered the Narrows at the same time and the race was declared a draw. Both ships ended the race as they started, side by side. This was hailed as a remarkable feat and the story became part of Newfoundland's wonderful heritage of sea stories.

The *Fanny Bloomer* ended its days in England. In 1870, Captain Arthur Jackman took the *Fanny Bloomer* with a cargo of seal oil and skins bound for Liverpool. The vessel was sold there and spent the remainder of its years carrying coal between Wales and Waterford, Ireland.

One of the most exceptional cross-country races in Newfoundland's history took place in June 1916. The race involved a race between the *Newfoundland Express* (informally called the *Newfie Bullet*) and the sealing vessel the *Sagonia*, from Port aux Basques to St. John's. The officers and crew of the *Sagonia*, while socializing with the engineer and crew of the *Newfoundland Express* at Port aux Basques, argued that their ship could travel from Port aux Basques to St. John's a lot faster than the railway train. The railway men strongly disagreed with the seamen, who in response challenged them to a cross-country race. The railway men accepted the challenge and rules were drawn up for the race. Because the participants were scheduled to leave hours apart, it was agreed that the winner would be determined by the time it took each vessel to travel from Port aux Basques to St. John's. The *Newfoundland Express* began its cross-country trip at 1:00 p.m. on Friday, June 9th, and arrived in St. John's next day at 7:30 p.m. The total traveling time for the *Newfoundland Express* was thirty and a half hours. The *Sagonia* left a few hours after the *Newfoundland Express* and arrived 2:50

a.m. on Sunday and recorded a travel time of thirty-three and a half hours.

The clear winner of this unique cross-country race was the *Newfoundland Express*.

Chapter 13: Sixty-five Trapped Inside Inferno

Some people never even got out of bed. One old lady was lying in her bed with one hand clutching a one dollar bill and the other a set of rosary beads. Other patients were partly out of bed; others kneeling in a praying position and there was one woman with her hands folded across her chest. Most of them were burned beyond recognition.

Fire Chief William Baker, *The Emerson - Hull Home Enquiry*, 1948

On a daily basis in St. John's, thousands of cars drive past a building located at the corner of Springdale and New Gower Streets, completely unaware of the long night of horror that took place there when sixty-five people struggled for survival inside a firestorm that was quickly swallowing up the entire building. Some perished inside the hellhole, while others met death by jumping through the upstairs windows to the sidewalks below.

The date was February 10, 1948, and the building was the Hull Home. This tragedy happened just six years after the Knights of Columbus (K of C) fire, which took place on Harvey Road on December 12, 1942. The shock and horror of that conflagration was still fresh in the minds and hearts of all Newfoundlanders.

In that tragedy, the St. John's City Council had failed to enforce its own building regulations. Their negligence contributed to the loss of ninety-nine lives. The Dunfield Enquiry determined that the city neglected to enforce *Section 44 of the*

St. John's Act, passed in 1925, which required developers to submit building plans to the council before a building permit could be issued. The Hull Home was bound by this same law, to submit building plans to cover the conversion of the building into a seniors' home, but they failed to do so.

Because of the enormity of the K of C tragedy and the widespread publicity that accompanied it, it seemed not only unlikely, but impossible, that the same mistake would be repeated. Yet, the important lessons learned after one of Newfoundland's worst tragedies were quickly forgotten. The aftermath of the Hull Home tragedy disclosed that city council had again failed to enforce its own regulations and, like 1942, misfortune followed.[1]

It was one of the coldest days experienced that winter. Thirty-four men and women perished in this holocaust, compared to the ninety-nine souls lost in the K of C fire. The two disasters, which occurred in such close proximity in time to each other, were a severe shock to Newfoundlanders everywhere. How did the fire start? Who or what caused it? Was it arson or negligence? These were some of the questions that the judicial enquiry delved into during the dramatic series of hearings that followed.

The Hull Home was a privately operated residence for seniors. The many witnesses parading before the hearing provided multiple versions of the level of care given, the conditions at the home and the possible cause of the fire.

The Hull family, operators of the home, was severely criticized during the hearing but were also well-defended. The city's building inspector, the fire chief and an ex-patient of the home gave evidence suggesting the Hulls were negligent and exploited their tenants for financial gain.

---

[1] For more on the Knights of Columbus Fire, 1942, see *Newfoundland Disasters*, Jack Fitzgerald, Creative Publishers.

Other witnesses including a nurse, a painter, two Salvation Army officers and an ex-patient indicated the Hulls were responsible people who were providing a desperately needed service in the city at reasonable rates for people with nowhere else to turn.

Isaac Hull and his wife were well-qualified to operate a boarding house or nursing home. Mr. Hull had operated the Salvation Army Hostel and Soup Kitchen in St. John's from 1929 to 1934. His wife had twelve years' experience in practical nursing at the Anchorage Home, which was operated by the Salvation Army. Most of her experience was in dealing with maternity and tuberculosis patients.

Shortly after their marriage in 1934, the Hulls began taking boarders into their home. In 1936, they leased the second and third floors of the Noah Building to expand their operations. This new residence became known as the Hull Home. The building was constructed in 1910 by Kaleem Noah and it was still in the hands of the Noah family in 1948. It was a three-storey concrete structure with a wood interior and built at the western intersection of New Gower and Springdale Streets.

There were no written agreements between the landlord and tenant, only a verbal arrangement that the monthly rental rate would be sixty-five dollars. The first floor of the building was occupied by F.W. Wylie, a commercial agent. Wylie's furnace supplied the heat for the full building and Hull paid $300 annually to cover his share of the heating costs.

At first, the Hull Home operated as a boarding home catering to working people in the city. In addition, the Hulls took care of the children of unmarried mothers until adoptions could be arranged.

The good reputation of the Hull Home spread rapidly and the Department of Public Health and Welfare, desperately in need of adequate accommodations for clients with special needs, began referring clients to it. Other referrals followed from the Department of Public Health and Welfare, which sent advanced cases of tuberculosis from the sanatorium. The Hulls increased their staff to include three practical nurses and a char-woman.[2] A doctor visited the home weekly and it evolved from a boarding house into an unlicensed nursing home.

The daily cost for staying at the home ranged between $1.50 and $2.50. This compared with $3.02 daily for patients at the sanatorium, $1.53 at the old age home, Sudbury Street and $1.98 at the Hospital for Mental and Nervous Diseases. The Department of Public Health and Welfare provided dressings, medicine, pyjamas and other bed garments for patients when requested by Mr. Hull.

The home expanded to include two homes adjacent to and west of the Noah Building on New Gower Street, which became known as the Hull Annex. Even with the addition, the Hulls continued to have a waiting list of clients looking for accommodations.

When it first opened, the Hull family occupied an apartment on the second floor of the three-storey building. During June 1947, Mrs. Hull became ill and had to lessen her activity in the operation of the home. Her involvement was reduced to advising her husband and visiting the home once or twice a week after she moved out of the building to live in their Allandale Road residence. Mr. Hull maintained a room at the home and spent most of his nights there.

On the day tragedy struck, there were forty-three people living at the Hull Home, and twenty-two others in the Annex. This included Mr. Hull and Howard Pike, a seventeen-year-old student at Prince of Wales College. Eighteen boarders suffered from tuberculosis, eight experienced psychiatric problems and seventeen were senior citizens. Hull acted as cook for the

[2] Soon after, the number of cleaning staff was increased to three.

Annex and used an oil range in the kitchen. This same stove became the focus for the accusations of negligence.

At the Emerson Enquiry, Hull recounted the events leading up to the outbreak of the fire. He said:

> I got up at 6:45 a.m., got dressed and went to the kitchen to turn on the range. I waited a few minutes before dropping a lighted match on to the range, and then turned it down from high to medium. I did not look at it before lighting it. There was nobody in the kitchen with me at the time. I then went over to the Annex to light the coal stove. After that I called Mrs. Mouland who slept in the Annex.
>
> As I was going through the backyard returning to the main building, I was met by one of the patients, Nellie Quick, who said, 'Mr. Hull there is something wrong with the stove.'

Mr. Hull pointed out that the patient in question was never allowed to touch the stove and that he was not too concerned about the problem. Hull investigated her complaint and when he got to the kitchen was alarmed to witness flames rising up around the kettle on the stove and shooting up from behind it. The fire was spreading rapidly and Hull made a snap judgement call. He chose to leave the building immediately to get help. He said there was no time for him to go upstairs to wake the patients. Before leaving he went to the bottom of the stairway and shouted a warning to the others. While doing this he encountered Howard Pike and sent him to call the fire department.

The call was received at the fire hall at 7:02 a.m. and by 7:03 a.m. District Chief William Baker and six firemen were on their way to the scene in a fully equipped Bickle firetruck.

The West End Fire Station was located on New Gower Street, just a short distance from the Hull Home. The truck was equipped with a hose, a booster pump, two ladders, a 200-pound life net and some other smaller firefighting equipment. At 7:06 a.m. another alarm went in to the Central Fire Station located at Fort Townshend near Bonaventure Avenue. From there District Fire Chief Caddigan, in a similar truck, responded to the call. The fire was already out of control.

Baker described the scene that greeted him as the firetruck approached the scene. He said:

> We could see flames coming out of the windows on the eastern portion of the building. When we got there, we could see people at the windows, trapped. I ordered two ladders to be put up right away. These people seemed to be calm although some seemed ready to jump.

Caddigan described a similar scene. He recalled that while passing Long's Hill going down Queen's Road:

> I could see flames jumping twenty feet or more into the air. I remarked to the driver that it must be the Horwood Lumber Company. When we got there, the first thing I noticed was the people in the top-flat window. I ordered the men to raise the ladders. At that time one ladder was already up and some people were coming down. The back of the building was a mass of flames and volumes of smoke were pouring out on the Springdale Street side.

Jean Murphy (nee Baird) was a teenage student at St. Patrick's Convent School and lived across the street from the

Hull Home. She recalled being awakened at around 7:05 a.m. by a strong smell of smoke. She jumped from her bed thinking her own house was on fire. She was so horrified by what she witnessed through her window that she ran to a backroom and refused to come out until she was assured the fire was out.

What Jean had witnessed was the terrified people jumping from the third-storey windows of the flaming Hull Home building, some of them to their deaths on the sidewalk below. Jean passed away in 2013 and memories of this horrific scene had haunted her for a lifetime.

During the period when firemen had just arrived and were sweeping into action, panic was setting in among the residents trapped inside. Daisy Miller, one of four trapped in a second-storey room, was awakened by the strong smell of smoke. She rushed to open her room door but was forced to retreat because of the smoke and flames. She could hear the roar of the fire gushing up the staircase and realized residents in the room were trapped. She broke a window to call for help and saw Hull and Pike standing below. They encouraged her to jump, which she did, but not before making a futile attempt to rescue Mrs. Sheppard, a blind roommate. She recalled, "I was really scared. I got out on the ledge and jumped. Two men were there to catch me. I did not hear any shouting or screaming inside before I jumped and I did not hear anyone sound an alarm."

One of the men who caught Miss Miller was Walter Carew of Flatrock. Carew was on his way to work at the Newfoundland Fuel and Engineering Company and had stopped to watch the fire. He recalled, "I saw three men in another window. One of them jumped and was killed. Miss Miller jumped just before the flames broke through in her room. We caught her."

Margaret Gale, a patient in the same room with Daisy Miller, remembered her crying out "Fire! Fire!" while smashing out the window. She recalled the feeling of terror that seized her mind and body as the room became hot and the smoke began encircling her. She witnessed Daisy jump from the window. When she attempted to do the same, she heard someone warn her not to jump but to use the stairs instead. She already knew that was impossible because the flames and smoke were spreading too rapidly.

Mrs. Power, who was in the same room, joined Daisy at the window and both got out onto the ledge. They were praying aloud until they summoned up enough courage to jump to the pavement below. They survived, but Miss Power later died in the sanatorium from a combination of tuberculosis and the injuries sustained in the jump.

William Wall was trapped on the top floor of the building. He first learned of the fire when one of the patients shouted that the building was on fire. He went to his room door and noticed the smoke ascending the stairway. From there he went to the window where he saw flames shooting up outside. He could see Hull on the sidewalk kicking at the door, trying to open it. He said that on many occasions the inmates had discussed among themselves the possibility of a fire and how they would deal with it. Based on these talks, his first move was to toss his mattress out the window in anticipation of having something below to cushion a jump from the window. Fortunately, the firemen reached him in time and managed to rescue him. As firemen removed him, he recognized the screaming of his friend, Mr. Starkes, whose words were inaudible, but sounded like, "I am burning, smothering or something like that."

Alice Connors was twenty-three years old and was among the survivors. She described the unfolding events inside the Hull Home that terrible day. She said:

I didn't pay much attention when I first smelled smoke. A patient noticed it first and when I got up and

I saw smoke coming up the stairs, I woke up patients in my room and then I went across the hall to Bill Wall's room. As I did, I heard Mr. Wiscombe yell, 'We're gone this time.'

When Connors entered the room the patients were crying and praying. Smoke was trailing behind her, which added to the fear of the patients in the room. Mrs. Alice Wiscombe was bedridden and Mary Agnes Lambe, from Placentia, was sitting on her bed and said, "If the firemen can't get up to us we are gone." All Alice Connors could do to help was to encourage the occupants to move over to Mr. Wall's room on the front of the building facing New Gower Street and hope to be rescued by the firemen. She left, but nobody followed her and they all perished in the flames. Alice Connors managed to get outside onto a window ledge where firemen used a ladder to bring her to safety.

Isabel King, a twenty-six-year-old medical patient, was so shaken and terrified that she couldn't remember her name or how old she was. She was able to recall her jump from the third-storey window and that the three doors in her room were blocked. Two had sideboards in front of them, while the third was in flames. Isabel was the only patient in her room to escape the inferno.

Chief Caddigan had taken two firemen to the Annex where they forced open an entrance. Some patients were frightened by the sudden intrusion into the building and attempted to avoid them. Caddigan calmed them down and quickly organized an orderly evacuation of the Annex.

Meanwhile, severe frost was hampering firefighters and medical teams. The fire hoses actually froze to the streets. Fire Superintendent Vivian suffered frostbite to his hands and feet and Police Chief Strange suffered frostbite to his ears. Despite this problem, both men remained on the job until the fire was extinguished. Vivian completed his duties at the site before leaving to seek medical attention for frostbite. He felt certain the building had been burning for at least fifteen minutes before the firemen got there.

Chief Baker, after inspecting the building with Vivian, described their findings:

> Some people never even got out of bed. One old lady was lying in her bed with one hand clutching a one dollar bill and the other a set of rosary beads. Other patients were partly out of bed; others kneeling in a praying position and there was one woman with her hands folded across her chest. Most of them were burned beyond recognition.

Dr. Ed Sharpe, who completed all the victims' death certificates, said that while the bodies were badly burned, all victims had actually died of smoke inhalation.

Caddigan believed that the recent painting of the building had contributed to the rapid spread of the fire. Vivian speculated it was a surface fire which, "… reached the ceiling then spread underneath. It did not burn through the floor. The draft from the stairway took it up the walls and it roared through to the top flat, having the draft with it, it had to go, creating a terrific heat."

The second and third floors were completely gutted. Streams of water carried charred wood and debris down the stairs. Vivian described the scene:

> One could see on the inside rooms some with mattresses drenched and solidly frozen, and others had whispers of smouldering excelsior from the mattresses

scattered around. One room on the second floor had two beds hardly touched by flames. All the walls were charred and in many cases were burned through. In one spot the roof sagged dangerously and many of the uprights of the floors were nearly burnt out. In the intense frost icicles hung from the ceilings and continued to drip. The rooms all lay open when the walls burned through revealing charred bureaus, scorched clothing and in the kitchen, the blackened stove.

When firemen attempted to remove one of the bodies from a bed, the mattress suddenly ignited and had to be extinguished by the men.

Just eleven days after the fire, on February 21st, the Emerson Judicial Enquiry got underway in the number two courtroom in St. John's. There was a high degree of public interest into the investigation and when Chairman Sir Edward Emerson called the session to order, the courtroom was filled to capacity. Harry Carter acted for the Crown; E.J. Phelan, K.C., and city engineer Jack Grant represented the city. Isaac Hull was represented by one of the city's top lawyers, Jimmy Higgins, who in later years served as chief justice.

The first revelation at the Enquiry revealed that the city's building inspector and fire superintendent had issued several warnings in 1944 to Hull regarding his operation. Had these warnings been followed up and acted upon, the tragedy could have been avoided. That report had originated four years before the fire, but investigators found it difficult to locate due to bureaucratic buck passing at city hall.

The city building inspector, F.M. Cahill, and fire superintendent, Vivian, had prepared the report following a routine inspection in 1944. Mrs. Hull was present throughout that inspection and resented being told that the stove, later found to be the source of the fire, had to be repaired. She responded, "I am capable of looking after my own affairs."

The same report included some alarming details about the architectural structure and logistical details of the building. It noted that the building was divided into two wings, each with one exit and doors opening inward. Just four years before at the K of C fire, doors opening inward were a contributing factor to the deaths of many people. Laws forbidding such a practice were already passed by council. The fact that the stairway was only two feet, six inches wide in places and the building inside was constructed of wood concerned the officials.

A stunning disclosure at the Enquiry noted:

> Unknown to council, this building was also occupied as a hospital and infirmary for the aged and infirm. There are thirty-five inmates in the building, [excluding the Annex] including mental cases, chronic TB cases and people of advanced age.

The same report included a warning that the kitchen range which was an oil burning unit was close enough to the wall to scorch the wallpaper and the range itself was leaking. Recommendations had been made:

To have a fire escape erected at the rear of the building.

All exit doors changed to open outwards.

A fire shield was to be placed at the back of the kitchen range and repairs were to be made to the oil burning unit in the kitchen and its carburetor was to be replaced.

Other recommendations made included:

The removal of an oil stove partly blocking the doorway and stairway.

An exterior staircase to be built.

The chimneys to be cleaned.

Vivian and Cahill were stunned by the landlord's negligence to assure the safety of the building's occupants. Overcrowding was immediately noticeable. In one room they found seven people. The wall behind the stove had signs of previously being affected by flames four or five times. A review of building documents required by city council for an establishment of its size alarmed the officials. They discovered that dwelling plans had not been submitted as the law demanded, neither had there been applications for occupancy or alterations. The chief of police was notified of the state of affairs at the Hull Home. Despite the lessons learned by the K of C Enquiry, lethargy had once again set in, and as a result another needless and tragic loss of life occurred.

After receiving the earlier inspection report, city council made no direct follow-up with the Hulls. The contents of that report were published in local papers and council sent a copy to the Department of Public Health and Welfare.

The Department of Health and Welfare followed up with their own inspection but took no action. After the tragedy, Hull said he did not act on the recommendations, "… because in view of the department's inspection and the fact the government had sent even more patients," he had assumed they considered the home in fit condition to operate.

Crown prosecutor Carter was more than surprised to learn that council made no effort to enforce the recommendations for fire escapes. Emerson was equally as upset and stressed that the city solicitor had advised the council to act on the recommendations and still they were ignored. The city had agreed to send The Department of Health and Welfare's suggestion to Hull but neglected to do so. There was no official effort by any party to encourage Hull to act on the recommendations.

The stove in the Hull Home was the focus of much of the Enquiry. Emerson called several oil burner mechanics as witnesses and their testimony showed a long history of trouble and neglect with the stove. F. Oakley testified he had sold a duo-thermo unit to Hull in 1942 and several weeks later was called in to make adjustments to it. At that time the carburetor cover was missing. He said, "I replaced the valves and some other parts. This was unusual because the valves usually last as long as the stove."

Gordon Whitten, also a repairman, was called in two weeks later to examine the stove. He told investigators:

> There was only one screw left in the oil control valve. The trip valve was tied down to keep it open. This allowed a lot more oil than usual to flow. Some of the fuel supply pipes were also leaking. I warned Hull of the danger of tampering with the carburetor.

Three months later, Whitten was again called in to repair the stove and found the carburetor was leaking oil from the main intake valve which was cross threaded and badly split. He explained, "It showed signs of being forced. The main float was also bent and I fixed it all."

F.G. Wylie, whose firm occupied part of the building, testified that during 1946 he experienced problems with oil dripping from Hull's kitchen into his office. He noted, "It was so bad that we had to move goods and place a pan beneath it to catch it."

Mr. H. Heale, who like Gordon Whitten was an oil mechanic with Monroe Machinery, expressed the view that the firm had received an unusual number of calls to repair the stove at the Hull Home. He told investigators:

Under extraordinary conditions flames could get outside the stove through water pipe holes. This happens as a result of high temperatures, drafts and excessive gases caused by excessive oil and other things.

William Daniels and George Royle, both oil burner mechanics, testified that they had been called to repair the stove at the Hull Home on many occasions. Daniels believed:

The chances of fire escaping through the open space at the water pipe connections were extremely remote because oil fires always went away from air. This is shown when the lid of an oil stove is lifted and the flames go down away from the air.

Daniels recalled that his inspection of the stove showed:

All connections of the stove were tight and there was no indication of an explosion in the stove. However, it was possible that external heat atomized the fuel in the fuel tank, itself lifting the lid with a slight puff. There were indications this had happened.

His conclusion was that the fire was caused by excessive heat from the funnel igniting some dishcloths on back of the stove and these had dropped to the floor.

Mr. Royle had repaired the stove after council's inspection in 1946 and recalled that it had been leaking. When he disconnected the carburetor, he found that it was not screwed on to the angle iron connecting it to the stove and the screws were missing. There was an unscrewed cover left over the carburetor. Although he considered it to be a piece of careless work, he felt it was not necessarily dangerous and did not make any changes. He was called in again in 1947 to examine the stove because the fuel lines between the tank and carburetor were plugged. This problem was resolved.

Hull, age forty-four, appeared as a witness dressed in a neat brown suit with a matching brown shirt. He was of medium height, had thinning brown hair and wore bandages on his hand to cover injuries received in the fire. He acknowledged that the Hull Home had been inspected by Vivian and Cahill but explained, "I understand they had made recommendations but had not made them to me. I read about them in the paper."

He denied Cahill's claim that the wallpaper behind the stove had been scorched. In the days that followed, other witnesses also challenged Cahill's findings. As a result of the report in the newspapers at that time, Hull had requested Dominion Distributors, agents for the stove, to repair it. He took no additional action because he said he was waiting to hear from city council. Hull insisted he never did hear from the official body and neither did he go out of his way to inquire about the matter.

Throughout the questioning session, Hull appeared very nervous and twisted a pencil in his hand, sometimes tapping it on the witness box rail. His eyes constantly flickered back and forth. He told the Enquiry that when he first witnessed the fire in the kitchen, he attempted to fill a bucket with water but the smoke and flames forced him from the building. He said, "I shouted, 'Fire! Fire!' repeatedly, as I left." He added that he helped evacuate patients from the Annex.

Fire Chief Caddigan surprised the Enquiry when he testified that he and two firemen had to break open the entrance to the Annex and organize the evacuation of all the tenants of that building.

Howard Pike described how he became aware of the fire. He said:

Nellie Quick slept on a mattress in the dining room. There was no bed; the mattress was on the floor. On the morning of the fire, Nellie woke me up saying, 'Look Pike, there's something wrong with the stove.' I could see the stove from where I slept and I could see the flames coming up around the kettle and behind the stove. That was about 6:45 a.m. I jumped out of bed partly dressed over my pyjamas and ran out of the room. I met Hull at the head of the stairs. He told me to call the fire department.

Pike called the fire department from a phone in the hallway and then attempted to get upstairs to alert the others. The heavy smoke pouring through the hall drove him back. While running out of the building, he heard Hull shouting, "Fire!" and watched him trying to catch Stephen West, who had jumped from a second-storey window.

Mr. H. Bennett provided the Enquiry with background information on life inside the Hull Home. After admitting he had no use for the Hulls, he explained why he felt tenants were not properly looked after. He said the food was very poor and badly cooked. He testified, "The meals were meagre with only a cup of tea and two slices of bread for breakfast and watery soup for lunch."

Bennett had first entered the Hull Home as a patient and when recovered, he took on some work around the building. He helped with the cooking in the Annex, filled the oil tank and lit the oil stove. He added, "Sometimes the oil control valve leaked. Hull often took it off and tried to fix it. When he couldn't, he gave it to me to take to a repair shop. It was leaking so bad that the kitchen canvas was soaked in oil."

Clayton Hiscock, a patient, said he was awakened by another patient who shouted, "She's gone this time for sure!" Hiscock said:

We closed the door and smashed open the window. Hull and Pike were on the sidewalk and they yelled for us to jump. I said it's just as well to die here as it is to kill ourselves down there. Just as the smoke and the fire began to fill up our room, the firemen appeared at our window on a ladder and we were rescued.

When asked about the treatment of tenants provided at the home, Hiscock said:

It wasn't good and it wasn't bad. Sometimes we got enough food and sometimes we didn't. Some patients complained to Mrs. Parsons, one of the nurses, about this. We couldn't get fresh meat, only beans and soup. Our rooms were cold. I once asked for bed clothes and they gave me a quilt.

Jean Parsons had several years' experience as a practical nurse at the Twillingate Hospital before joining the staff at the Hull Home. Her account of meals there conflicted with other witnesses. She testified that the food at the home was good. She said the mid-day meal included a choice of tomato juice or soup, plus meat and a choice of vegetables including cabbage, potatoes, turnip or carrot. Also served were tea and a dessert. Miss Parsons said:

As a rule the evening meals offered salt or canned fish, fruit, jam, cheese, biscuits, and bread, toasted, if desired. The night lunch offered a choice of milk or eggnog. I never heard any complaints about the food from any of the patients.

A practical nurse at that time earned ninety dollars a month.

Major Sainsbury, a Salvation Army officer and former probation officer with the Department of Public Health and Welfare, said she visited the home several times per week. She refuted some of the criticisms levelled at the home by other witnesses. "First," she said, "the food was good, ample, and cooked well." She claimed, "There were no signs of scorch marks on the kitchen walls" and suggested these could have been marks left by dirty water.[3]

Sainsbury testified that she had never seen more than four beds in one room and had never encountered a locked room. She admitted that after the publication of council's report, everyone seemed to realize the potential danger from fire, but no one seemed to know who had the responsibility. She said Hull had informed her that he had discussed the matter with Mrs. Noah, the owner of the building.

Mr. R. Cave, the contractor called in to paint the interior of the home after council's inspection, testified that there were no scorch marks on the kitchen walls.

More evidence supporting Hull's position came from Annie Hicks, a patient in the Annex. She testified that there were no rooms in the Annex that held seven people. Salvation Army officer Captain Mouland, who was in charge of the Annex, said there were never seven people to a room in the Annex and the only locked door in that area was the luggage room. He, too, said there were no scorch marks on the kitchen walls. Captain Mouland suggested that claims of seven in a room were likely due to patients visiting each other.

[3] In another court case involving the negligence of a twelve-year-old child on Blackhead Road who perished due to lack of medical attention, the mother of the child testified that Major Sainsbury had asked her to lie to authorities and say that Sainsbury had visited the home in recent weeks. See *Newfoundland's Era of Corruption*, Jack Fitzgerald.

The issue of treatment of tuberculosis patients at the Hull Home was discussed. Hull pointed out that the health department's doctor, who visited the home weekly, had not given any general instructions for the care of those patients and because of this, the utensils used by these patients were washed with those used by the general population at the home. He explained that staff used a solution in water for cleaning walls and floors and added that no disinfectant was used on the walls because the doctor said they were clean enough.

In his findings, Emerson agreed that the Hull Home was inadequately staffed with just three cleaners but concluded the home was well-run. He found that the home was clean and the food was well-cooked and adequate. He noted the staff treated patients with sympathy and consideration. Emerson did not hold back in respect to the contributing factors that led to fire and the loss of so many lives. His final report laid the blame for the disaster on city council and the Department of Public Health and Welfare.

The Enquiry chairman determined that the Department of Public Health and Welfare was negligent by failing to take measures to minimize risks. City council, he pointed out, was negligent because it failed to use its authority to guard against the tragedy.

A positive note in the Emerson Report was the chairman's praise for the conduct of seventeen-year-old Howard Pike, the youngest person in the home. He wrote:

> Pike, after calling for the fire department, attempted to make his way upstairs to rescue the other patients. If some responsible leadership had been shown, Pike would have stayed and assisted in the evacuation of residents.

Notes

I was a pre-school aged child in 1948 and lived a short distance from the Hull Home. I recall walking over to the scene the next morning with friends my age. What stands out in my memory to this day is the smell of smoke, fire hoses on the streets, crowds standing around, and the bitter frost. By then, the fire was out but still smouldering, the injured taken to hospital and firemen were still searching the ruins for the dead. The number of dead in the tragedy was not known at that time but people were comparing it to the Knights of Columbus fire just six years before. I was not surprised to learn in later years that it was one of the coldest days of that year, a fact which hindered the firefighting operation. I know it was the bitter frost that shortened our stay at the scene. We hurried back to our homes and the warmth and comfort of a kitchen stove fire. Like the K of C disaster, the inferno at the Hull Home was embedded into the minds of people for a lifetime.

Jack Fitzgerald

Chapter 14: Blizzards, Cyclones, Hurricanes and Avalanches

The Great Blizzard of 1868

Stories of blizzards are not uncommon in Newfoundland history. However, the level of devastation experienced and the number of lives lost cause some to stand out more than others. The blizzard that hit Newfoundland on February 3, 1868, was one of the worst storms in decades and within twenty-four hours had claimed almost thirty lives. The winter that year had been most severe and the poor were hardest hit. On February 3rd, thirty people lost their lives between Heart's Content and Harbour Grace. The deep snow covering the forests and the biting temperature of winter created a major challenge to men trying to gather firewood to heat their homes. People were running out of food and many took to the streets to seek charitable help from their neighbours. All thirty men and women who perished in the blizzard were either in the woods attempting to get wood or on the streets in nearby communities begging for food for their families.

The Newfoundlander, February 7, 1868, observed:

> Remembering the present conditions of so many of our poor, it is much to be feared that WANT was in most cases the evil that drove those unhappy victims from their houses on that fatal day. The weather was such that even the best fed and clothed who were long exposed to it would have succumbed and it is easy to understand how soon such hardship would prostrate those who perhaps for weeks or months had been without either food or clothing, half sufficiently for nature's demand in this type of winter.

The *Daily News* reported on February 15, 1868, that, "It has all been but impossible, except upon occasional days, for the poor to face the woods, so great is the depth of snow and so inclement the weather."

The *Harbour Grace Standard* of February 8, 1868, stated that: "Prior to the storm there were many poor creatures in town that day soliciting charity. Some lost their lives trying to get home."

The great blizzard struck on the afternoon of February 3, 1868, and people rushed to get to their homes. Those in the woods became lost in the blinding, swirling snow and those who had tried to walk from Harbour Grace to their homes perished. In the area of Riverhead two men, Smith and Quilty, were rescued but died hours later in their homes. Other victims identified were: Joe Drover, Joe Hussey, Jane Mercer, Grace Lundrigan, Jean Baird and John Coombs from Lower Island Cove. The *Daily News* identified another victim in the following manner, "A man belonging to Mr. Rorke of Carbonear, also perished." On February 4th, search parties went out into the woods and highways in search of those lost. By Friday they had found the bodies of all thirty missing people.

According to H.M. Mosdell, the blizzards of 1868 also brought death and destruction in Green Bay. About forty people in this area lost their lives to the great blizzards of January and February 1868. That winter was extremely cold and stormy. Three men left Fogo for Twillingate and became trapped in the storm. They were never heard from again. In the area between Joe Batt's Arm and Fogo, a man named Randell perished and his friend, Harold Green, lost both legs to frostbite. John Young and his two sons were trapped on a slab of ice overnight and when rescuers arrived next morning the two boys had perished.

Mr. J. Budgell, his wife and four children, left the upper part of the bay for Tilt Cove just before the storm struck. The next day rescuers came upon the grizzly sight of Mr. Budgell frozen to death with oars in hand. Mrs. Budgell held her baby in her arms, both frozen to death. The lifeless bodies of the three other children were found locked in each other's arms.

H. Lawrence and T. Sweeney of Fortune Harbour died when their boat became trapped in a slab of ice and sank. Both men drowned. Three boat crews driven off of the land by the storm were never heard from again. Two other boat crews from New Bay Head and one from Exploits Burnt Island also disappeared. Four men drowned at sea on a trip from Fogo to Little Fogo Island. Eleven fishermen from Twillingate and Fortune Harbour were also lost in the storm and never heard from again.

A unique aspect of the storm of 1868 was that for generations after any major winter storm that claimed one or more lives was called 'Coombs Day.' This was synonymous with the Coombs family name because, in 1868, the Coombs family of Upper Island Cove lost three family members to the killer blizzard. Rescuers did not locate the bodies of John Coombs and his teenage children, Mary and Richard, until a week after the storm struck. The name originated in Upper Island Cove and spread throughout Newfoundland.

The Great Gale of 1846

In 1846, one of the worst windstorms to hit Newfoundland in over thirty years struck. The hurricane-force winds were accompanied by a high tide. The Native Hall in St. John's was totally devastated by the wind. The timber that fell from the hall killed a five-year-old boy and his twenty-year-old sister. King's Bridge and Job's Bridge were destroyed and St. Thomas's Church was moved from its foundation.

The great gale of 1846 also claimed many lives and caused shipwrecks. In Burin forty-six men and eleven boats were lost in the storm. The *Shamrock*, after sailing from St. John's, was lost with all its crew off Cape St. Mary's. Captain Joseph Kean and his entire crew were lost off Cape Ballard.

The great gale of September 19, 1907, also resulted in loss of life and widespread devastation of property. It was in that storm that the *Effie* was lost with its sixteen-man crew. Other shipwrecks include: the *Jubilee*, the *Evelyn*, the *Harold T.*, the *Olive Branch*, the *M. Myler*, the *Snorr* at Bonavista, the *Hetty* at Harbour Grace, the *Fanny* at Grate's Cove, the *Ella Jane* at Old Perlican, the *Duchess* at Freshwater Bay, the *Mary Ellen* at Red Head Cove; and the *Lena*, *Mary Jane* and *Robert* at La Scie. Twenty-nine schooners were lost at Twillingate, seven lost at Musgrave Harbour, five at Tickle Cove, five at Keels, four at Newtown, four at Eastern Tickle and four at Fogo. By the time the storm ended ninety ships were lost.[1]

Tsunami at St. Shott's

June 26, 1864, was a red letter day in St. Shott's, near Trepassey. On this day, a curious and rather awe-inspiring natural phenomenon known as a tsunami struck the community. It was an unnatural kind of day. People in the area believed threatening weather was imminent, though what kind they were not prepared to say.

---

[1] Months before the Hon. Joseph R. Smallwood suffered a stroke, he had invited me to co-author a book with him dealing with an interesting aspect of the early settlement of Newfoundland. We discussed the project over breakfast at a hotel in St. Lawrence, then drove to his Roache's Line home to plan it.

Smallwood was interested in chronicling the story of the hardships, battles and lives lost by the first settlers to this country. He believed that much blood was shed by these settlers in just getting to know the climate and geography of the land. The examples he mentioned included the great windstorm that struck Conception Bay in 1775. The fishermen were so unprepared that by the time the storm ended 300 people had drowned and dozens of boats sunk. That loss is only matched by another great storm which struck on May 31, 1858, when 300 French fishermen were drowned and an undetermined number of boats went to the bottom of the ocean.

At 7:00 p.m., to the surprise and consternation of people in St. Shott's, the sea suddenly began to recede from the shore. It was obviously no mere ebb of the tide, as the waterline went out and out and out until it was nearly 1,000 feet from the shore. The sea retreated so far that it completely exposed the wreck of the British warship HMS *Comus*, hitherto lying submerged in five fathoms of water.

The water went out over 250 yards beyond the wreck of the *Comus* which was seen to good advantage, guns, shot and bolts being plainly visible. Then, as suddenly as it retreated, the sea returned with great force and speed after about ten minutes and poured in to St. Shott's filling up the Gut with gravel and large stones, overturning several boats and sinking one.

In endeavoring to explain the cause of this phenomenon, the *The Newfoundlander* in July 1946 said:

No doubt, a severe submarine volcanic eruption has taken place somewhere not very remote from the Southern Shore. On the 27th, it was remarked by everyone that the sky had an unusual appearance. It was very sultry, there was a dark, leaden smoke, which seemed to envelope everything and there were loud peals of thunder and vivid flashes of lightning at the same time. Nothing of the kind ever happened there before. Masters of ships in port say that the sky looked like it did in places where they experienced earthquakes.

Cyclone Hits Lumsden

In addition to blizzards and hurricanes, Newfoundlanders sometimes faced the ravages of the dreaded cyclone. During late June 1930, a cyclone took the community of Lumsden by surprise. Before the day was over every one of the 100 houses in the community were seriously damaged, most windows were smashed and ten people were in the water struggling to survive.

The cyclone struck at around 3:00 p.m. on the last Thursday of June. People sensed a sudden change coming when the skies darkened and it seemed that nightfall had come early. This was followed by a storm with hail as large as snowballs, which struck homes with tremendous force. Every home facing north had its windows smashed, and all homes suffered damage. The wind swirled around the community tearing clapboard and roofs off the houses. Fishermen rushed to their wharves to secure their boats. During the battle against the storm, several skiffs and a motorboat capsized, tossing ten men into the water. Wilf Goodyear managed to save seven of the men. The three men who died in the storm were: Baxter Goodyear, Sam Goodyear and Ron Cuff. The Newfoundland Government sent the *Prospero* with a load of building materials to help the community rebuild.

Newfoundland was a harsh place to settle and a challenging country to survive in. Yet, early settlers survived hardship of getting here and faced even greater challenges to settle and build the country. The people of the Battery in 1921 and again in 1959 displayed the same kind of courage and perseverance as the early settlers. This is a testament to the strength and character of the people of Newfoundland, helping make it the island it is today.

Avalanche in St. John's and Other Weather Calamities

A winter storm that struck St. John's on Sunday, February 15, 1959, was described in the St. John's *Daily News* next morning as, "All but unheard of in this part of the world." The slight snowfall that began falling at 5:00 p.m. the previous day appeared to be just another snowstorm with fifty mph winds expected, but by 3:00 a.m. next morning it had ripened into a raging blizzard with hurricane-force winds recorded at 135 mph. These were the type of winds that Newfoundlanders expected to witness only in the province's Wreckhouse area, located on the west coast.

Throughout Sunday, February 15th, radio and television news reports warned of a winter's storm with fifty mph winds approaching Newfoundland from the Maritimes. The storm moved across the province dumping eight inches of snow on Corner Brook and Gander. However, around 5:00 p.m., as it hit the Avalon Peninsula, the winds had increased to ninety mph. People were settling in for just another winter storm and were not expecting the storm of a lifetime. Most people in eastern Newfoundland were not yet aware of its increasing ferocity.

Near midnight the storm had escalated into a blizzard with hurricane-force winds. Radio and television stations had been knocked off the air. The exception was VOUS, the American station at Fort Pepperrell, St. John's, which reported on the storm for a few hours before they, too, were forced off the air. For the next twenty-four hours the only connection Newfoundland had with the outside world was an underwater cable to the mainland. When the storm subsided, VOAR, a radio station operated by the Seventh Day Adventist Church, allowed CJON the use of its tower on Merrymeeting Road, so it could at least broadcast to the St. John's audience. VOAR was operating three days a week at that time.

The biting southeast wind savaged the Avalon and by 3:00 a.m. the wind force was recorded at 135 mph. Because power had been cut off, the population was not aware of the destruction and death that had already visited St. John's. City streets were deserted during the storm and many cars were buried under snow in the city and on the Conception Bay Highway. Stranded motorists sought refuge in hotels and many were given shelter in the homes of strangers. Colony Cabs on Kings

Bridge Road allowed twenty stranded persons to wait out the storm in their taxi stand. Memorial Stadium left its doors open all night for any stranded persons wishing to take refuge. About fifty people availed of the shelter, but it proved to be an uncomfortable night. The emergency power went off near 3:00 a.m. and they were without heat for the rest of the night. At least they were sheltered from the bitterly cold winds outside.

Canadian National Railway (CNR) cancelled its train services, airports were shut down and the St. John's Fire Department was snowbound. Blown transformers left the Avalon Peninsula in darkness and the U.S.A.F Base at St. John's declared a state of emergency. The city's two daily newspapers, *The Daily News* and *The Evening Telegram*, were forced to suspend operations due to lack of power. The U.S.A.F at Red Cliff, which had measured the hurricane force winds at 135 mph, reported this was a record. The previous record was 116 mph.

Meanwhile, the hurricane tore roofs off city homes, smashed plate glass windows and demolished neon signs. The roof of a home on Forest Road, owned by Charles Summers, was ripped from the house and hurled almost 200 feet away into a backyard. Part of the structure of Bishop's College, located on Pennywell Road, went crashing to the ground. A two-storey house on the corner of Topsail Road and Molloy's Lane was ripped away and carried by the winds for over 100 feet. Pieces of timber went flying into the windows of nearby homes. A piece of clapboard torn from a home on Gilbert Street smashed into Mary Whelan's store window on Casey Street.

During the height of the blizzard vandals broke into St. Theresa's School on Mundy Pond Road and almost completely destroyed it. They turned on the fire hose and left it running all night. By morning the school was flooded. Windows were beaten out, filing cabinets were broken open and the contents strewn around, pictures were taken from the walls and smashed and furniture was broken.

Still unknown to the general population was that a terrible tragedy was unfolding in the Battery at the entrance to St. John's Harbour. Five people were already dead and thirteen others were buried beneath tons of snow. A family trapped in a house hit twice by a snow slide held each other and prayed throughout the night. They feared the next slide would carry them down into the freezing harbour waters below. Drifts of snow twenty-one feet high made it impossible for outsiders, who may have become aware of the battle for survival, to get to the scene. The RNC made an attempt but their vehicles became stranded in the snow. The people of the Battery, as they did many times before in the hour of need, came together to help each other. Lead by Ray Riche, a rescue party of fifty men was formed and they worked in the blinding blizzard throughout the night to rescue those buried beneath the snow. While the Battery men fought the elements, Mrs. Riche brewed tea and made sandwiches for the workers.

Earlier in the night, as the storm was building and steadily reducing visibility, people rested in their homes feeling protected from the ravages of the wind and snow swirling around them. The increasing snow fall was steadily adding to the winter's accumulation on a 200-foot slope above the Outer Battery and the potential for disaster was growing. The word 'avalanche' was not yet on anybody's mind.

Near 1:00 a.m. the winds intensified and a blizzard with hurricane-force winds was battering the area. Windows rattled, dishes in cupboards moved. The Battery was now completely isolated from the rest of the city. Suddenly at 1:05 a.m. people were shocked out of their sleep by a loud explosion, which some described as being like, "Fifty tons of dynamite exploding at the same time." Battery resident Alex Wells told *The Evening*

Telegram, "It was louder than any clap of thunder when it hit, my wife and I jumped at least three feet high." The night of terror at the Battery had started.

The explosion heard by residents was the sound of an avalanche. The tons of snow above the community came sliding down the hill bringing death and devastation as it moved towards the harbour waters below. The force of the moving snow rocketed two houses fifty feet downhill, ripped the top storey off another house, demolished several other homes and lifted a young girl from her bed, carrying her 200 feet, where she miraculously landed on a neighbour's front step.

Two teenaged girls were trapped beneath the snow for hours, one pinned beneath a kitchen stove, the second under a floor. Eleven people trapped in one house prayed all night to be rescued. Another slide would have likely taken them into the ocean below.

There were two slides. The initial one was followed by the disastrous avalanche. Three families of Garlands, totaling eleven men, women and children were trapped in the home of the senior Garland. They prayed for several hours to be rescued as snow slid past the roof and into the rolling sea below.

Alex Wells and six others in his home escaped without injury. They were saved from sliding into the ocean by the two-storey house behind them, owned by Jim Pearcey. The avalanche carried Pearcey and Clar Wells' home a distance of fifty feet where their slide was halted by crashing into other homes. Alex's home collided with Pearcey's. One of the people in Alex's home that night was Ralph Barnes. He was dressing to join Alex and the others in an effort to help neighbours when he heard a young girl crying. He looked out the window and saw a young girl's head protruding from a bank of snow on a fishing flake in front of Alex Wells' house.

Ralph rushed out the door to the rescue of the child and fought through a whirlwind of snow to get to her. He recalled,

"She gripped me tightly and was trembling with terror." The child was Sharon Pearcey, who had been thrown from her bed a distance of 200 feet, where Barnes rescued her. While Alex and Barnes were leaving their house they were approached by Clar Pearcey, son of neighbour Jim Pearcey, and asked if they would help him find his brother Charlie, who was still trapped in the house. Clar said he knew where they could find him. Barnes later noted that, "We didn't know where to look when we got to Pearcey's. It was in ruins and it was impossible to see anything because of the storm." The men followed Clar into the ruins and succeeded in digging out Charlie.

Meanwhile, the rescue effort shifted to the home of Alex's brother, Clar. Alex heard someone crying out for help. The blizzard made it impossible to see anything, so Wells and Barnes followed the sound. It led them to the buried home of Clar Wells. Others were already there and trying to dig their way into the house. Alex heard the cry again and along with Noseworthy went to a small opening beneath the rubble of the house. They cleared the opening and succeeded in rescuing Clar, his wife Beatrice and their daughter, Winnie.

A third Wells brother, Otto, battled the storm to rescue his family of five from their home after it had been crushed by the avalanche. Art Wells, who in the 1990s coached the Youth Bowling League Teams at Plaza Bowl in St. John's, has never forgotten the terror of that night. He had been out sliding down the hill with his brothers and friends earlier in the night. Art says there was nothing special about the storm at that time, "… it was like any other snowstorm. It didn't stop us. There was a lot of wind and snow but everyone was having fun."

By midnight, Art and his brothers, Austin and Derek, were sleeping in their beds. They were awakened by a loud noise only to find that snow was filling up their room. Art's infant sister, Cynthia, who was in a crib near a window, was knocked from her crib and ended up beneath a bed. They cleared the snow and rescued her. By then Otto Wells was aware of the avalanche and he gathered his family together to evacuate the house.

Otto was concerned that if they tried to get to a neighbour's house another slide could hit and bury them all. He got a long piece of rope to secure his house to the twine store. This would serve as a safety line for his family. One end of the rope was secured to the Wells' house and the other was tied around the stomach of Art Wells, who made his way through the blizzard to the twine store, which was located nearby, where he quickly secured the rope. Then Otto Wells, his wife and remaining three children made their way to safety holding the rope tightly all the way.

Art Wells and several of his friends were sent to the Red Cross on Plymouth Road the next morning to report the disaster and to seek help. Art recalls that the bodies recovered that day were stored in the twine shed, where he and his family had waited out the storm. When the road was cleared later in the day, the bodies were taken to the city morgue.

Meanwhile, Ralph Barnes had returned to the Pearcey house after learning that people were trapped inside. At the same time, Ray Riche arrived and to get through had to cut a hole through a roof which had blown off a house and was now blocking the road. Inside the Pearcey home only the sullen and ominous sound of the howling winds greeted the workers shouts of, "Anyone there? Are you okay?"

"Perhaps they are unconscious," one worker said. Riche led the men inside the house to search. The number of rescue workers increased to sixty and throughout the night and early morning they battled the biting sub-zero temperatures and hurricane-force blizzard winds. There were a few people still alive and praying for someone to come rescue them. One of these was Clar Wells' daughter, Ruth, who was trapped beneath a burning stove; another was Ruth's friend, sixteen-year-old Shirley Noseworthy, a visitor to the home that night, who was trapped a few feet away beneath the snow and rubble of the house. At about 3:00 a.m., they located Ruth and succeeded in getting her out from under the stove and to a nearby house. She was badly burned and later taken to a hospital. The weather reached its peak at this time and the rescue team had to retreat to homes away from the path of the avalanche. Visibility was zero and the men had no way of knowing whether another slide was imminent. Throughout the night, sleep and relaxation eluded them.

At 7:30 a.m. with the blizzard continuing, the rescue workers went out again to battle the elements in search of survivors. Weather conditions were so deteriorated that the police were still unable to get help into the Battery. William Earle Sr. was among the rescue team that morning. He described the team as a very spirited and determined group of men. Mr. Earle recalled, "That around 11:30 a.m. we heard a cry for help that led us to Clar Wells' house and Shirley Noseworthy."

In addition to spending a terrorizing night buried in nearly twenty feet of snow, Shirley (Noseworthy) Eales suffered frostbite to both legs. However, she never lost hope that she would be rescued and attributed her optimism to her faith in God. Interviewed almost twenty years later by Ken Meeker, CBC News, Shirley said, "The last thing I remembered was Ruth Wells walking in front of the kitchen stove. The lights blinked once. They blinked one more time then it was total darkness. I heard a big bang like thunder and then screaming. It seemed like I went down a shutey-shute about twenty feet."

The avalanche was followed by a great deal of screaming and crying. She said, "It seemed like it went on for hours before it settled down." Things then became eerily silent. She was trapped from the waist down and used her hands to remove snow from around her face, which enabled her to breathe.

Bill Earles recalled, "When we started digging through the snow, we heard her faint voice say, 'I'm freezing. You're knocking the snow down on top of me.' We passed down a blanket for her to wrap around herself."

Miraculously, she had survived nearly eleven hours buried beneath the house and crushing snow, trapped between the floor and a rock. Just ten feet from the young girl, they found the body of seventy-six-year-old Mrs. S. Vincent, mother-in-law of Jim Pearcey, buried beneath a mattress under eight feet of snow.

It was an emotional time for the Battery men when they found Mr. And Mrs. Jim Pearcey. The avalanche had struck the house with such force and surprise that the couple were killed in their sleep. The Pearceys were found in bed with Jim holding his arm around his wife. After removing the two bodies, the search continued. The police arrived around mid-morning and some of the searchers were able to rest.

The last body recovered from the avalanche was that of nineteen-year-old Ted Wells at 1:45 p.m. Several of his classmates from St. Michael's School laboured courageously throughout the long rescue effort with hopes of finding their friend alive. They repeatedly comforted each other by saying, "Ah, Ted will be all right." Rescue worker William Earle said they found the body of Ted Wells crushed by the roof that fell upon him. When the search was all over, three people had been rescued from the Pearcey home and six from the Wells home. The Garland house was not seriously damaged and all those trapped inside, eleven in total, including four children, were safely rescued from the place. Alex Wells told an *Evening Telegram* reporter, "What a night. We were frightened all of us were about what happened. And we didn't know what else would happen. Never again ... please!"

One hundred-year-old Isaiah Dawe was taken from his home in the Lower Battery but died later that day at the old

General Hospital. In addition to the destruction of the Wells and Pearcey homes, a home owned by Walter Morgan was pushed by the crushing snow into the back of another house and was almost totally demolished.

By Monday afternoon, when the search had ended and the shock of the experience was setting in, a group gathered at a fish loft in the Lower Battery to discuss the tragedy, destruction and their own futures. These were the eight men hardest hit by the avalanche. Several houses not completely destroyed were for the time being uninhabitable. *The Evening Telegram* organized a fund to help victims restart their lives. Trustees appointed were Harold Lake, Raymond Riche and Douglas Hunt. Meanwhile, the storm had taken another life. By 3:00 p.m., in a car buried beneath snow on the Memorial Stadium parking lot, four people had been found.

Co-manager of Memorial Stadium, Walter Reynolds, told reporters that others trapped on the parking lot had taken refuge in the stadium where the doors remained unlocked throughout the storm. At 7:00 a.m., two men and two girls left their car on the parking lot and entered the stadium. They had no idea that four others were still inside a car on the lot.

The discovery of the four people was made by two men who went to the parking lot to dig out their own car. They found that the hood of the car was buried beneath snow but the doors could be opened. The motor had been left on most of the night. Three of the occupants survived after being treated at hospital, but seventeen-year-old Shirley Lush of St. John's died of carbon-monoxide poisoning.

When the storm ended on Monday afternoon, temperatures dropped to five degrees Fahrenheit. Mayor Harry Mews encouraged residents to help emergency efforts by clearing snow from sidewalks, foundations, roofs and coal chutes. The public responded and men, women and children using only shovels completely cleared Hagerty Street and John Street. People were shoveling on every street in the city. The scene on the streets of St. John's resembled that of the far North. Snowshoes, which people had stored for years, were taken out and used. Skis also became a common means of transportation.

The city was faced with the problem of reopening streets, which had been buried in up to twenty-one feet high snow drifts. Assistance in the way of snow clearing equipment was given by the R.C.A.F at Torbay. A supervisor with the city told reporters, "When we saw what had to be done and the condition of the streets after the storm, we did not know where to start. Some drifts were twenty-one feet high and if it had not been for the extra snow blowers loaned by the R.C.A.F, we could not have done half as much as we have." Twenty-four hours after the end of the blizzard a single cut had been made through only twenty streets and roads in the city.

Meanwhile, another crisis was developing. A rainstorm with sixty-five mph winds struck on Thursday. While it took much of the snow away, it caused more severe problems for the city and its residents. Mayor Harry Mews and Attorney General Leslie R. Curtis issued an order for cars to stay off the streets and people to stay in their homes unless they had to go out. Casual city workers were called in to assist with the emergency. In many cases, council workers were assigned specific streets. They were required to remain on-site and try to avert blockages and flooding. Downtown restaurants did booming business with workers unable or not wanting to return home for lunch.

Mayor Harry Mew's patience was tested by an irate lady who called him on the morning after the blizzard, while the mayor was still mobilizing resources to deal with the emergency situation, and demanded that he explain why her street had not yet been cleared. Mayor Mews patiently explained that a crisis had hit the city and before terminating the conversation advised the lady to, "Please wait." The mayor praised the response of city workers to the emergency situation saying, "They have risen to the occasion magnificently. Every demand that we have made upon them to work long hours in poor weather conditions, they have accepted."

The heavy rain falling on top of the snow created torrential flooding that ran down streets like rivers; flooding on Water Street and Duckworth Street was as high as two feet in places. City council workers had to use a small boat on Forest Road adjacent to the Anglican Cemetery to free a catch basin. Only snow clearing equipment and emergency vehicles, along with a few busses, were permitted to use the streets and they moved at a snail's pace.

Neighbourhood kids in the Cabot Street and Flower Hill area built a dam of snow at the top of Flower Hill, where it intersected with Cabot Street. Dino Caul, from Caul's Lane, was on his way up the hill with his shovel to join in the mischief when the dam broke. The force of the water knocked him off his feet and carried him downhill to the Monroe Street intersection. Harry Constantine and Mike (Dinty) Hearn came to his aid and pulled him out of the river of water as it flowed downward past Roberts Grocery Store (now Flower Hill Convenience Store).

Telegraph and telephone lines that had been restored after the blizzard went down again on Thursday, February 19th, and communications with mainland Canada were knocked out for most of the day. The Newfoundland Light and Power Company faced major problems when trying to restore electricity to the city. St. John's had been thrown into darkness during the blizzard when the switches at the Gould's Switching Station were thrown by the storm. Attempts to correct the problem from St. John's were unsuccessful, so the company sent a team of men to the Goulds to make the repairs.

The company ploughs were unable to make it through the heavy drifts blocking the Goulds Highway. Finally, the company sent two men on foot equipped with snowshoes to do the job. After a twelve-hour blackout the two men succeeded in restoring power to the capital city. The few stores that managed to open after the blizzard had line-ups of people looking for lamps, heaters and candles. The Newfoundland Light and Power Company had used every available man during the storm to work on damaged lines feeding individual homes.

The CNR dispatched a rotary plough to open railway lines between St. John's and Clarenville. The plough encountered fifteen-foot-high snow drifts, which blocked the railway line. The line was cleared and a passenger train stranded at Clarenville managed to get to St. John's with its weary passengers. Meanwhile, the R.C.A.F managed to clear the runways at Torbay and flights began arriving.

There were many critics of city council for not being prepared to deal with the hurricane-blizzard. Both of the city's daily newspapers responded to the criticism in editorials. The *Daily News* noted that in earlier years there was no urgency attached to keeping city streets open for motor traffic. In 1921, a severe winter storm disrupted city services. However, the drifts remained on the roads for two weeks before being removed by council. Another major storm struck at the end of March 1938 and continued unabated for eighty hours. The snow remained piled in great drifts until, "... melted by the spring sun." Soon after, city council adopted a policy to keep streets open to traffic during the winter season.

The Daily News editorial noted that St. John's by 1959 had developed into a modern city and was an important distributing centre for the province. It stated, "That imposes a heavier burden on the municipal government in dealing with heavy snowfalls." Many new miles of street had been added to the city after Confederation.

The editorial continued, "It would be quite impossible to keep in hand for such emergencies as that of last weekend a supply of equipment equal to the task of complete restoration of traffic facilities in a day or two. This last snowstorm comes under the heading of a phenomenon and it would be unreasonable to ask of the council more than it is trying to do."

The Evening Telegram editorial responded to criticisms that the city had not equipped itself to take care of winter storms stating:

> At the same time, there is criticism that snow removal costs are too high, that further charges to cover such costs should not be made. The best outlook would seem to be that of the city fathers, who have acquired equipment to take care of normal needs, have found methods to cope with emergencies without making the permanent investment for additional equipment.

One city resident obviously didn't agree with some of the praise being heaped upon citizens, politicians and public employees as being heroic in their response to the storm. He or she put their thoughts in a letter published in *The Evening Telegram* under the heading, "Heroic Deeds":

> Sir:
> Permit me to take this opportunity to congratulate all citizens of St. John's, and especially those wintering in Florida, on the way in which we have responded to the current crisis. The heroic efforts of our city council, who by the use of large quantities of radio and television time, to say nothing of snow-ploughs, have made

it possible to walk from one end of our fair city to the other without sinking beyond our knees in snow, especially if one wears snowshoes.

The special regulation requiring all automobiles unless engaged in work of great urgency to keep off the streets is the greatest thing since Confederation. One cannot but admire the zeal with which large numbers of private cars, beer trucks, etc., are pursuing their errands of mercy. The pedestrians have also entered into the spirit of the thing, and even grandfathers can be seen leaping the snow banks like goats (and with glad shouts) out of the paths of heroic emergency vehicles.

An interview with some of these pedestrians should be of great interest to students of rare and forgotten old Newfoundland dialect. Citizens will be overjoyed to learn that all the hot air generated in public service announcements, instructions and regulations is to be dedicated into the greatest snow blower of all time, by which means it will be possible to clear all snow in a few hours, and have enough left over to heat the city for the rest of the winter.

Finally, do not be downhearted if you cannot get fresh milk for your kids. Beer is being delivered, so to paraphrase Marie Antoinette, "Let them drink beer."

Sgd. The Abominable Snowman

Earlier Blizzards

The 1959 avalanche was not the first to strike the Battery. On February 8th, 1921, a blizzard battered St. John's and caused an avalanche at the Battery that devastated and buried houses, pushing stages and flakes into St. John's Harbour. Fortunately, there was no loss of life but residents spent a night in terror. There may have been loss of life if some of the buried homes had been occupied. At that time, some homes in the Lower Battery area were only used during summer months by fishermen from St. John's.

As in 1959, the people of the Battery were isolated from the city by the storm and depended on each other to survive. Hardest hit was the family of Alf Wells. At 11:00 p.m. on the night of the blizzard, Wells was alarmed after hearing a rumbling sound above the noise of the storm. Instinctively, he thought "Avalanche!" and warned his wife that they had to vacate the home immediately. However, the snow hit the Wells home before they could get out of bed.

The avalanche struck the house with such force that the ceiling collapsed, consequently trapping Mr. and Mrs. Wells in a sitting position in their bed. Wells struggled and freed himself. He was unable to stand because the roof had come down on the floor. One part of it was held up by a partition. This gave him room to rescue his wife and two children, an infant and a two-year-old boy.

Once outside the house visibility was zero. The storm encircled the family as Alf Wells moved them down a slope to his brother's house only to discover that it too had been devastated. His brother and family had taken up refuge in their father's home next door. Mrs. Alf Wells had suffered a severe back injury when the snow crushed her home and even the short distance to his father's house was a major battle for the family. They remained with Alf's father until the storm ended and then moved Mrs. Wells and the children to the home of Henry Abbott.

When the storm subsided next morning the community learned that twelve houses had been buried beneath snow during the avalanche. The home of G. Rogers was carried 100 feet from its foundation and several flakes and stages were carried into the St. John's Harbour. The avalanche left the home of Moses Pearcey with only one room habitable. The Pearcey family found shelter in that room until the storm ended the next morning. Families affected by the 1921 avalanche included the Wells, Pearcey, Edgecombe, Rodgers, and Morris family.

Not far away from the Battery in Quidi Vidi Village, blizzard-force winds ripped the roof off George Cooke's fishing stage and tossed it 100 feet away. It struck a man, who escaped with his life only because a corner of the roof became lodged on a boundary stone set up by the Admiralty many years before.

The 1921 storm sparked public controversy over the way the city handled snow clearing. Joseph R. Smallwood, then a twenty-one-year-old journalist, suggested the city consider contracting out the job, so council could better budget for winter expenditures related to storms. It was at this time that a novel idea was proposed to use the World War I Mark A Tank (nicknamed the Whippet), owned by Silverlock's Garage on Springdale Street, to clear the main streets. A letter to *The Evening Telegram* on February 11, 1921, thought it was a good idea and stated:

> Mr. R.G. Silverlock, so I understand, has taken up the new and novel idea of bringing the Whippet Tank in play for the purpose of doing the trick, for which if he should succeed will save quite a lot of expense to the Council, as the present mode of doing the work is a very expensive proposition.

In this era, there was no policy in place to keep streets clear of snow for motor traffic. Sometimes snow would remain piled up on city streets before being removed and if snow fell late in March, it would be left for the hot sun of spring to melt. The city's snow clearing operation was comprised of some horse-drawn carts that held a few hundred pounds of snow. City workers would fill these carts and the snow would be taken and dumped in the St. John's Harbour.

Silverlock felt his tank could flatten the snow along the main city streets in a couple of days. The idea caught public attention and when the tank rolled onto Water Street on February 8, 1921, hundreds of people turned out to witness the historic event. This marked the first time in the city's history that a motorized vehicle would be used for snow clearing. City council watched with interest because, if successful, the idea could save the city money and improve things for business establishments in St. John's.

For most of the day on February 8th, Silverlock's mechanic, John Churchill, worked on preparing the tank to test its capabilities in snow clearing. By 5:00 p.m. he had the motor running and moved the Whippet onto Water Street. Records are not clear on who the driver of the tank was, but it made its way only a few hundred feet and then stalled. Silverlock decided to leave it there for the night and resume the snow clearing early the next morning.

The driver of a Whippet tank was regarded as a prodigy by the military. These were difficult and dangerous machines. Driving a Whippet was compared to driving two tanks at once. The air inside was always polluted due to the exhaust pipes that led to the side. In battle Whippet crews wore gas masks to avoid carbon monoxide poisoning from its engine.

Churchill, assisted by another mechanic, worked on the Whippet next morning until it was in good running order. Meanwhile, word had spread throughout the city and hundreds turned up to watch the tank do its work. As it moved slowly along Water Street near the courthouse, an excited crowd followed. The Whippet remained around for many years and then was left parked in front of the courthouse. When World War

II broke out it was scrapped and the metal was sent to England to use in the war effort.

There were other avalanches in Newfoundland history including one in Distress Cove on the Cape Shore. That tragedy struck on March 12, 1863, and claimed the lives of two brothers, John and William Foley. The men had been duck hunting when the avalanche struck and buried them under tons of snow.

Winter scene on Water Street, St. John's. *Panl*

The Monkey's Puzzle in St. John's was the row of housing shown here, which ran from Water Street at the foot of Temperance Street up to Battery Road. *Panl*

A sealing ship stuck in the ice. *Panl*

Seal hunters working on the ice. *Panl*

A glimpse of St. John's Harbour when it was "iced in". *Panl*

St. John's Harbour in winter. *City of St. John's Archives*

The *Iceland* stuck in ice. *Panl*

Military Road, St. John's after a storm. The old street car railing is visible.
City of St. John's Archives

Clearing the way for the electric street cars along the railings near the corner of Prescott and Water Streets. *City of St. John's Archives*

St. Johns Harbour in winter. *City of St. John's Archives*

283

City residents testing the ice on St. Johns Harbour. *City of St. John's Archives*

Acknowledgements

I acknowledge with sincere appreciation the help and encouragement of the following people during the writing and publishing preparation for this book. In particular I would like to thank Bob Rumsey for reviewing the manuscript, Maurice Fitzgerald for the cover design and photograph editing and Don Morgan for the final manuscript editing and invaluable advice. I am also grateful for the professional work and advice provided by Pam Dooley, Joanne Snook-Hann and Todd Manning, of Creative Publishers in guiding *Jack Fitzgerald's Treasury of Newfoundland Stories Volume I* along the road to its final publication. Special thanks to Donna Francis of Creative for her encouragement, support and accessibility when needed. Also the staffs at the Provincial Archives of Newfoundland and Labrador, the A.C Hunter Library (Newfoundland Collection), the Queen Elizabeth II Library, MUN, Centre of Newfoundland Studies, MUN and the City of St. John's Archives. I must also acknowledge the late Dr. Bobbi Robertson, who decades ago guided me through the entire collection of records kept by the Newfoundland Historical Society in the old Colonial Building, and the help provided at that time by my friend and co-worker, Richard "Dick" Hartery.

Bibliography

Official Documents:

Supreme Court Trial Records, Newfoundland Supreme Court Registry, St. John's, Newfoundland.

Colonial Secretary's Letters, GN 2/1/2, vol. 2, 1752-1759.

The Record of the Judicial Proceedings held by His Majesty's Justices of the Peace for the District of Trinity in the Island of Newfoundland, 1753-1774.

Colonial Secretary's Records, GN13, Attorney-General/Justice, 1. Department Records, 2. Newfoundland Constabulary, 6. Her Majesty's Penitentiary. Newfoundland Archives, St. John's.

*Colonial Secretary's Letters, GN 2/1/2, vol. 2, 1752-1759.*Newfoundland Archives.

Books:

Prowse, Judge D. K. W. *A History of Newfoundland.* Macmillan and Company, London and New York, 1895.

Fitzgerald, Jack, *Too Many Parties, Too Many Pals*, Jesperson Publishing, 1982.

Convicted, Jesperson Publishing, 1983.

Rogues and Branding Irons, Jesperson Publishing, 1987.

Jack Fitzgerald, *The Jack Ford Story*, Creative Publishers, 2007.

Jack Fitzgerald, *Newfoundland Disasters*, Creative Publishers, 2005.

Where Angels Fear to Tread, Creative Publishers, 1995.

Smallwood, Hon. Joseph R. , *Newfoundland Miscellany*. Newfoundland Book Publishers, 1967.

And *Encyclopedia of Newfoundland*, Volumes 1,5,6. Newfoundland Book Publishers.

Interviews:

Dr. Bobbie Robertson, Newfoundland Historical Society, 1986.

Hon. Joseph R. Smallwood, Premier of Newfoundland, interviewed in 1983 and 1984.

Dr. Douglas Paulse, Director of Forensic Psychiatry, Waterford Hospital, St. John's, Newfoundland, March and July 1987

Newspapers and Publications:

The Evening Telegram, St. John's, Nfld.; *The Daily News*, St. John's, Newfoundland; Grand Falls *Advertiser* (1959, 1969, 1971); *Western Star*, Corner Brook, Newfoundland, 1959, 1960. *The Royal Gazette*, St. John's, Newfoundland, ; *The Newfoundlander*, St. John's, Newfoundland. *The Patriot*, St. John's, Newfoundland; *Harbour Grace Standard*, Hansard, Province of Newfoundland, 1959-1960; *Toronto Daily Star*, February-March 1960; *Montreal Star*, March 1960; *Montreal Gazette*, March 1960; *Calgary Herald*, March 1960; *Regina Post*, March 1960. *Catholic Cadet Corps Magazine*, 1920s collection.

JACK FITZGERALD was born in St. John's and educated at Holy Cross School, Bishop Eustace High School (New Jersey), the College of Trades and Technology and Memorial University. During his career he has been a journalist, a feature writer and political columnist with the St. John's *Daily News*; a reporter and public affairs writer with CJON and VOCM news services; and editor of *The Newfoundland Herald* and the *Newfoundland Chronicle*. During the Smallwood administration, he was Assistant Director of Public Relations with the Government of Newfoundland and Labrador.